Social Class and Family Life

SOCIAL CLASS AND

FAMILY LIFE

DONALD GILBERT McKINLEY

THE FREE PRESS, *New York*
COLLIER-MACMILLAN LIMITED, *London*

In my craft or sullen art
Exercised in the still night
When only the moon rages
And the lovers lie abed
With all their griefs in their arms,
I labour by singing light
Not for ambition or bread
Or the strut and trade of charms
On the ivory stages
But for the common wages
Of their most secret heart.

Not for the proud man apart
From the raging moon I write
On these spindrift pages
Nor for the towering dead
With their nightingales and psalms
But for the lovers, their arms
Round the griefs of the ages,
Who pay no praise or wages
Nor heed my craft or art.
                    —DYLAN THOMAS
                    In My Craft or Sullen Art

▪ ACKNOWLEDGMENTS

Many have helped me in the development of this book. Perhaps a study of the bibliography will give the reader some idea of my intellectual indebtedness. There are, however, other individuals and organizations to whom I would like to express my personal gratitude.

Above all, the scope and system of Talcott Parsons' ideas have provided a stimulating and also a liberating framework for thought. Its frequent use and resulting stimulation led me to broader and, what are for me and I hope to the reader, quite interesting perspectives on new problems. I also want to thank him for many helpful and provocative conversations.

I am indebted, too, to fathers, and the students and staffs of several high schools and institutions in the Boston area. Without their trust and intellectual curiosity much of the data in this book would not have been available to me.

The facilities and financial support given by the National Institutes of Health, by Harvard University, and by the University of Pennsylvania in the early and unstructured stages of my work were welcome assistance. Also, during this rather unpromising phase I had numerous encouraging and enlightening discussions with Dr. Daniel Funkenstein and Professor Alex Inkeles.

For aid in the later phase I am especially indebted to two very able and helpful people whose contributions were sometimes clerical, sometimes editorial, and sometimes of a theoretically and critical nature. They are Robert W. Rogers and Barbara B. Brown.

I suppose most writers see their problem differently at the end and I would like to deal with one point which will possibly help the reader. Although Chapter I is entitled "An Introduction to the Problem," in many ways I now feel the summary (pp. 241-247) in the final chapter outlines my basic thesis in a clearer fashion and makes the progress of the book more meaningful. With that in mind perhaps the reader, especially those with some familiarity with the family and society as fields of study, will find his appetite whetted if he turns there and sees how the story ends.

For permission to reprint "In My Craft or Sullen Art," from *The Collected Poems of Dylan Thomas,* I wish to thank J. M. Dent & Sons Ltd., and the trustees of the Dylan Thomas Estate, and New Directions, Publishers. Copyright 1957 by New Directions.

Finally, I wish to thank the publishers who have given permission to reprint material from their published works: Basic Books, Inc., Columbia University Press; Harper & Row; Holt, Rinehart and Winston, Inc.; Indiana University; The Macmillan Company; The University of Michigan Institute for Social Research; Oxford University Press, Inc.; Princeton University Press; Routledge & Kegan Paul Ltd.; The Rural Sociological Society; and John Wiley & Sons, Inc.

DONALD G. McKINLEY

New York
December 1963

Foreword

In this book Donald McKinley has made an important and welcome contribution to the understanding of one of the most central and at the same time controversial fields of social science. In doing so he has presented what is to date probably the fullest and most careful and analytical review of the literature yet to appear, and has made important independent contributions through his own original research.

The book goes far to destroy a myth which for about a generation has had considerable currency in sociology and anthropology; namely, the myth of the free and permissive lower class culture in American society which could be set over against the allegedly more restrictive middle class. The main field of the controversy of course has concerned the family in relation to child training functions. Here McKinley mobilizes an indeed imposing body of evidence that the discipline imposed on lower class children tends to be significantly more severe than for their middle class counterparts. This type of evidence may be supplemented from another field by Lipset's now well-known material on working class authoritarianism in political matters.

The picture which emerges is that on the higher class levels the primary accent is on training for independence and the assumption of responsibility. It matches the relatively early and extensive emancipation of the child from the tutelage of his family and the exposure to highly competitive achievement pressures, especially in the school. The principal sanctions are the attitudes of approval and disapproval or disappointment. The lower the class level, the less realistic do higher achievement expectations become for the majority. As a matter of realistic adaptation to disadvantaged conditions there tends to be greater emphasis on negative sanctions and the maintenance of at least a respectable conformity with community standards. A strikng fact is the increase in resort to physical punishment as the level of socioeconomic status falls.

Upon this background, Dr. McKinley analyzes with great sophistication the sense in which the phenomena of lower class deviance, in the broadest sense, may be interpreted as reactions to the strains imposed on the members of handicapped groups in a society characterized by high pressure to individual achievement. He presents an unusually happy combination of empirical comprehensiveness and rigor with the creative use of available theoretical tools.

Dr. McKinley has become so impressed with the severity of the pressures to which lower class members (and perhaps the middle class) are subjected in the American type of society that he suggests that absolute limits of human capacity to cope with conditions of strain and demands for achievement have possibly been exceeded over a rather wide front. The seriousness of the social problems involved is clearly beyond question, and the author is to be commended for delineating them in such a clear and forceful fashion. At the same time it seems to me the conclusion about absolute limits, in both a biological and psychosocial sense, are premature; the sociologist's obligation is to push analysis in terms of the environmental factors as far as possible before claiming to define their limits.

In any case, Dr. McKinley has posed this issue in especially sharp form. He thereby leaves a new legacy of, to me, unsolved problems. It is noteworthy how greatly the field of controversy has shifted from the problems from which the study took its departure. This type of shift of fields of controversy is one of the best indices of the progress of a discipline.

TALCOTT PARSONS

Contents

Social Class and Family Life

CHAPTER 1

An Introduction to the Problem

THE PROBLEM AND THE GENERAL FOCUS

In this study we will be primarily interested in the social setting of the family and the ways in which this setting influences the structure of behavior that occurs within the family. To make our discussion meaningful, it is necessary to outline the structure of the social setting, the significant behavior in the family, and some theoretical position explaining how the one influences the other; the problem becomes, "What structural features and processes of society are significant influences on important aspects of behavior occurring in the family?"

Generally, we believe that family behavior responds to, and is structured by, extrafamilial aspects of the society. (It appears that the line of development of the family, historically and cross-culturally, has been from a protosociety based almost exclusively on kinship. As society became more differentiated and specialized, the kinship structure became somewhat simpler and made adjustments to the changes in extrafamilial society.) We recognize, however, that the strains and demands of the personalities formed in a particular family influence what occurs in that family. We also recognize that the family as a system has needs and exerts certain pressures on society, thus determining to some extent the direction of society's development.

Casual observation and careful scientific study reveal the variability in the family and in kinship structure in diverse social settings. The contrasts in the nature of the family in rural and urban areas, in different cultures, and in different social classes attract great interest, and require some theoretical and generally comprehensible

1

explanation. The careful observer also sees that different kinds of personalities are typical of different settings.

Several types of explanation are offered for these observed facts. A psychological inclination leads the theorist to link them rather simply: the difference between families in different social settings is a consequence of different personalities "naturally" gravitating to or being created in these different social settings. Families are not simply collections of personalities, however, and the role structure of the family itself must be explained. As will be seen, this view does not mean we reject psychological explanations.

Often the family or the kinship structure is also explained as a manifestation of the "values" or cultures that exist in different social realms. On occasion, however, "values" are simply abstractions based on the very behavior patterns that they are supposed to explain. Such "values" may serve as useful concepts for ordering many observations, but they take on a certain tautological quality—a quality characteristic of the concept of "instinct" in psychology in the early twentieth century.

Though we will frequently rely on cultural and psychological levels of explanation, our orientation and main focus are sociological; that is, we will attempt to explain the role structure and emotional climate of the family in various segments of industrial society as consequences of the nature of the family's position in the social structure. Social structure is very complex, and a family can hold many positions by virtue of its relation to the many aspects of society. This complexity requires some kind of simplification, and we have chosen to focus on variability in status or class placement. We shall use this detailed analysis of the class-determined structure of the family and the psychological responses of family members as a point of departure for a statement about a second basic interest, the origin of subcultures in various classes. We shall also examine in detail the father's experiences in the particular occupation that confers upon him and his family a certain status in the society.

By "culture" (which we discuss at length later in this chapter) we mean, very briefly, the more abstract and ideal standards of action that are shared by a group or society. By "status" we mean, in general, the rank a person occupies in the reward (possessions, esteem, money, etc.) or power structure of society. The rewards and positions of power are a social unit's "resources." Interaction tends to develop among individuals and families of like status, and gradually norms (rather specific rules, or standards, of action) emerge from these social relationships. We shall call these patterned norms attached to status groups their "subcultures." We shall generally take the view that systems of interaction and the subcultures developed constitute a multibonded status community or "class." These are our theoretical definitions of "culture," "status," "subculture," and "class." We will not adhere precisely to these definitions each time we use the terms, however, for they have a number of other legitimate meanings. From time to time we borrow these other meanings.

The Family in Complex Societies

One condition basic to our study is the social setting of the family. What is the structure of this setting? It is influenced by the degree of social complexity of the society, and other factors come into play—geographic, ethnic, and political. A review of all these conditions and their influence on the family would give helpful understanding, but such a review is beyond the scope of this study.

We have chosen to focus on status, and this is not arbitrary. Basically, it is the paramount significance of the economic system and the importance of occupations (and their differentiated rewards) in modern society that lead us to focus on "achieved" class status and to slight these other conditions.

Perhaps a brief comparison of the family and the influences that impinge upon it in simple and in modern societies will provide some picture of the special conditions that impinge on the modern family and of how the modern family differs in its social context from the family in less complex societies. This contrasting picture will help make clear why we frame the problem as we do. Basically, our problem does not emerge except in those societies where rather diverse institutional activities are carried out independently of the family. The problem is particularly significant in those societies where the activities independent of family behavior have developed into diversely rewarded occupations. We plan to study the ways in which these diversities in rewards received by the father in his occupation feed back into and influence family life. This feedback results in the emergence of particular styles of life (subcultures) and patterns of family behavior in the different social classes.

Any society must come to terms with its physical environment, and it does this through the development of certain tools and the organization of tasks among its members. In primitive societies where economic activities are carried out within a kinship structure, the technology and the ecology—and the way these influence the allocation of tasks according to age and sex—are intimately bound up with the ways in which the various other activities and functions

of the family are carried out. Thus, Firth's and Homans' studies of
Tikopia (1936 and 1950, respectively) demonstrate how a particular environment, interacting with a given allocation of tasks to cope
with this environment, results in predictable patterns of responses,
sentiments, and strains within the family or kinship group. Also,
Murdock's studies of various societies would appear to support his
making (for further analysis) the following assumption:

> Our twelfth assumption is that the forms of social structure [really
> kinship structure] are not determined by kinship patterns [that is, other
> kinship patterns of a specific nature] or terminology, or influenced in any
> major degree by them, but are created by forces external to social organi-
> zation, especially by economic factors. It is assumed herewith, for example,
> that the available sources of food and the techniques of procuring it affect
> the sex division of labor and the relative statuses of the sexes, predisposing
> peoples to particular rules of residence, which can eventuate in the for-
> mation of extended families, clans, and sibs. (Murdock, 1949, p. 137.)

In modern differentiated society this direction of influence continues, but the relationship between kin systems and economic activities is rather different. First, it seems the nuclear family has developed in response to the requirement for mobility, geographically and
socially, in a society in which economic activities are dominant. It is
just not possible for extended families and lineages to move in toto
in response to varying occupational demands in various areas. Partially as a consequence of these demands, a kin group has resulted—
the nuclear family—which structures itself around one person engaged
in the economic complex. In addition to these structural consequences, the economic emphasis conditions the roles and emotional
patterns of the family (Parsons, 1954, pp. 89-103, 177-196).

It would appear that economic factors influence the family in
two additional ways. The work situation and its emotional climate
and social structure influence, to an important extent, the *personality* of the husband-father and the way in which he plays his roles
in the family. Furthermore, the evaluation of the worth of his occupational activity places him in a certain position in society with
regard to the economic and social power he enjoys and the esteem
or social approval he and his family receive. Variation in these social
dimensions opens and closes the door to a multitude of "life
chances," and requires a number of basic adjustive responses within
the nuclear family.

Thus, the family in modern society is structurally rather isolated
—especially from the occupational system. It is the father's direct
involvement in both the kin system and the status-generating eco-

nomic system that leads us to focus on the father's role as a link between the private life of the family and the public arena of achieved status.

Processes in the Family

Just as it is not feasible to discuss all of the social factors that influence the family, so it is also difficult to analyze adequately all that takes place in the family group in response to those factors. In this work we will touch on many things—peer-group activity, infidelity, the reproductive function, and crime and love as responses to status and manifestations of the different classes' subcultures. Our interest focuses on certain factors within the family, however—predominantly, the structure of authority, the sources of emotional support for the child, the process of socialization—and on their consequences for the child. We are also interested in the child's occupational choice and the class conditions influencing the development of his adult sexual role.

The common patterns of authority, of emotions in the family, and of techniques of socialization will also be analyzed as modes of adjustment to the strains or advantages of life in different statuses in society. These characteristic responses by families have characteristic consequences—different kinds of children, displaying special needs and personalities.

The Meaning of "Status"

The focus of this work is the relationship between status and family roles. As "status" is usually used in discussions of family behavior, it refers to wealth and prestige in the society-wide system of stratification. Our use is somewhat different. *First,* we use status to refer to the individual's (or any social unit's) rank as recipient in the differential distribution of several social resources. That is, how much does this unit get of the things wanted in the society or of those things which provide power to get the things desired? An individual or group holds not just one general status (as Warner might classically have felt); he holds different ranks, each rank in relation to different rewards (power, wealth, esteem, etc.). *Second,* the individual holds not just one general status in the broader society but a number of statuses, each in a different social system or group (in the work situation, in general society in its expressive activities, in general society in its political activities, in the gang, etc.).

These explicitly made distinctions in rank or status are used to investigate special associations between status and behavior (Chap. 7). The explicit recognition that a social unit can hold various statuses also leads us occasionally to look at the influence of the interaction among statuses (e.g., Lenski, 1954). Our approach will attempt to indicate the way in which certain patterns of statuses can lead to an emphasis on special activities as compensation for low achieved status. It is felt that there are various behavior systems or institutions (family, work, political activity, etc.) in which approval and rewards of different types can be won. In a society some activities—in industrial society probably occupational activities—are considered the most important. As a result of certain social realities, not every individual can achieve status in these activities. Given this situation, alienated groups introduce alternate standards of evaluation according to which achievements in other activities are regarded as equally valid or more valid measures of human worth, although the alienated may have some reservations about the alternate standards. The alternate standards may be rejected by those who are successful within the presently dominant value system (those who have vested interests); emotional commitments, social estrangements, and possibly conflict ensue. This may be one key to the emergence of subcultures and social change.

This discussion has a familiar ring: it suggests psychological and social-structural explanations of Marx's theory of social conflict and change—the theory that thesis in conflict with antithesis produces a new synthesis.

The Level of Personality

Social experiences, values, and norms become internalized in idiosyncratic ways for each person. The personality system is the level on which these experiences, values, and norms are internalized, and are fused with motivations residing in human physiology. We will review several concepts at this level that we find useful to our discussion. This is not a study of personalities in a sociocultural milieu, however, and we must again simplify greatly. We will choose those psychological concepts which are central to our analysis and most predictive of behavior within our theoretical scheme.

We will use personality concepts to explain how culture and the social position impinge on the personality system, mold certain motivations, and in turn feed back certain sentiments into both the social system and the culture. In this way we will attempt to show how new norms arise in deviant subcultures from these sentiments and how established subcultural norms are sustained. These norms concern behavior both inside and outside the family.

The Need for Approval (A Form of Status). There is an intimate and preverbal association in infancy between love and approval by others and the satisfaction of basic needs. We would maintain that this results in approval by others operating as a psychological need for all "normally" socialized individuals. Such a general statement must recognize the phenomena associated with the concept of reference group; that is, each of us picks and chooses what standards he will recognize, whom he will identify with, and whom he will try to please. Part of our discussion will attempt to explain this "choice."

In addition to this psychological need for approval originating in the early parent-child relationship, we see that society takes an active hand. It defines approval and social status as desirable ends in themselves. If approval and status were not desired states, social control and therefore society could not function. Approval results in various satisfactions, and disapproval results in dissatisfaction. Without this correlation, control over one's associates would be difficult and organized human behavior nearly impossible. It should also be recognized that certain rewards (money, power, possessions) are not only rewards in themselves but also symbolize human approval.

Responses to Few Rewards and Little Approval. A second basic position is that a blocking of satisfaction (a frustration) will most commonly result in some attempt to achieve satisfaction in some other way. If a person is "controlled" by others, then the alternative routes are limited by these other individuals. This restriction on alternate methods may result in attempts to gain satisfaction in a nonnormative manner in this area of behavior at the expense of other individuals and their needs (aggression and crime). This nonnormative (illegitimate) behavior will generally be directed toward individuals or expressed in situations where other individuals are least able to retaliate. (The individual whose satisfactions are blocked may, in a certain area, also respond by attempts to gain satisfaction in some alternative activity that is not illegitimate—only variant.)

Low status then results in a blocking of satisfaction in three ways: (1) it denies the individual a sense of worth and approval, (2) it denies him certain nonpsychic rewards (such as material wealth) and facilities that are consequences of approval by society, and (3) it means others have greater control over him, thus limiting his alternate routes to satisfaction.

High status is not pure advantage, however. It may introduce tension, isolation, and exposure to criticism; and the individual in lower status may enjoy a certain "freedom" from responsibility, as well as the dependent security often found in low status. Nevertheless, we will attempt to show that in the long run greater satisfaction is obtained at high status.

Deprivation and lack of power also result in other psychological responses which we feel are somewhat less common and less central to our theory. Anxiety, regression, and submission—responses that will be discussed in Chap. 4—help explain behavior in different strata of society.

A Definition of "Culture"

We are interested to an important extent in the effects of status on family behavior. Status is essentially a ranking, and the social rewards and facilities associated with the rank define and legitimize the status. To make our discussion meaningful, we must then make clear the norms (standards) by which people are judged to have succeeded or failed—are ranked and rewarded—in a society. Knowing the standard, we can begin to make predictions about behavior in various status levels. Can one standard be found in industrial America, or are there several basic standards? We will argue that there is in a society one dominant and unifying standard or set of values—its culture—by which individuals, roles, and groups are evaluated. In American society this ethos or evaluative guide seems to be a somewhat secularized Protestant ethic which focuses on a this-worldly solution to adaptive problems, on a postponement of gratification in the pursuit of this solution, and on a pursuit of an assurance of a sense of personal worth. The reader may ask, "Is there only one unifying standard?" and "Is a secularized Protestant ethic the dominant culture and evaluative standard in American society?" We will postpone a marshalling of evidence and discussion of the assumptions which would answer this question until later (Chap. 3).

A THEORETICAL PERSPECTIVE: PARSONS' SYSTEMS OF ACTION

Our attempt to relate two aspects of the social system (social status and family) and our propensity to rely also on cultural and psychological concepts require some theoretical view which will meaningfully relate the concepts involved to each other. Parsons' general theory of action seems most valuable for our purposes. To understand Parsons' approach some statement is required regarding his theory not only of society as a whole but also of human action as composed of various systems of action.

With regard to the position of Parsons in understanding a social phenomenon, Gouldner states:

Parsons' assumption is that it is impossible to understand adequately any single pattern except by referring it to some larger systemic whole. He therefore assumes that the *whole* system must be conceptually constituted prior to the investigation and analysis of specific patterns. In consequence, Parsons is led forthwith to the analysis of the *total* anatomy of social systems in an effort to identify their constituent elements and relationships. This presumably makes it possible to refer any given problematic pattern in a systematic manner to all the component structures constituting the system. (Gouldner, in Gross, ed., 1959, pp. 244-245.)

This general orientation of understanding the whole situation is carried one step further in the analysis of societal phenomena, which must, in turn, be placed and given meaning in some over-all "system of human action." To accomplish this, other systems of action are introduced: the cultural system, the personality system, and the neurobiological organism. These three levels of behavior, as well as the social system, are within the system of human action, for the basic concern of this theory is the development of a statement of how behavior is organized (sanctioned, i.e., rewarded and punished, or controlled) through symbols and communication. Thus certain physical and geographical forces are treated as givens or conditions that modify the systems of action but are not of focal concern.

The Cultural System

These systems form a hierarchy of symbolic control from the cultural system down to the organism.[1] Thus the cultural system, as we have said, is a highly abstract and over-all statement about truth, the good society, and beauty. Being so abstract and inclusive, the cultural system is the most enduring of the levels of normative organization, and it fosters integration of various subsystems; that is, it allows and takes into account certain subcultural modifications while exercising control over them. It exercises control over the other systems (through various agents of social control) by operating as

---

1. There is also some influence operating in the opposite direction. The sense organs communicate realities and stresses on the biophysical level. The symbolic standards (ideals or culture) of any system of human action can never be fully realized, for there are certain realities (demands from levels lower in the system of symbolic control) which qualify the ideals and make their complete achievement impossible.

a set of standards for individuals in their sanctioning of other individuals in the system, through their personal commitment to it, and through their efforts to specify desirable behavior in various situations in light of this over-all guide. (Culture and the control it exercises are discussed more fully in Chap. 3.)

The Social System

Certain statements of values which are part of the cultural system focus on social behavior (man's relationship to man), and thus certain cultural values are also social values. These values are made more concrete within the social system: there is further specification about what should be done at various social structural levels, from the more inclusive and public of these levels to the more limited and private. These social levels are (1) the societal level, (2) the institutional level, (3) the managerial level, and (4) the technical or primary level (Parsons, 1959, pp. 3–38).

For the technical or primary level "the crucial point is the involvement of individuals with one another in cooperative activities which involve physical presence, at least part of the time, and direct cooperation in physical manipulations of the environment, whether the manipulations be primarily 'technological' or 'symbolic' or 'communicative.' " Most social behavior in primitive societies takes place at this level.

Provided that the society is largely an ascriptive society—that is, that statuses, resources, and rewards are largely determined by kinship or tradition—it can function at this level. However, with complexity and differentiation of activity, and with mobility of individuals and "resources," a higher level of organization arises. This is the level of organization referred to by the terms "administration" and, in the language of much sociological analysis, "bureaucracy." At this level, as at all social levels, four basic functional problems arise; certain subsystems (possibly at the primary or quasi-managerial level) arise to meet those problems. Thus, cliques among factory workers or the personnel department in a large factory may develop to cope with certain problems (e.g., of an integrative or tension-management nature). Presently we will discuss these four functional problems.

A higher and still more inclusive level is the "institutional" level. The board of trustees of a university is an example of an organization on this level. In this situation the society and its values as well as those of the university are coordinated in an attempt to guide the course of the university in a way advantageous for the society as a whole and for education as an institution.

The fourth level is the "societal" level, and it is perhaps at this level that the polity characteristically comes into play in a complex society. In the more advanced societies basic values and *broad* social control are expressed and actualized through such terms and social behavior as "the American way of life," "democracy," and "communism." Such over-all values were previously expressed through the religious institution; they still are in less differentiated (sacred) societies.

Social norms, as we have tried to show, vary in their specificity: on the cultural level they are most general, on the primary level most specific. Not only is there this variation in regard to specificity, but there is also variation in regard to the focus of their functional concern: they try to deal with different functional problems. What are these functions within society or any social system (for these functions appear at each structural level)?[2] Parsons states:

Let me start with the proposition that all social systems are organized, in the sense that they are structurally differentiated, about two major axes. When these axes are dichotomized, they define four major "functional problems," with respect to which they differentiate. These four fundamental functional categories apply at all four levels of structural organization. . . . The first of the two major axes of differentiation is perhaps most generally characterized as that between the "external" and the "internal" references. The first set of functions tends to specialize with reference to the mediation of relations between the system and the situation external to it; the second, as seen in these terms, is concerned with the maintenance of the stability of pattern of the units and of the integrative adjustments of the units to one another. . . . The second axis of differentiation . . . is analogous to the differentiation between means and ends in terms of action as such. (Parsons, 1959, pp. 5-6.)

Though there are semantic and philosophical problems about means and ends (thus, sexual activity might be viewed as an end in itself or as a means for reproduction only), means (or "the instrumental") generally have to do with methods or patterns of action to achieve some goal, and ends (or "the consummatory") have to do with those actions which are gratifying or lead to more immediate gratification and consumption within a particular means-

2. It is of course difficult to define concepts such as function in any neat way which the writer can consistently and easily abide by in later discussion. However, we generally mean by "function" the basic needs of the society and its socially organized attempts to meet these needs.

end chain of behavior. If one views means and ends as qualitative dichotomies relating only to individual behavior this definition may seem rather strange. In Chap. 9 we deal with some of the difficulties involved in this qualitative and largely psychological use of "means" and "ends" in analyzing human behavior. We are inclined to consider means and ends, instrumental and consummatory, as matters of degree and as polar terms referring to a continuum of action. We try to clarify this also in Chap. 10.

When these axes bisect each other, four quadrants are delimited and four basic functional problems of a system, which are the focus of specialized activity, are defined:

Quadrants	Functional Problem
External-instrumental	The problem of making realistic adjustments to the demands of the external environment or situation with regard to the means required to achieve certain goals and to maintain the system (the adaptive problem).
External-consummatory	The problem of deciding upon basic overall goals and of controlling and organizing the system's units in pursuit and consumption of the social goal (the goal attainment problem).[3]
Internal-instrumental	The problem of developing and maintaining certain controlling norms and handling certain problems of personal motivation in order that the system may continue to operate effectively (the pattern maintenance and tension management problem).
Internal-consummatory	The problem of social integration and of developing emotional solidarity through expressive interaction and feeling of common goals (the integrative problem).

These various structural levels of society and functional problems in society (or any social system) must "communicate" with each other in some way. Certain mechanisms (symbols and attitudes),

3. This definition is gleaned from several sources and it perhaps illustrates the ambiguity of some concepts in the theory of action as proposed by Parsons and others. The goal attainment function is certainly consummatory in nature and yet in many ways "controlling and organizing the system's units in pursuit . . . of the social goal" has a very instrumental tone. Perhaps these opposing qualities result from the attempts of action theorists to make this analytical definition too close to the nature of actual political behavior. Or this supposed contradiction may be resolved when we recognize that each functional division at a societal level has within it processes at a more specialized subsystem level characteristic of the other three functional activities.

such as money, power, and emotional commitment, act as communicating ties. Through these mechanisms (in an abstract sense very much as in economic theory) pass certain "resources" and "products"; that is, each unit is tied to the others by consuming their output and in turn producing some desired product (the socialized child, tires, votes) for some other subsystem or level.

The Personality System

Symbolic statements and other experiences are internalized and operate to control or guide the individual. That is, general cultural values, norms, and social objects (the organization of experiences associated with an individual) are introjected and form the socialized aspect of the personality. When these are combined with motivations derived from a neurobiological level, they produce the actual behavior of the individual. Thus, to understand an important part of the structure and functioning of the personality one must understand the structure of the cultural and social processes the individual has internalized. Nevertheless, the personality is itself a system and must be analyzed as a system attempting to maintain itself in equilibrium through selection and organization of these external influences.

The Problem in the Light
of Parsons' Approach

In summary, let us see if we can state our problem in the light of Parsons' method of analysis, for it seems the most complete for our purposes, and it greatly influences our orientation. It provides a conceptual ordering and structure (almost a typology) of factors which interact with the parent-child relations in the family and which at least should be kept in mind and if possible should be dealt with. It enables the analyst to see family behavior as predominantly a part of a subsystem of action with a particular focus, "solving" for the social system certain problems which originate in the biological and psychological nature of man. (We will not usually outline our ideas specifically in terms of its concepts, however, for we are not always certain what some terms and dimensions, e.g., consummatory, mean.)

Given the fact that American society is guided by some cultural system that is used to evaluate and reward units (individuals, occupational roles, ethnic groups, etc.), what are the consequences of placement in differently evaluated positions within primarily the adaptive subsystem (the system of activities that is organized largely in occupational roles)? We will maintain that the norms or values of this subsystem are the predominant values in American society. Our question is, "What are the consequences of this placement for the way in which parents, particularly the father, carry out certain functions (especially socialization) in the family?" Since many of the parents' functions are in the nature of socialization through a manipulation of sanctions, is the parents' access to sanctions of various kinds (resources) influenced by their status and does it in turn influence the resulting product returned to society, the socialized child? This may be a clarifying way of looking at this question, and it is certainly an interesting way to do so.

A FINAL STATEMENT

This is not simply a report of a research project, though the author's research and empirical conclusions are frequently relied upon and are first reported here. It is primarily a theoretical and practical statement, about a certain area of human behavior, that attempts closure or temporary resolution. This closure sometimes requires our referring to the data of others; at other times we freely (but, it is hoped, intelligently) reinterpret the data of others; and at still other times our interpretations are supported by ordinary (but critically analyzed) observation. In regard to this last, the reader is asked to exercise charitable forbearance.

CHAPTER 2

Family Behavior and Social Status

A comprehensive review of the social influences on family behavior should not limit its scope to a discussion of the influences of status only. However, if any treatment is to be thorough, some limits must be established, and for this reason we will focus on social status. We would like to study other variables, such as those which reveal themselves cross-culturally (Murdock, 1949), technology and the economic system (Linton and Kardiner, 1947), values and positions of particular ethnic groups (Frazier, 1939), and special kinship structures (Malinowski, 1927). Consideration of these variables would be necessary in making an over-all and systematic presentation of the interaction of the kinship system and other functionally specialized institutions or subsystems of the society. The literature reviewed and the ideas proposed here, however, constitute an attempt to give a picture of behavior in different spheres of family activity in the various classes of society.

This broad but brief chapter is intended merely to orient the reader; many of the ideas discussed here will be examined in greater detail later. The factors discussed here are those that our later theory must take into account and in part explain. Here we will discuss certain important functions of the family—certain important things that the family does for society and for its members as individuals. We will then discuss the way in which the family operates and is structured to carry out those functions in different social classes.

Perhaps no mode of study is so helpful as the comparative one. It gives us perspective on *our own* way of living and looking at things, to which we are especially strongly committed in such an intimate and anxiously emotional sphere of life as the family. It offers an approach where study through controlled research is difficult or impossible. Presenting the strikingly different ways in which people go about their lives, it allows the observer to study these exotic variations and to reach a common-sense understanding of them.

IMPORTANT FUNCTIONS OF THE FAMILY
IN DIFFERENTIATED SOCIETIES

In our introductory discussion of the family in simple and complex societies, we focused on that activity (the economic) that we consider the independent or causal variable. We stressed how our problem arises as it does only in a highly differentiated and industrially oriented society. To highlight this we showed the contrast in the family's relationship to economic activity in these two types of societies. Despite the sharp differentiation between family and work in the United States, the family does continue to operate as an economic unit through household tasks and consumption.[1]

Several functions, however, continue to be carried out by the family in much the same way in differentiated societies as they were in simple societies. These functions are the personality-maintenance function, the status-conferring function, and the socializing function. Let us look at these to give our treatment of the family some conceptual setting.

Personality-maintenance Function

The family remains the dominant social situation in which an individual can be himself. Within the family he can regress (move back to less formal and less rationally controlled behavior): he can love with greater freedom and express hostility with less fear of crushing consequences, and it might even be said that the family is a social situation in which he can hate more freely.

In this emotionally charged situation, with its ascriptive (in a general sense, inherited) and stable base, he experiences a certain security, and escapes from the rational, transient, and impersonal modes that characterize many relationships in general society. These

1. Certain political functions influence the structure and behavior within kin groups. The need to institutionalize power, to control and coordinate activity, and to secure some sovereignty over a land area have a direct influence on the kinship structure in primitive societies. This influence is very indirect in modern society, however. The family does continue to have "political" problems of its own, though no institutionalized political activities are carried out from a kinship base. (In America even traditionally political families such as the Tafts, Roosevelts, or their lowly parallels in Middletowns—must, despite the behind-the-scenes activities that result from their ascribed positions of political influence, maintain those positions by means of acquired political skill or by obtaining votes.)

modes are particularly pervasive in urban society. Work activities are almost never carried out in kin or family groups, with their highly personal nature. Even the kinship group is limited in scope, for it is the dominant ideal in American society that new nuclear families establish their residences separately from the natal families of both spouses. Also, in the urban industrial society the community setting of the family is often completely changed; that is, the family may move and become relatively isolated from past emotionally meaningful associations.[2]

This function of providing an emotional haven, however, is also carried out by the family in primitive societies to an important degree: the individual in any society is continually being pried loose from emotionally meaningful social situations of his earlier life, he can never completely escape from the need to recapture the gratifications of those past situations, and the family fulfills this need.

The marital family presents one group in which these regressive tugs may be responded to and expressed in accepted and adult ways. For the adult, the spouse is not only a purely sexual object, but also an emotional-erotic object through which he both gratifies regressive needs and achieves mature fulfillment of his sexual role.

Parents and siblings may offer the child an ascriptive emotional haven—one in which he is valued because he is who he is. Relative to the outside world, there is less focus on his performance.

The child also functions in the maintenance of the adult personality, by providing suitable situations in which the parent may vicariously relive certain childhood experiences. The child may be a suitable companion in childish activity—play and talk—that is explained as amusing the child. Progeny also serve to validate the parent's sexuality and adult status. The child is also a suitable *alter* toward whom the adult can play the parental role—and the parental role is one whose authority and responsibility is enhancing in the eyes of the individual and of society. Finally, the child, like the spouse, is an individual the parent can love—sometimes emotionally, sometimes quasi-erotically—or hate; tensions and hostilities are released in interaction and in the process of socialization of the child.

---

2. Elizabeth Bott, in the study we will review, shows what occurs in the nuclear family that moves to a new community. The conditions described in that study perhaps help to explain certain modern phenomena: the attempts to capture emotional intimacy in rather fluid situations through sexual attraction (dating, going steady) and through earlier marriages; the decreasing percentage of unmarried; and, above all, the "togetherness" theme of the contemporary American family.

The Status-conferring Function

The family locates people within society. Though this placement is generally termed the "status-conferring function," perhaps it would be better to use the term "position-conferring function": individuals are located by the family not just in terms of class-ranking (our "status"), but also in terms of ethnic group, region, community, and even more limited social categories. One is born the *son* of a *lawyer,* the daughter of the *town drunk,* the son of a *white* migrant laborer.

This is a largely unnoticed but very important function (and without it the problem of interest to us would largely evaporate), for it provides a stability and predictability to our own lives and to society as a whole. One can imagine the emotional and organizational turmoil if each morning or month or year individuals moved or were shuffled about to meet some rational criteria of the best possible arrangement of individuals in familial or primary groups. If our interest were divorce or desertion, we might ask what social and psychological pressures operating on individuals lead them to dissolve these ascriptive ties. Instead, our problem will be to understand by what behavioral means varying social and psychological pressures are adjusted to within the ascriptive bond of the family— for it is this ascriptive bond that is the heart of its placement function.

The Socializing Function

The family, above all, creates socialized personalities—it socializes both child and adult. The human personality is a consequence of both biology and social experiences. The family is that group which seems, in terms of present social organization, best suited for pressuring the child—sometimes patiently, sometimes forcefully—to meet those standards of behavior and sentiments that are considered appropriate for the full human being occupying a certain age position. Emotional dependence and involvement are required to bring about this development, and if the child, through the intense relationships of infancy and childhood, did not come to need the approval and love of his parents and socializers in general, then the problem of socialization would be greatly magnified. This touches the core of our interest.

Finally, the adult does not arrive in the marital relationship as a complete product or personality that then acts out certain motivations if properly maintained. In family situations adults also continue to learn through practice how to be husbands, wives, daughters-in-law, fathers, mothers. Experience does not merely tell them what they should and should not do in various circumstances; it probably reconditions their motivations so that their sentiments become more consistent with the social roles they are required to play. Such changes come about through the expressions of expectations on the part of relatives, in-laws, neighbors, spouses, and children. Adults are also socialized in the family.

The fulfillment of these functions interacts with and influences the fulfillment of other functions. Thus the reproductive function is not simply a biological process but one conditioned by status and its attendant problems of maintaining the personality.

CLASSES AND THEIR VALUES IN AMERICAN SOCIETY

Before we attempt to discuss in very great detail the influence of status on these functions and (later in this chapter) the influence of status on various patterns within the family in different classes, we will present a rather broad discussion of the general class structure in America. We recognize that the decision about the number, boundaries, and characteristics of American classes is somewhat arbitrary. The scheme chosen (see Table 1), seems the most useful

Table 1
Social Classes in Urban America[a]

Class Name	Approximate Per Cent of Population	Typical Occupational Roles	Typical (Kahl, 1957)[a] Values
Upper class	1-2	Ambassador, major executives	"Graceful[b] living"
Upper middle class	10	Minor executive, high school teacher	"Career"
Lower middle class	22	Bookkeeper, photographer, clerk	"Respectability"
Working class	46	Electrician, bus driver	"Security" and "getting by"
Lower class	20	Longshoreman, laborer, the erratically employed and chronically unemployed	"Getting kicks"

a. Much of our discussion of values in this chapter depends on Kahl's careful statement (1957, pp. 184-220).

b. This is probably truer of the upper levels of this class. The lower levels of this stratum are probably quite career-oriented also.

for the purposes of the discussion in this chapter, for it focuses on urban American society. It divides society into five classes (which are very rough equivalents of the five classes of Hollingshead's system, which we later use), and certain typical values and distinctions allocated to these classes by Kahl are similar to the kinds of distinctions that we wish to discuss and explain.

Table 1 shows the percentage of the population, typical occupations and typical values (modes of life) that seem dominant in the various classes in urban American society. This table is presented to give the reader a framework within which to place the ideas that follow in this work. We do not always use these same five class levels in later sections, for other studies and their terminologies must be introduced.

"Graceful living" is a phrase that seems to capture the basic theme that prevails in many activities considered characteristic of the upper classes. The upper-class individual lives life in its broadest scope, but with a grace and taste that communicate to others that he is in control of the situation and of himself. The development of these capacities and the prevalence of social situations where they may be realized are probably possible only in the more favored levels of society. There the emotional climate (a sense of security and confidence as a consequence of deference received) and material resources allow the individuals of this class to act with such poised control.

Skills in consumption (tasteful dress, knowledge of secluded vacation places, etc.) and skills in public service (patronage of the arts, leadership in civic and charity groups, etc.) replace skills in specifically occupational areas. Skilled consumption and generous public service—traditions developed by and inherited from the nobilities and aristocracies of Western society—are appropriate activities and symbols of elite status in modern American society. In contemporary society, however, this style can frequently be developed only after the sacrifices of some "career-oriented" (see below) forebear have provided the individual with the necessary resources and social advantages.

The "career" orientation is probably dominant in the next stratum of society, the upper middle class. Success, specifically occupational success, becomes a kind of compulsive drive for the members of this class. It is a compulsive drive that is equally puzzling to the "libidinal" slum dweller and the aristocratic individual.

Two important things may be said about the upper middle class, with its career or success orientation. First, here more than in any other class the personal philosophies and commitments of the various actors result in a fusion of work and family or private life. The home becomes a kind of second office, where colleagues and business associates are entertained and business decisions are made, implicitly or explicitly. To some extent, the wife becomes a social and emotional assistant in the trials experienced by the husband in the work world. Second, the career orientation is probably the dominant set of values in American and industrial society; that is, this orientation and its values are sufficiently strong in complex societies to bring persons on the lower levels and on the elite level to question their own casual attitudes toward work. We shall discuss the dominance of these values at length in Chap. 3, attempting to give it added meaning and to substantiate this latter point.

The philosophy of "respectability" probably typifies the lower middle class; that is, the concern of the members of this class is not with "productivity," which is the concern of the members of the class just above, but rather with traditional morality. In the eyes of the upper strata, the members of this class are fearful and unimaginative conformists; in the eyes of the lower strata, the "get nowhere and get no fun out of life either." In certain respects this may be true, but their conformity, their morality, and their responsibility in work give them a status and respectability much greater than have people on lower levels. They may as adults also enjoy greater freedom from the striving occupational demands on members of the upper middle class.

This emphasis on morality infuses life in the lower-middle-class family. It creates certain attitudes toward play, sex, and duties at school and work. It is probably a necessary precursor to an emphasis on "productivity"; that is, a puritanical emphasis on respectability and morality by the adult generation places a block on libidinal expression by the child, who, as a result, seriously attends to his school work and is relatively isolated from affectionate and holding peers. Using Freudian dynamics, the child sublimates and is perhaps on the way to becoming a productive and upwardly mobile member of the class above. In this way, lower-middle-class parents may live out their inhibited desires for active achievement through their children: "Do well and your folks will be proud of you."

The struggles to "get by" at a reasonable level of living and to obtain some security characteristically occupy the life of the member of the working class—the skilled and regularly occupied blue-collar worker. The occupational barrier or gulf between blue- and white-collar skills and manners makes mobility dreams and "career" orientations somewhat unrealistic for the member of this class. The worker's goals and interests develop in response to the realities of the situation, and the husband-father and the family focus on such matters as paying off debts regularly, keeping out of difficulty with various forms of social authority, and planning in terms of a regular pay check each week or so. This philosophy of life makes possible certain luxuries or activities such as redecoration, occasional trips, a second television set, or another child. These everyday concerns influence the philosophies passed on to children and the manner in which the family attempts to instill these philosophies.

If one is at the bottom of the heap (in the lower class)—if he is defined by self, family, and, most importantly, by society as immoral, unintelligent, irresponsible, and unproductive—certain attitudes toward work, morals, and social authority are likely to develop. And if it appears that the place in society of one's friends, family, and self will remain much as it is at present, certain psychological modes of adjustment emerge on the individual level and certain norms arise on the social group level. With time they become inherited and working traditions in certain social groups and control the individual to a degree, whatever *personal* experience and inclination may be. One becomes apathetic to those areas of life (voting, work, respectability, and sexual morality) that are considered the serious business of life for other social strata. If certain areas of life lose their emotional salience, others gain. One lives considerably more for the present, the physical, the emotional—life is lived to get kicks. Drinking, dancing, exciting movies, sexual adventures, physical conflict, horseplay, sports, and gossip about scandals and love affairs all weave a kind of riotously rich and disorganized tapestry out of the demands of the situation and the "libido."

This picture can be exaggerated, as it often is by members of the higher levels of society to secure their own moral respectability and justify their exploitative (emotional and economic) relationships with members of this class. There is a great deal of organized and responsible behavior on the part of the lowest stratum.

In addition, the conditions that produce a predisposition to apathy in regard to the "serious" realms of an industrial society may be so overwhelming that dancing, lovemaking, and conflict are also paled by apathy. For example, if one has been imprisoned twice, perhaps once unjustly, for assault with a deadly weapon, then one may turn to the apathetic security of television and its violence as a better and safer substitute.

THE QUALITY AND BREADTH OF KIN
TIES IN DIFFERENT CLASSES

The previous section has focused on the characteristic occupations and philosophies of life of the different strata in industrial

America. We will now present the traditional findings and views on the relationship between family behavior and social status; our own theoretical statement, to be presented later, must not be in conflict with these findings and views, and it should also provide a new understanding of and perspective on them.

This shift in interest requires a shift in terminology. If our discussion is to be succinct, we should deal only with the three classes or ranges of status (the upper class, the upper middle class, and the lower class), for they reveal most clearly the kinship differences about which we want to talk. These are the differences between patterns inherited more from the past (the upper- and lower-class family) and those patterns which are considered modern, progressive, and suitable for successful living in an industrial society (the mobile upper middle class).

The general ideal in American society is a nuclear family (the parents and their children only) living alone in their own residence. Ideally, the family should be complete, and it is preferable that no additional individuals, such as roomers or relatives, should reside in the home. This is quite in contrast with other societies, where a father or another member may divide his time between one residence and several others (Gough, 1960) or where additional relatives, though they may cause added problems, are on the whole considered economic and emotional assets and warmly welcomed (as in the traditional Chinese family). Nevertheless, it is considered desirable that ties with closer relatives be maintained through visiting, favors, and letters (Reiss, 1960). These standards are conformed to in varying degrees by the different classes. We feel that this variation can be tied to the life situations and the traditions inherited and maintained in the diverse strata.

The general picture regarding the strength of these family ties is presented in a number of sources (Warner and Lunt, 1941; Davis, Gardner, and Gardner, 1941; Bott, 1957; Hollingshead and Redlich, 1958, esp. pp. 69-134). This picture indicates that the kinship ties, obligations, and interests are somewhat more extended in the classes at the two extremes than they are in the middle.

The Upper-class Kinship Pattern

The upper-class individual finds in his inherited status and name both a source of power and an agent of control over his behavior: his membership in the family group is a definite asset in his relations outside the family, but each member of the kinship group guardedly controls other members in their leisure activities, occupations, and choice of marriage partners so that this asset will not be reduced in value by status-lowering activities.

There is especially great concern with the sexual and emotional relationships between upper-class males and girls of somewhat lower status. That this is a special problem might be true for a number of reasons. The girl may be more appealing than girls of his own class because she makes fewer demands for accomplishment and can operate as a stronger regressive focus. She also may exchange her special beauty, charm, and physical appeal for her lover's higher social position, or her charm may be a consequence of an almost conscious decision to be as pleasing as possible. By contrast, the high-status girl is less impressed by her male equal, presents herself as less flexible to his emotional needs, and is thus less appealing, on an emotional and quasi-erotic level at least.

In upper-class families, common economic endeavors (family trust funds, family businesses, land and property held jointly) result in an intertwining of interests and controls that give pragmatic nourishment to the emotional ties that already exist. The matter of who will eventually inherit what leads to control over younger generations (relatively speaking) by the older generations who still retain economic power. The upper class appears to exercise stronger authority over children (especially into adulthood) because compliance brings both emotional and material rewards. By contrast, the lower classes may have less to offer both emotionally (their approval may be less important due to their lower status) and materially. Though the control may appear more severe, it is perhaps this factor that makes it actually less effective and more burdensome for the adult child to accept.

Table 2
Relative Economic Contribution of Spouses at Different Social Class Levels (New Haven, 1950)

Social Class Level	Median Class Income with Employment of Husband Only (in Dollars)	Median Income with Two Spouses Employed (in Dollars)	Per Cent Increase in Total Income When Wife Works	Per Cent Wives Working
I[a]	10,000	15,000	50	8
II	6,500	10,000	53	18
III	4,930	7,540	53	28
IV	3,810	5,763	52	37
V	2,660	4,350	64	48

a. It is felt that the figures for Class I and perhaps those for Class II are greatly influenced by Yale University faculty and staff's creating rather large proportions of relatively low-paid Class I men and relatively more competent and highly paid wives than would be true of the typical Class I.

Source: Compiled from various sections of A. Hollingshead and F. Redlich, *Social Class and Mental Illness* (New York: John Wiley and Sons, Inc., 1958).

Table 3

Data Relevant to Socialization Function and Its Distribution by Social Class*

General Class Level	Per Cent Mothers Who Work[a]	Number of Children per Family[a]	Per Cent Mothers Rated High on Warmth to Child[b]	Per Cent Mothers Showing Some Rejection of Child[b]	Per Cent Fathers Rated High on Warmth to Child[b]	Average "Power" Score of Father[c]	Per Cent Families with Marked Paternal Authority (Germany)[d]	Per Cent Families with Marked Maternal Authority (Germany)[d]
Upper	4	1.7	51	24	60	45	53	0
Upper middle class							30	16
Middle	10	3.4				36	25	10
Working	18	4.0	37	40	56	28	14	33
Lower	41	4.7 (est.)					25	29

*The reader should be aware of the fact that the strata of society referred to by such terms as "middle (class)" is only roughly comparable from study to study. For the precise range of status that is covered by each figure, the original study should be consulted. We are interested here in noticing several trends.

a. A. Hollingshead and F. Redlich, *Social Class and Mental Illness* (New York: John Wiley and Sons, Inc., 1958).

b. R. Sears, E. Maccoby, and H. Levin, *Patterns of Child Rearing* (New York: Harper & Row, Publishers, 1957), p. 426.

c. Fred L. Strodtbeck, "Family Interaction, Values, and Achievement," in *Talent and Society* (Princeton: D. Van Nostrand Co., Inc., 1958), pp. 135-194. A high score denotes high power over mother and son.

d. René König, "Family and Authority: The German Father in 1955," *The Sociological Review*, July, 1957, pp. 107-127.

There may also be a stronger patriarchal pattern in the upper classes, because the higher-strata father is generally more adequate as a person (at least as society evaluates him) and contributes successfully to the family income and prestige without his wife's working. Our interpretation of this relationship between power and economic competence is supported by a study of Tables 2 and 3. We see the father exercising greater power in those classes where his contribution is high in an absolute sense and high relative to his wife's and where the likelihood of the wife's working is low.

The Lower-class Kinship Pattern

Perhaps because of lack of interest, perhaps because of incapacity, families in the lower class are much less likely than are those in the higher social strata to entertain in the home or socially interact as a unit with nonkin. It appears from a number of extensive observations that the kinship system, operating through matrilineal ties, acts as a system of economic and emotional security (Frazier, 1939, and Bott, 1957). It operates through the mother rather than through the father, because she seems to be more kin-oriented and more responsible for her children's and kin's welfare, and is (as shown in Tables 2 and 3) often an important economic provider. Matriarchy becomes even more pronounced among Negroes. Traditions inherited from the period of slavery, the limited power of the Negro male in society, and even the greater discrimination in hiring and discharging Negro men than Negro women, all contribute to matriarchy among Negroes. Elizabeth Bott's study also shows that it is not simply social class tradition and values that influence the extent to which kin are *emotionally recognized* (considered emotionally significant to the person) but rather a number of interacting factors (often associated with social class) and the extent of kin networks possible. Bott lists these social factors as follows:

1. Economic ties among kin
2. Residence and physical accessibility of kin
3. Frequency and intensity of contact of the relatives among themselves
4. Attitudes towards connecting relatives (e.g., the attitude towards an aunt creates or prevents contacts with her children)
5. Perceived similarities and differences in social status among relatives (Bott, 1957, p. 122)

Though Bott tends to minimize the association with social class, there does seem to be a characteristic pattern appearing in her report of the lower strata: the pattern of closer kin ties.[3] The relatives act as an economic cushion when unemployment, health problems, or untimely death occur, and they do occur at this level more frequently.

The higher rates of death, desertion, and divorce in the families of the lower class and the closer mingling of kin are reflected in the figures in Table 4, which show the resulting structure of residential groupings. (See also Table 27 in Chap. 6.)

Table 4
Per Cent Distribution of Family Types in the Lower Class
(New Haven, 1950)

	Per Cent
Nuclear (parents and children)	44
Stem (3 or 4 generations)	23
Broken nuclear (1 parent only)	18
Married couples (no children), widows, and widowers	11
Mixed (common-law, in-laws, etc.)	4

Source: A. Hollingshead and F. Redlich, *Social Class and Mental Illness* (New York: John Wiley & Sons, Inc., 1958), p. 124.

The Upper-middle-class Kinship Pattern

In contrast to the lower class, the upper middle class seems ideally responsive in structure to the demands of an occupation- and achievement-oriented society. A study by Hollingshead and Redlich (1958, pp. 91-92 and 101-102) shows that approximately 90 to 95 per cent of the families were complete nuclear families in this class in New Haven. Also, we observe (Table 3) the middle-class father midway between the upper-class father and the lower-class father in the degree of authority exercised.

Table 3 also shows that, in general, parents of higher status are warmer toward their children. The possible reason for this in terms of social class and its consequences for the family and for the child will be dealt with later.

3. This pattern may become weaker at the lower levels as all classes in the American population become more geographically mobile. However, even when there is lower class mobility, there seems to be greater movement in kin units. It is, after all, probably easier to find four suitable jobs of a semiskilled nature for four brothers in a new community than for four brothers with highly placed and specialized occupations.

THE RELATIONSHIP BETWEEN SUBCULTURAL
VALUES AND SOCIAL CLASS

In this chapter we have described values characteristic of the various classes and, briefly, patterns of family life. The next question comes easily. What causes these particular values and patterns to exist at the various levels? They are not just "naturally" the characteristic values of their respective classes. Rather, their origin and maintenance should be explained. It appears to this writer that the various subcultures emerge and become common in a particular level of society, and develop into special configurations, because of three conditions. First, the *preexisting subculture* and special circumstances of a given social class incline the individuals in that class to act in characteristic ways by operating as definitions of expected behavior in the socialization process and in adulthood. Second, the various *social classes recruit individuals* who already behave in ways typical of that class. And third, individuals in a particular society are ranked and rewarded according to *certain cultural standards and not others;* thus, varying subcultural configurations or orderings of strata are created as the criteria change from society to society and as individuals and groups adjust to their status in a particular value system. It is the cultural standards of American society which will occupy us in the next chapter.

CHAPTER 3

The Ethos of Industrial America

Christian, wouldst thou in grace excel?
Wouldst thou enlarge thy store?
Use what thou hast with liberal zeal,
and God will give thee more.

Let not they sacred talents lie
concealed beneath the ground.
But bless they fellow Christian by
the Treasures thou hast found.
—ELIZA ELLIS, 1831
Framed sampler, Homestead Hotel, Evanston, Ill.

THE DOMINANT CULTURE AND ITS HISTORICAL ROOTS

Our position is that the ranking of people in society by a certain set of standards and the resulting differences in how they are rewarded both have a significant influence on how the individuals of the different classes act. What is the dominant cultural standard in America, an industrial society, by which individuals are judged and rewarded? In the present chapter we shall try to answer this and to discuss briefly some of its history. This is something of a detour but a necessary one. It will give us added understanding concerning who is at the top and why—and why others are in the lower strata of society. It will also allow us to predict the particular pattern of responses characteristic of a class, given the cultural standards or ethos of the society.

The Basic Theme

Our view is that the basic theme of the American cultural system is control of the social and physical environment and the manifes-

29

tation of this mastery in high productivity. This includes not simply maximizaton of production of material goods but of personal services, skills, and satisfactions. Traditions, specific moral norms, ascribed roles, and traditional allocations of rewards are all sacrificed in the interest of rational and efficient production in great quantity of a large number of resources. For American society the word "freedom" conveys this rational pursuit of a large number of relatively unspecified goals. According to this ethos, "freedom" also implies that there are few institutionalized restrictions on *who* may pursue these goals and on what *means* they may use to pursue them.

It might be protested that if individuals can pursue so many different values in so many different rational ways there is no general theme. It appears to this analyst, however, that the pluralism is itself a general principle. That is, the fact that there are relatively few limitations on who can pursue what and on the means of pursuit, except for the expectation that the pursuit be efficient and directed toward the goal of maximizing the amount of resources available to the society, is itself an ethos. Our morality "forces" us to be free.

This position should not be given an extreme interpretation. Thus, Durkheim's discussion (1933) of the ethical basis within which business contracts must be developed has significance here: it is recognized that there are very binding moral conditions within which this rational activity must be conducted. Relative to other societies, however, the conditions are fewer in number and less specifically outlined.

In achievement-oriented (that is, oriented toward bringing about increasingly efficient mastery over the physical and social environment) American society, this ethos seems to derive from Protestantism. This is Protestantism not as Americans now think of it but as it was proposed by early European spokesmen for that religious movement. Let us discuss its historical roots and its relationship to capitalism and the American cultural system in the twentieth century.

Pre-Reformation Elements

In our understanding of the central importance of Protestantism in Western industrial society, we are greatly indebted to Weber (1930). His analysis of the relationship between capitalism and Protestantism reveals that Protestantism was not simply a parochial religious protest but actually a culmination of several broad cultural trends or threads in Western thought.

There are important elements of Greek philosophy and values in Christianity in general, and these seem to have been emphasized in Protestantism. The emphasis in Greek thought on rationality in science and theology and the focus on rational mastery of oneself and the environment were brought over into Protestantism.

Such themes as the imperatives to go beyond passive obedience to God's will, to actively work to change this world, and to bring about the Kingdom of God on earth are Protestant manifestations of this approach to life (Bellah, 1959, and Weber, 1930).

Greek philosophical thought, especially Platonic philosophy, fostered a view which sharply separated the domains of the spirit and of the flesh. Not only was there this rather sharp dichotomy, but the view was that the latter as a realm of being and as a realm of human activity and interest was much more base. In Christianity and especially ascetic Protestantism this developed into a view that the pleasures of the flesh were evil and the instrument of the devil.[1] Pleasure was therefore to be replaced by work and the accomplishment of God's will. This suggests the concept of sublimation and Freud's forceful insight that civilized achievement is gained at the expense of "eros" or libidinal pleasure. Though Freud's insight probably has universal application, it is perhaps much truer in Western society and much less true in those societies where civilized activity consists of inherited traditions and a refinement of libidinal pleasure itself.

Judaism is also an inextricable part of Protestantism. The Judaic focus on one supreme God who is personally aware of one's deeds and misdeeds contributes to the modern emphases on devotion to higher callings and on responsible self-control in daily activities. Not merely aware, the Judaic God punishes and rewards, not according to chance or personal impulse, but according to one's actions and devotion to God's commands. God, much like the rational market system, is just.[2]

1. It is interesting to see how such broad and abstract themes of life get translated into moral standards of parental action. Thus Miller and Swanson (1958), in a review of American child-rearing literature, found that fairly severe sanctions and restraints were recommended to parents to prevent genital fondling by their young children in the eighteenth and nineteenth centuries. By the middle of the twentieth century, however, some change had occurred, and mothers were advised to distract the child with a toy or some activity whenever such behavior was observed. Generally, this would be interpreted as more permissive (and more likely to lead to development of a healthier attitude toward body pleasure). This writer, however, wonders if such antiseptic parental behavior is really wise, since it may almost define out of psychic existence the realms of body pleasure and psychosexuality for the child. One wonders, then, if the same puritanical attitudes and themes are not still at work in modern disguise.

2. This interpretation of God seems also to structure our psychiatrically influ-

Though Protestantism was a rejection of many aspects of Catholicism, it was still basically Christian, and thus, it derived many of its principles from early Christianity. Perhaps most relevant for our interest here was the emphasis on the equality and fate of each individual soul. This posture both in early Christianity and in Greek thought probably paved the way for individualism in later developments of Western society. It is this individualistic interpretation of life and afterlife that makes it possible for the person "freely" to choose his own goals and his own means of achieving these goals.[3] This approach seems characteristic of American society, and is alien to an ascriptive, traditional, and unchanging approach to the choice of means and goals. It is an approach which allows the individual to act to an important degree in his own interest. But in so doing, ideally he brings about changes in society which maximize the resources made available to society.

The contribution of classical Rome to the development of rational society and Protestantism was its system of secular laws. It emphasized that the state was composed, to an important extent, of free and unincorporated individuals. As citizens they were equally subject to a universally applicable set of laws. This relatively greater standardization of expectations and sanctions, which Western society has inherited, makes possible the development of innovating and contractual agreements or exchanges between any two individuals or units in the social body. Ideally, no special rules impede maximum freedom in the development of rational agreements which will maximize production and mastery of the environment.

As an outgrowth of this view, and probably not only for humanitarian reasons but also in the interests of efficiency, American society, especially its more liberal elements, judges some types of discrimination in public and economic activities to be reprehensible. Racial discrimination does, after all, introduce "irrational" elements

---

enced definition of the good parent. Even in such intimate spheres of life as parenthood, personal desire should be replaced by rationality and justice. Kohn (1959) finds that middle-class American parents do punish in a manner parallel to this conception of God. Working-class parents punish like gods dominated by personal impulse.

3. It is this individualistic ethos in American society that has probably impeded the development of theories of social systems. In contrast, the psychology of the individual has considerable popular support, and even sociology tends to have an individualistic bent. It should be pointed out that Protestantism, especially in its early Calvinistic form, does not unqualifiedly accept the idea of freedom for the individual soul. Rather, the individual soul has a predestined and unchangeable fate. In Chap. 8 we discuss predestination as an ascriptive state which might have led to motivations for achieved success among certain Protestant groups.

into what would otherwise be rational and efficient contractual arrangements between individuals of whatever color.

Thus the cultural heritage of European society provided values similar to American views, and it provided several crucial elements in the development of a near-Protestant ethic: the concept of a supreme God who was personally aware of one's devotion to His laws and who rewarded justly; an emphasis on rational thought as a tool in an active effort to understand and thus control oneself and the environment; an attitude of respect toward universal legal rules before which all were equally judged ("government by law"); and the interpretation that individuals' essential beings are equal in ways independent of their position in the corporate state.

Calvinist Elements

Given these conditions, what special position did Protestantism offer, and how does it relate in its secular form to modern American values? Weber (1930) and many sociological analysts of the values of modern industrial society view Calvin's statement of Protestantism as the most crucial one in the origin of capitalism and the development of a rationalistic approach to everyday activities. Much of the core of Calvinistic Protestantism was not truly new to Christian theology. Rather, it was the stress on certain views and the motivational implications of their unique combination by Calvinists that gave it force. These views are clearly stated in this quotation:

The propositions are, schematically, as follows: (1) There is a single, absolutely transcendental God, creator and governor of the world, whose attributes and grounds of action are, apart from Revelation, completely beyond the reach of finite human understanding. (2) This God has predestined all human souls, for reasons totally beyond possible human comprehension, either to eternal salvation or to "eternal sin and death." This decree stands from and for eternity and human will or faith can have no influence on it. (3) God for His own inscrutable reasons has created the world and placed man in it solely for the increase of His glory. (4) To this end He has decreed that man, regardless of whether predestined to salvation or damnation, shall labor to establish the Kingdom of God on Earth, and shall be subject to His revealed law in doing so. (5) The things of this world, human nature and the flesh, are, left to themselves, irreparably lost in "sin and death" from which there is no escape except by divine grace. (Parsons, 1949, p. 522.)

The orientation tends to project the personal isolation and responsibility characteristic of secular individualism onto the cosmic level. Just as one cannot really lose oneself in others, so also the individual exists on the fleshly and human level and cannot expect spiritual union with God. Passive meditation and obedience will not link him with the Holy Spirit. Instead, he must actively work to bring about the Kingdom of God on this earth. Two choices have then been made: (1) active mastery of the natural and social environment rather than passivity, and (2) a concern for this world and its everyday challenges rather than for the world of the spirit or the afterlife.

Since God cannot be "intuited" by spiritual union he can only be served as a willing and effective worker. Effective service requires a knowledge of God's works. This theological position leads to a secular emphasis on empirical "facts" and general laws of nature and human behavior rather than on intuited wisdom, on education rather than on meditation, and on various forms of science (Merton, 1949, pp. 329-346). A choice has been made in a third area of human concern.

In Calvin's view the individual's mortal fate was predetermined by God. One's soul was either of the elect or of the damned. The individual could not, either by good works or by sacred ritual, change his destiny; a kind of fatalism could have resulted had the moral posture allowed passivity and submission. The general interpretation is that predestination when combined with a demand for active mastery had certain results: great anxiety and strong motivations arose to understand one's fate.

The anxiety led to a modification of Calvinistic theology by Calvin's followers: an interpretation emerged which stated that though a person's fate was predetermined he could gain knowledge of this fate by looking for signs of his destiny. Success in secular activities, which would bring about God's Kingdom on Earth, was taken as divine evidence and reassurance of one's good standing among the elect. Thus one must constantly strive, through rational control of personal desires and knowledge of natural laws, toward this-worldly success.

These attitudes were combined with a kind of individualism which was in some degree peculiar to Protestantism but which also derived from early Christianity. This individualism emphasized a fear of others who might be of the damned or who might seduce one into sinful actions which would be evidence that the actor himself was damned. It also emphasized the moral imperative that the serious demands of God take precedence over personal motives of pleasure or pride, as well as over the traditionally meaningful loyalties to friends, family, and community. This produced an anxious inner loneliness which neither "many acquaintances but few friends" nor success seemed (nor presently seems) to still.

One must serve God rationally and in an informed manner, he must reject or place in a lower order of importance the demands of self and others. He must act consistently to bring about God's Kingdom on Earth and to reaffirm his elect position by success in individualistic enterprises. In Weber's interpretation success in the rationally organized and serious business of business seemed ideally suited to salve the anxious psychological consequences of Calvinism.

Success meant material affluence, but this was a wealth that could not be used for charity, for the fate of the poor was evidence of their own slothfulness, their damned souls, and God's will.[4] Also, compassion for the poor was dangerously close to passion and other forms of impeding human emotional ties. Nor could this wealth be used for the dangerous pursuit of pleasure. Unlike Catholicism in its position of some tolerance and understanding toward the weaknesses and delights of the senses, Protestantism looked upon pleasure as in nearly constant conflict with God's work and will. Pleasure could not be allowed, for it might reveal that one's soul was damned. Economic resources could only be accumulated and reinvested. In this way, economic power was constantly available for further economic development (mastery and change of the natural environment and economic organization).

In summary, certain choices were made which led to anxiety about one's real worth, questioning of the value and/or morality and trustworthiness of intimate quasi-erotic loyalties and of compassion, deemphasis of most human institutions and the community in its various forms. There resulted a strong focus on the economic institution and an emphasis on the maximization of individual success and "productivity" in bringing about the good society (God's earthly Kingdom).

Secularization of Protestant Elements

Does this adequately characterize the cultural values of industrial American society? Taken by itself and without qualifying explanations it may seem a rather extreme statement. The position taken here is that compared with the cultures of other societies (for instance, of traditional India or Spain), these choices in a secular

4. A later secular statement in the form of Social Darwinism held that the poor were poor as a consequence of the operation of natural laws (survival of the fittest); in this manner the neglect of the needy was rationalized.

form characterize the dominant ethos of our industrial society. An examination of some aspects of American society in its beginnings will help us understand how these choices have been modified in America.

The basic modification of the moral standard has been its secularization. Part of the secularization took place in Europe itself. The economic views and political philosophies to support these views developed by Adam Smith, John Locke, and the Utilitarians provided an explicitly theology-free statement of the moral importance of rationality, individualism, free enterprise, and hard work. John Locke, particularly, spelled out the moral and political consequences of rationality and individualism. These ideas became the progressive ideas of the time of the American Revolution (Northrup, 1947, esp. pp. 66-164). They gave justification for and structure to the new American society.

In Locke's view, society and the government were composed of innately independent individuals.

. . . all men are naturally in . . . a state of perfect freedom to order their actions, and dispose of their possessions and persons as they think fit, within the bounds of the law of Nature, without asking leave or depending upon the will of any other man. (Locke, 1887, p. 192.)

But societies and governments do arise, for

[Man is] willing to quit [the state of Nature] which, however free, is full of fears and continual dangers; and it is not without reason that he seeks out and is willing to join in society with others who are already united, or have a mind to unite for the mutual preservation of their lives, liberties, and estates, which I call by the general name—property. (p. 256.)

From this perspective a commonwealth is created for "the preservation of property" and to protect the individual from others. Thus, society, rather than being given and structured from the very beginning by man's *ascribed* biological nature and psychosocial dependency (the view of Aristotle and modern sociology), was *achieved* through the rational efforts of originally independent persons in order to protect their private interests.

Another perspective held by Locke led to an emphasis on and provided intellectual and moral justification for personal choices, tolerance of varying minority views, and a deemphasis of political organization in the new society. Because each individual was innately free and rational and reached his "truth" by way of direct communication between his inner mental being and God, all must recognize the views and needs of others.

This was certainly a philosophical position favorable to the needs of a society moving in the direction of high economic and cultural development and diversification. This general position also provided a favorable base for American political values, which maintain that "all men are born free and equal" and that the government originates in "the consent of the governed." The state's function is not to bring into fruition, through power and coordination, a people's noblest goals. Its primary purpose, rather, is to constrain and inhibit both private offenses and a high concentration of public power. Absolute power corrupts, and it must be divided to create various fairly autonomous sources of power (the Federal system) and the three branches of government.

Though these secular ideas developed in a bourgeois Protestant Europe, their acceptance and resulting influence were more marked in America. Having come alive at this intellectual and philosophical point in Western culture, America was at the same time saturated by this perspective and then somewhat isolated from later moderating and reacting ideas which developed in Europe after Locke and the Utilitarians. In America no powerful working tradition of society as an organic hierarchically structured system existed to dilute this cultural theme. Further, this individualistic emphasis on economic effort and rational mastery was particularly suited to an economically underdeveloped and potentially wealthy nation of successful individuals.

The rather specifically Protestant definition of the "will of God," "God's laws," and predestination required secularization because America's newly recruited citizens were not largely ascetic Protestants who would accept these parochial teachings. They were often the religiously alienated, members of persecuted religious sects and Jews, Roman Catholics, Eastern Orthodox, and various nonascetic Protestants. The Kingdom of God on Earth became "democracy" and the "American way of life." Responding to God's calling came to mean responding secularly to the morality of success.

The deemphasis of traditional norms, of the organic social body, of the compassionate and quasi-erotic primary group ties, of the mystery and beauty of the inner spirit; and the emphasis (to a greater extent than in industrial Europe) on impersonal mastery, rational economic endeavor, and success, was and is probably a consequence of the migration of particular individuals to America. They were, after all, individuals who were largely willing to give up the highly developed and subtle values of Europe. They were also willing to give up the intimate ties to country, village, friends, and family in the pursuit of a "better way of life." It was a way of life which had few binding traditions, statuses, and goals compared with the European way of life, and it was the way of life of a society which deemphasized personal ties and emphasized social and geographical mobility ("Go West young man") in the interest of economic progress. The ethos was probably exaggerated by some of the immigrants themselves and in response to them. Thus, in their attempt to prove themselves acceptable Americans the immigrants developed values which were caricatures of American values of rationality and individualistic goals. Also, coming as they did from diverse cultures, it was perhaps necessary, if sharp cultural conflict was to be avoided, for even greater tolerance and freedom in the choice of means and ends in the pursuit of the good life to be introduced into the American ethos.

The general picture we are trying to draw seems to be one seen by early European travelers in America. De Tocqueville in 1840 wrote:

To evade the bondage of system and habit, of family maxims, class opinions, and, in some degree, of national prejudices; to accept tradition only as a means of information, and existing facts only as a lesson used in doing otherwise and doing better; to seek the reason of things for one's self, and in one's self alone; to tend to results without being bound to means, and to aim at the substance through the form—such are the principal characteristics of what I shall call the philosophical method of the Americans. . . .

The practice which obtains among the Americans of fixing the standard of judgment in themselves alone leads to other habits of mind. As they perceive that they succeed in resolving without assistance all the little difficulties which their practical life presents, they readily conclude that everything in the world may be explained, and that nothing in it transcends the limits of the understanding. Thus they fall to denying what they cannot comprehend; which leaves them but little faith for whatever is extraordinary, and an almost insurmountable distaste for whatever is supernatural. (De Tocqueville, 1947, pp. 251-252.)

It may seem to the reader that certain salient themes of American society have been ignored. Such motifs as violence, other orientedness as opposed to the inner loneliness we spoke of, and the pursuit of pleasure and sensuality come to mind. We shall try to relate them all to the dominant ethos we have outlined, for they undoubtedly exist in American society. It is the view here, however, that they manifest themselves in particular ways which can be fit into the position that the dominant ethos is productive mastery of the environment.

THE DOMINANT CULTURE IN CONTEMPORARY AMERICA

It is the dominant theme that we are interested in, for its values take precedence over or bring into question other values held; and it is the basic theme which is used by people to evaluate and reward. It also holds a position of legitimacy: individuals in positions of control are committed to it, and others not committed to it must generally deal with it and adjust to it. Our definition does not require that all or even most people accept it as their personal standard. Nearly all must, however, recognize its normative power in the society.

As it impinges on the adult male in American society, the value system seems to be this: each person must prove himself basically worthy of approval by acting as an instrument of some higher goal through productive effort—especially in his occupation—which will indirectly bring about a somewhat undefined better society or life for all. (Even the "good" society is undefined because it itself should remain a flexible instrument for achieving the "good life.") In an almost Calvinistic sense this effort is required of all, for no one is good (not even the white Anglo-Saxon Protestant of an old elite family) until he proves himself *productive*. And to be productive means to create resources which will allow individuals or groups in this complex and differentiated society to choose, fairly autonomously, their own goals.[5]

Behavior as a Consequence of This Value Orientation

This value posture may result in an anxious postponement in choice of goals ("Americans don't know how to enjoy life") and an anxious preoccupation with activity and productiveness ("Americans don't know how to relax"). For individuals without the required position and the know-how of productiveness, it may lead to

5. That certain studies such as North and Hatt's ("Jobs and Occupations: A Popular Evaluation," *Opinion News,* September 1, 1947, pp. 3-13) show certain occupations such as state governor or Supreme Court Justice ranking higher than more "productive" occupations such as factory owner may only reflect the American political philosophy. This philosophy holds that the government is to act primarily as a moral referee and control over the dominant activity—the production and organization of goods and services. Holding this position of control would be given higher status, but primarily by virtue of the services provided to the economic activities.

goallessness and normlessness (Merton, 1949, pp. 125-149)—a rather thorough and hostile alienation from society. This is perhaps most characteristic of the lower levels of the urban proletariat (Meier and Bell, 1959).

The dominant orientation results in individuals behaving in a number of ways considered by informal observers to be typically American (busy, restless, rootless, driven, "materialistic," or better, "productivistic"). Let us give some formal order to these observations:

1. A person must *achieve* by "effort," which means *postponing* certain *pleasures* of the senses.
2. The person as an instrument of some future goal may indulge himself, but primarily with the idea of increased ability to produce. Thus leisure may be pursued actively, but it becomes recreative rather than simple pleasure. After all, all work and no play would make Jack unproductive.

In this way leisure is consumed and pleasure sought in a conspicuous and rather anxious manner in industrial America. The new emphasis on consumption may also reflect the institutionalization of productive norms. People now "just naturally" work hard within a very efficient social organization. This produces the affluence we see, and also the problem of what to do with the affluence (Galbraith, 1958). With our deemphasis on the general human community it is difficult to invest it in public needs (parks, schools, and public rituals); with our skepticism of the moral worth of compassionate charity it cannot be used too copiously to rehabilitate those "lost souls" at the bottom of the social heap. Nor can it all be reinvested economically, for that would only increase the wealth and postpone a solution. We have had to make an uneasy peace in the last twenty or forty years with consumption and pleasure. It must be not only a "healthy" and rehabilitating pleasure but one which will consume the products of the market and sustain the productive processes and motivations. Perhaps such expensive and vigorous leisure as skiing is most typical of this new trend. We "work" at pleasure (the mock drama and seriousness of sailing or baseball). Those directly interpersonal pleasures which might occupy leisure—such as goalless loafing, visiting, social rituals, and extrafamilial eroticism—seem either to be decreasingly indulged in or to be engaged in covertly and with considerable concern. Such libidinal and social pleasures seem less normatively organized and more ego-alien in our culture than in, say, traditional Latin cultures.

3. As an instrument of this future and general goal, the individual need not always respond to the needs and feelings of his kin or particular friends. (William F. Whyte's "college boys" recognize this, and thus are distinguished from his "corner boys.") He is a private individual answering a higher duty or more general value system. This does not mean that he can be antisocial or even asocial, for a productive role requires smooth and pleasant interaction. This obligation is found in such concepts as "other-directed" and "the organization man." He must not, however, love too much or hate too much, for such emotions are demanding and are personal indulgences. They can be disruptive and can impede efficiency. He must be pleasant, *well adjusted*, and cooperative.

And still there continues the haunting concern about one's basic goodness or social worth, a concern which is a secular parallel to anxiety about the fate of one's immortal soul. Striving to contribute to the society through success in achieved roles helps allay this concern.

4. Devoted effort is not enough, however. A person must be rational, skilled ("a person needs an education"), and neither foolish nor sentimental. This would seem to mean that a person must act to maximize resources even at the expense of certain traditional sentiments and beliefs which are ends in themselves but restrain productivity.

We are not saying that these are the personal values of all or a majority of the American population. They merely form the major measuring rod for all. Neither do we mean that they are the only values, for numerous ascriptive qualities act as evaluative bases, and many individuals pursue goals of a variant nature with some social support and reward (F. Kluckhohn, 1950).

Evidence in Support of This Statement

What kinds of contemporary evidence can we offer to support such a broad outline? The writer would first appeal to the reader's sense of the reasonableness of the outline; that is, it fits in with numerous experiences and with literature, fictional and nonfictional, including the analyses of Western and American society and culture made by such writers as de Tocqueville, Weber, Mead, Kluckhohn and Kluckhohn (1946), Handlin, and Parsons and White (1961). Let us, however, present a line of thinking and then some evidence which will lend some precise empirical support to our position. Whatever social class and status may be, they seem to be a ranking of people from the most highly esteemed and rewarded to the least esteemed and rewarded. If we can determine the basis of this ranking in American society perhaps we will have a clue to the dominant values, the ethos.

We have maintained that efficient and productive activity for the development of a good society is the dominant value in American society. This activity is carried out in American society largely in the occupational role. If our position is correct, then the occupation held should be the major basis of class placement, for it is an indicator of the contribution of the individual to society.[6]

A study by Hollingshead and Redlich provides some evidence. They and their workers judged social class position on the basis of a large number of details gained through observation and interviews. These rankings correlated 0.94 with a combined index of education, residence, and occupation (Hollingshead and Redlich, 1958, p. 394). These rankings when correlated with each of the variables of the combination produced the figures in Table 5. We see occupation to be the most important contributor to the combination and to be the variable most highly correlated with placement.

Table 5
Judged Class Correlation with Individual Variables

Judged class with residence	.69
Judged class with education	.78
Judged class with occupation	.88

Source: A. Hollingshead and F. Redlich, *Social Class and Mental Illness* (New York: John Wiley and Sons, Inc., 1958), p. 394.

Even Warner, who suggests (Warner and Lunt, 1942) that the importance of occupation and economic position in the stratification system has been overstated, gives evidence for the importance of occupation. He finds that occupation correlated 0.91 with social class as determined by "evaluated participation," which took into account prestige and patterns of social interaction. Correlation with the Evaluated Participation Index was increased to only 0.97 when

6. A critic might take the position that the occupational role only provides the best predictor of power and the resulting ability to change power to esteem. This esteem is not necessarily forced or "bought" through one's position but rather eventually becomes legitimized by an educational effort to change the basis of esteem to match the basis of power. Thus the bourgeoisie of Western Europe developed a value-base which rivaled and eventually dominated the landed aristocracy's.

education, source of income, amount of income, dwelling area, and house type were combined into an index (Warner et al., 1949, pp. 167-168).

Similarly, Centers, whose interests are devoted to revealing other types of relationships, says:

By far the largest differences in adolescent attitudes with respect to labor and collectivism are found in relation to parental occupational stratification, and the lower the occupational level, the greater is the incidence of pro-labor and collectivist views. (Centers, 1953, p. 369.)

A thorough study by Kahl and Davis (1955), using the method of factor analysis, shows the central importance of occupation among nineteen different measures of socioeconomic status. The factor which accounted for most of the variability in an individual's status was highly associated with or defined by several measures of the individual's occupation. Association of variability in status with education was slightly lower, and with such things as the interviewers' ratings of subject, residence, place of residence, etc., it was considerably lower. This detailed study is perhaps the most crucial for our thesis that the occupational role is the prime determinant of social status and therefore the focal role in the culture's standard of evaluation.

A study by Bott (1954) also gives supporting evidence, although the study was made in Great Britain. The opinions of the general population should not be taken as final verification of sociological concepts, but here again there was very strong agreement among her subjects that occupation was the most important factor in placing a person in a social class.

We would not take the position unequivocally that these values, with their emphasis on occupation, are directly and solely derived from the Protestant ethic. This ethic could reasonably be considered a *post facto* theological and religious organization of ideas originating in secular social and cultural conditions. As a catalytic statement it gave, in turn, further impetus to the trends which originally gave it birth. It may be that such a set of values—the focus on individualism, on productive work, on means, and on relatively undefined future ends—results from exposure to fluid social situations, from exposure to varying sets of values, from the development of expanding control over the physical environment through science and technology, and as a consequence of liberation from ascriptive ties. These are generally the conditions of urban secular societies.

If we take the ranking of occupations as evidence of a nation's values, and if nations with different religions agree on the ranking of occupations, we then have evidence that a nation's religion is not crucial in determining its secular values. In fact, we observe that the populations of predominantly Protestant nations (Germany, Great Britain, New Zealand, and the United States) are in close agreement with the populations of non-Protestant (the Soviet Union) and non-Christian (Japan) nations on the prestige ranking of a number of occupations (Inkeles and Rossi, 1956). The prestige scores or ranks given to comparable occuptions in Japan and in the various Protestant societies all correlated over 0.90. This may indicate the emergence of a basic agreement between diverse industrialized societies with various religious pasts on the relative worth of diverse occupations. It is true that minor variations in ratings were obtained which were attributed to special cultural allegiances.

In terms of empirical evidence, in terms of detailed and sophisticated analyses, and in terms of everyday observation in this society, it appears reasonable, however, to regard a rather secularized Protestant ethic as the dominant value orientation in American society.

Contemporary Change of the Dominant Theme

There is a great deal of discussion in the literature on whether or not basic American values have changed. That is, has there been a movement from the nineteenth-century focus on the serious instrumental problems in life to a greater focus on problems of aesthetic expression, styles of life, and skills in consumption? In the writer's opinion, American society still evaluates its members in terms of, and gives control to those segments of the population who are concerned with, the "serious business" of production and the preparation and control of impulse necessary for this serious business. There may, however, be a new revolution in the offing. Individuals and groups like Frank Sinatra, the Beats, Ava Gardner, Elvis Presley, and a host of television, movie, rock 'n roll, and café society celebrities provide the "proletariat" not only with heroes and heroines, but also with skills for a new and gratifying way of life. These celebrities also teach the masses new skills which enable the latter as entertainers themselves to provide others with gratification. Their talent allows them, in turn, to accumulate considerable money and influence. Here one thinks of the numerous teen-age stars of lower-status ethnic group origin who have learned a particular skill by listening to and watching mass media. In a sense they may be the twentieth-century American parallel of Marx's progressive proletariat. That is, they have gotten hold of new abilities in the area that will count in the future just as the rising bourgeoisie "discovered" new skills that were to count for the future in industrial Europe.

This embryonic revolution may be abortive, however, for several reasons. First, it may not be possible for a society as complex and rationally organized as our own to operate effectively with a focus on expressive gratification. The affluence that makes possible these mass-produced and mass-consumed forms of expressive gratification also requires rationality and technical competence. (Of course, Americans may decide they are disinterested in mass-produced pleasure.) Second, the challenge of rising countries (the Soviet Union, China, etc.) which seem to be breaking out of an older era where traditional styles of life and not instrumental achievement were the focus, may make a dominant focus on this relaxation impossible.[7]

One might hypothesize that there is a circulation of elites within a society and a circulation of elite and powerful countries in terms of this instrumental-expressive dichotomy. As the lower classes within a society begin to focus on instrumental skills and become more powerful within the society, the country becomes relatively more powerful internationally. Meanwhile, the proletariat in other countries, bored with the instrumental focus of their societies, grasps new progressive skills in the expressive sphere and climb to positions of control. The country relaxes its attention to the pressing problems in the external and instrumental sphere and becomes less powerful internationally. One thinks here of "bread and circus" demands in classical Rome or Galbraith's analysis of America as an affluent society and its power position vis-à-vis the Soviet Union. In both cases, the general population might be viewed as weary of the trials and serious responsibilities of power and mastery of the environment. In the one case, refusal to attend to these matters and the focus on personal interests may have led directly to a diminution of imperial power. It could have similar results in the other.

Are America's values changing? With so broad a problem, and with so few well-controlled data, no answer comes easily. The truth of various interpretations may be determined, in the pragmatic American manner, more by their usefulness in explaining these and other problems.

7. The theme of expressive relaxation and consumption is now present, but that it can become the legitimately dominant one is another question. As stated earlier, this writer believes it now functions as an additional mode of achievement and mastery, as recreative in the interest of further and more productive effort, and as a solution to the excessively efficient institutionalized productivity of the society.

CODA

We have at some length discussed what is considered here the dominant standard of evaluation in American society. It is a standard which influences American family behavior directly in the sense that the child is socialized by norms of parent-child interaction developed out of a moral climate permeated by this standard. He is also socialized to accept and work toward the goals defined by this ethos. That is, our emphases on equality of the spouses and permissiveness in child rearing (let him develop his own ways of doing things in a nonpunitive atmosphere) draw on the themes of freedom and equality. The emphases on being active, getting educated, and "doing better than his folks did" focus on the themes of success and productive rational mastery of the environment. This is spelled out in interesting detail by Miller and Swanson (1958), but is not our central concern.

Our general interest is in explaining the influence of status (as it is determined by this ethos) on the individual's motivation and behavior, on the modes of family behavior, and on the emergence of subcultures. In the next chapter we turn to the motivational responses to differential evaluation and status.

CHAPTER 4

Psychological Responses to
Cultural Evaluation

"What is your work?"
"I'm a longshoreman. You know what that is—it's like an animal."
—From an interview with a father.

In this chapter we will try to show how different psychological responses can be expected as consequences of differences in status and the resulting differences in amounts of satisfaction. We will sometimes try to show how certain group or class norms develop in response to individually felt satisfaction or deprivation. This does tend to emphasize the level of psychological motivations in explaining social norms, and the writer recognizes that social processes operate somewhat independently of personal experiences to create new norms. Certain social processes and conditions relevant to the development of typical modes of action are discussed in the third section of this chapter, but in a rather incomplete manner. This incompleteness results partially from the state of sociological theory, partially from a desire to keep the presentation within manageable length.

SOCIAL REWARDS ENFORCE THE CULTURAL IDEAL

If the ideal exists that individuals should develop mastery over the environment and not rely on inherited roles and norms to define their behavior, how does America go about bringing this ideal into reality? Simply stated, by providing varying amounts of social resources or things wanted as rewards for behavior in accord with the ideal. It is a "sacred" belief in American society that people should be evaluated and rewarded not in terms of who they *are* but in terms of what they can *do*. This, very briefly, has been the kernel of the secular version of Calvin's doctrine throughout its circuitous history. We recognize that the ideal is not always practiced, for people are often ranked, hired, paid, and accepted on the basis of ascribed (inherited) qualities rather than on the basis of their actions. Nevertheless, the legitimate and powerful ideal is there. Those who are rich or poor, Negro or white, rural or urban subscribe to it on the level of ideals and act in accord with it to such a degree that it is increasingly characteristic of American society.

Types of Social Sanctions and Rewards

It would be desirable for us to present at this time a systematic statement of the kinds of resources available for use in rewarding and punishing people, for each kind of resource has its special consequences for the psyche. Later, we will try to develop this more thoroughly. Now, however, we will propose that there are four types of sanctions: material possessions (wealth in a material sense), interpersonal approval and disapproval (love, esteem, etc.), control over others (power and authority), and control over self (autonomy). The first three are the well-known wealth, honor, and power developed by Weber. The fourth, autonomy, is distinguished from power because power "looks down"; that is, "Who below me must act for my interests?" Autonomy "looks up" and "looks down." It asks, "How can I, while enjoying the benefits of membership in society, act independently of others for my own interest?" It is somewhat different from power and is very much like freedom.[1]

Psychological Responses as Intervening Variables

In this chapter and throughout this work we will look mainly at the psychological responses to social approval and disapproval. We do this for several reasons. First, we regard interpersonal evaluation as the most primitive and central condition of status. Other

1. The writer recognizes that though these resources are considered rewards, they (especially autonomy) are evaluated very differently in our society among different individuals, and among different societies. The absence of the resource in some cases may be even more rewarding than its presence. This is the basic point of Fromm's *Escape From Freedom* (1941). There he points out that in certain stressful periods people do not want freedom (autonomy). In fact, societies and individuals might be categorized or rated in terms of their degree of sensitivity to the presence or absence of each of these sanctions.

rewards are sometimes independent of it in creating status, but often wealth and power are themselves symbolic rewards resulting from social evaluation. We take this position because we view society as only secondarily an organization of power and economic exchange. It is primarily a moral order even in its contemporary mass form. Second, *social approval* is a particularly significant resource in understanding the structure and quality of *interpersonal* (social) relationships in the family, our basic interest. Later in this chapter and in Chapter 6 we will also discuss in detail the influence of degrees of autonomy on individual motivation and parental roles.

Only occasionally will we be able to talk about the special psychological consequences of variability in wealth or power. Many of the responses to little or much of these two would be similar to variations in the degree of approval, for two reasons. First, as stated earlier, they often indirectly signify degrees of interpersonal approval themselves. And second, many of the responses discussed in connection with approval or disapproval are really psychological responses to a wealth or poverty of social rewards, whatever their specific nature (e.g., approval, power, material possessions).

We must recognize, however, that the personal and group responses to being deprived of social power, for example, are somewhat different from the responses to being deprived of interpersonal approval or the other resources we have mentioned. And of course there is the further complication that special combinations of affluence or poverty of these various resources will bring about particular personal responses and the development of special subcultural norms. These particular norms develop to handle that group's special syndrome of statuses. Lenski's (1954) discussion of status crystallization and its influence on political attitudes and actions is an insightful beginning to discussion of this problem.[2]

TYPES OF PSYCHOLOGICAL RESPONSES TO SANCTIONS

We begin with the general position that deprivation of these social resources, and especially approval, is felt as frustrating and

2. It is also true that there are complexities in the structure of the deprivation which may very well influence the personal and subcultural responses that arise. Thus, some deprivations may be a result of specific obstacles to satisfaction in the form of norms, individuals, or physical conditions. Other dissatisfactions may result from a simple deficiency of the thing desired. Still others may result from various forms of personal conflict (approach-approach, avoidance-avoidance, and avoidance-approach) which make a satisfying choice difficult (Hilgard, 1957, pp. 176-179).

a threat to the individual's personality and security. We would then expect deprived individuals to respond in ways considered characteristic when frustration is felt—to exhibit aggression (extrapunitive, intropunitive, or displaced), regression to less differentiated or less "mature" behavior, restless anxiety, and problem-solving responses which are attempts to master the situation.[3]

Problem-solving behavior may be shown by individuals at all statuses who experience frustration. The position here is that it becomes characteristically less common when there has been a general past of deprivation and threat. Nevertheless, the deviant and innovating forms of behavior of individuals of low status who face many frustrating problems may be viewed as attempts to solve problems in creative and mastering ways.

Let us deal with each of the main responses in greater detail. We want to look at the psychological responses, and also, for illustrative purposes, to suggest some of the overt behavior which occurs in response to different levels of satisfaction. To simplify our discussion we will focus on the position and responses of the lower-status individual.

The individual's psychological response is not a direct and simple subjective response to objective conditions. The response is influenced by certain subjective frameworks within which the objective conditions are judged. Thus Stouffer et al. (1949) found that feelings of deprivation were felt strongly in those military units where promotions were greatest. Evidently the high rates of promotion set up certain expectations which the real rate could not satisfy. In those groups where the promotion rate was relatively low, satisfaction was higher. If we can extrapolate these findings to the societal level, they indicate that dissatisfaction is likely to be greatest in the lower levels of the most mobile societies, such as the societies of America and industrial Europe.

---

3. There are other forms of behavior considered important when frustration or deprivation of resources is felt: apathy, fantasy, and rigid stereotyped behavior (Knupfer, 1947). These are not central to our interest, however, and will not be discussed systematically.

We cannot assume that all behavior associated with status (e.g., aggression, apathy, conformity) is a consequence of satisfaction or frustration. Such behavior may be the basis of evaluation and precede the social status or ranking received by the individual. A more precise experimental design would make it possible to determine how much is the cause and how much is the consequence of the status of a social unit.

Aggression

"Frustration produces instigations to a number of different types of responses, one of which is an instigation to some form of aggression" (Miller, 1951, p. 483).

For the present we shall mean by aggression the expression of hostility *toward someone else*. Thus we would accept as a beginning the definition offered by Parsons:

"Aggression" will here be defined as the disposition on the part of an individual or collectivity to orient its action to goals which include a conscious or unconscious intention illegitimately to injure the interests of other individuals in the same system. The term illegitimately deliberately implies that the individual or collectivity in question is integrated, however imperfectly, in a moral order which defines reciprocal rights and obligations. The universality of the existence of a moral order in this sense is a cardinal thesis of modern social science. This is not to say that world society constitutes one integrated moral order in this sense; on the contrary the diversity of such order is a primary problem of integration but it is *not* as such the problem of aggression. Thus friction and hostility arising from lack of mutual understanding or mere thoughtlessness or insensitiveness to the position of the other party are not as such acts of aggression, although aggressive dispositions become attracted to these situations as fields of expression perhaps more readily than any others, because they are easier to rationalize.

The use of the term aggression here is thus narrower than in some psychological, particularly psychoanalytic, discussions. In particular "self-assertion" the "drive to master"—for example, of a technical skill—without meaningful hostility to others, will not be treated as aggression. It will not be an issue in the present analysis to decide as to whether on deeper psychological levels, aggression in the sense here meant, and nonaggressive self-assertion, or mastery, are fundamentally different or whether they derive from the same roots. On the level of *social behavior* the difference is fundamental, and that is what matters in the present context. (1954, p. 298.)

We modify Parsons' definition of aggression somewhat, feeling that the condition of "legitimacy" or "illegitimacy" is not always crucial. What is or is not legitimate is often a matter subjective interpretation. It depends on the mood and position of those involved or observing the acts. Our definition includes both conscious and unconscious, and legitimate and illegitimate "intentions to injure the interests of others." The definition is thus somewhat broader than Parsons', but not so broad as that of some psychoanalytic writers.

We are mainly interested in the causes of hostility and aggression in the family. We are not presenting a new idea in saying that certain intentions to injure the interests of others illegitimately are going to bring a response in kind.

What we will try to show in our discussion is that although some acts are defined "illegitimate" and others are defined "legitimate," both for the actor and the person to whom action is directed they are often psychologically equivalent. That is, control, punishment, and differential rewards (depriving social acts) even when accepted as legitimate produce resentment to some degree and create further dissatisfactions which find release in further hostile and depriving acts (attempts to injure the interests of others).

Legitimate and Quasi-legitimate
Problem-solving Responses

Given our culture's rather rationalistic bias and its view that problems should be solved by dealing with the external reality, it is not surprising that most of the popular and professional literature views this response as the most mature. The literature usually attempts to show that this approach offers, in the long run, the most satisfactory solution to problems met and frustrations felt. That is, the individual should develop, through careful thought and legitimate means, some new external situation which will meet his unchanged desires. But it is frequently just his and his subculture's inability to develop any adequate alternative to the external situation that has produced the original frustration. This would seem to be particularly true for the less knowledgeable and skilled lower-status person in industrial society.

His lack of skill and his inability to approach school and work in a successful way have led to lowered evaluation, fewer rewards, and status deprivation. Given this situation, the individual or group may develop certain illegal or nearly illegal innovations in the hope of achieving success. Merton (1949, pp. 125-149) in his discussion of anomie presents abstractly the possible responses to a lack of success among those of lower status in our achievement-oriented society. Though our basic line of thought follows Merton's somewhat, we propose here a rather different and simplified statement which will fit in with our theoretical discussion. In an achievement-oriented society those individuals who fail in the occupationally determined class system will turn to other roles for "achievement." This achievement will be sought not only in illegal achieved economic roles (e.g., crime, the syndicate), but also in the more ascribed roles regarding sex, the peer group, the "in-group," and the family. We will call this response "role compensation."

This line of thought suggests why lower-class behavior in these roles appears "exaggerated" to the eyes of the upper middle and upper classes. Such characteristics as masculinity, femininity, and patriotism, which in a traditional society are assumed without much question and acted out in a kind of relaxed naturalness, are matters of concern to the urban proletariat.

The importance of these roles and their forceful definition in the lower levels is also reflected in the working-class belief that those of the upper classes are frequently acting neither in ways appropriate to their sexual role nor patriotically. One is here reminded of various movements in this country concerned with national loyalty (e.g., America First movements and especially McCarthyism) which charged that certain elite groups (e.g., the State Department) were composed of effete Anglophiles and Communists.[4]

The bearing that role compensation has on behavior in the family at various levels of society will be our concern in the next chapter, and the way in which it fosters subculture themes will be our concern in Chap. 9.

Regression

Individuals who are frustrated respond not only with aggression and problem-solving behavior (what we call "role compensation"), but they also frequently regress (Barker, Dembo, and Lewin, 1941). In the terms of our general approach, we would say that regression is an attempt to move back into previous systems of behavior which in the individual's past provided greater status or rewards, given his abilities. Perhaps regression is only a special form of ascriptive role compensation in which the roles focused upon are those of past, gratifying organizations of life.

The regressive response to status-associated frustration may influence the forms of family life in different levels of society. If frustration is felt too strongly in adulthood, there may be a withdrawal

4. Many of Senator McCarthy's and his associates' charges that "security risks" riddled various governmental organizations were actually often predominantly charges that various sexual deviants (especially homosexuals) rather than actual Communist sympathizers played important roles in the government. The journalistic euphemism "security risk" distorted to some degree McCarthy's political dragon, for though homosexuals were perhaps in some degree risks, most citizens thought of the problem of political loyalty. (Even the New York *Times* felt more comfortable simply using the phrase without explaining it.)

from familial roles and a focus on premarital adolescent or even impulsive childhood ways. Even if the withdrawal is not complete ("going home to mother" or desertion), the familial role would be colored by such regressive interests.

Anxiety

Behaviorally, this psychological state is reflected in an excess of undirected movements, restlessness, muscular tenseness, and uneven and perhaps uncoordinated movements (Barker, Dembo, and Lewin, 1941). One might hypothesize that such a state results from a combination of attempts to solve the problem with the desire to strike out aggressively and yet to control the aggression. So long as none of these modes gains dominance, a kind of anxious indecision prevails. If our reasoning is valid, it would not be surprising if the anxious parent is most common in the lower middle levels, where there is lack of sufficient self-esteem and security to produce considerable motivation to aggress but also sufficient inhibitions and class norms against aggression to create some conflict and anxiety.

Our Focus

Our interest will lead us to focus, for several reasons, primarily on the psychological responses of aggression and role compensation. First, one of our primary interests is in explaining the variation in degrees of warmth and hostility expressed in the socialization process at different class levels. Simply stated, our hypothesis is that the greater punitiveness and the more common rejection of the child by parents in the urban lower classes is a consequence of the parents' greater frustration and stronger feelings of threat (see Tables 3 and 10). The parents' aggression is displaced from the frustrating system (the power and reward structure of industrial society) to the relatively powerless child. Second, since our interest is the degree of warmth or hostility in this *ascriptive group,* the family, these two responses to frustration—aggression and *ascriptive role* compensation—seem to be the two most salient responses in family behavior and especially socialization. They should, therefore, order more facts and predict more, within our domain of interest.

Aggression is a prominent response to frustration; the direction and degree of its expression are channeled by aspects of society's structure. Let us turn to this matter.

SOCIOLOGICAL CONDITIONS LEADING TO
EXTERNAL EXPRESSION OF AGGRESSION

Thus far we have looked at the psychological effect of the degrees of deprivation or satisfaction experienced at different status levels in society and have seen how these may help explain behavior (especially family behavior) at these different levels. Our approach has generally been that behavior characteristic of different levels is a consequence of many individuals' meeting certain socially structured conditions (the stratification system) and responding as *individuals*. Such an approach does ignore the importance of preexisting subcultures or norms regarding behavior. These patterns of norms may structure behavior relatively independently of the individual's experiences and motivations. This introduces us to a series of factors which we believe help explain not only the experiences which generate frustration and impulses to agress but also help explain *how the aggression generated is handled* by individuals or groups of individuals.

Aggression can be handled in different ways. It can be turned toward the frustrating person or displaced to some more vulnerable or less valued object. It can be dissipated through reasoning or working out some solution with the frustrating person in the area of discord. It can also be turned toward the self and reveal itself psychologically in feelings of guilt or depression; it can manifest itself behaviorally in repeated accidents or failures, in illness, or in suicide. These responses may be a type of displacement, or a judgment (at some psychic level) by the actor (i.e., the individual) that he is really responsible for his own problems.[5] This is not intended to be an exhaustive discussion of the dynamics of aggression, however; we now present the conditions that influence the manner in which aggression is handled in the different status levels.

Norms Regarding the Expression
of Aggression

As a consequence of certain personal experiences reflected on a group level, as a consequence of the selection of persons with varying degrees of emotional control, and as a consequence perhaps of

---

5. He may also attack or destroy "himself" as a means of attacking or destroying those introjections of certain social objects within himself held responsible for his frustrations.

the general direction of societal development at different social-class levels, there are preexisting norms regarding the appropriate manner or conditions in which aggression may be expressed. We feel that there is less acceptance of externally expressed aggression in the upper levels and more acceptance in the lower levels. This acceptance would then, in turn, be reflected in the varying degrees of aggression expressed in the parent-child relationship. Sociologically (or in terms of social structure and social interaction) this reliance on norms begs the question, to a degree, for our basic interest is in explaining why these varying norms or typical behavior arise at different status-levels.

The Structure of Society and the Expression of Aggression

There are structural features which bring about greater external expression of aggression in society and within the family at the lower levels. First, upper-status individuals, despite much social segregation of the classes and the normative control of laws and ethics, are in a more powerful position. This position allows them to express with greater security some aggression toward extrafamilial individuals at lower levels in social or work situations. By contrast, lower-status individuals may feel it emotionally "unprofitable" (Homans, 1961) to express aggression toward higher-status individuals. Their power and moral position make them vulnerable to strong sanctions. They may instead displace aggression to their equals or their family members, where psychic profit is more likely.

A second structural feature that influences the degree of aggression expressed within the family or among peers rests on something of a Marxian or Thrasymachian perspective. Many acts are not in an absolute sense aggressive or legitimate. They must be defined thus. In society "justice is the interest of the stronger" to some degree. That is, acts and modes of behavior, if they are beneficial to those in higher status (even though they may be to some degree exploitative of those in lower status), can, through the superstructure of law, education, and social ethics, be defined not as aggressive or exploitative but as ethical and just behavior.[6] On the other

6. See as an example the discussion of Social Darwinism in John Kenneth Galbraith's *The Affluent Society* (Boston: Houghton Mifflin Co., 1958, pp. 55-63). Also, one is reminded of a song that says if you are rich and don't work you are a bon vivant or playboy, but if you are poor and idle you are a bum. In line with this thinking, certain deviant behavior in the esteemed class is allowed and explained away as interesting eccentricity. Hostile arrogance and demands may be

hand, certain acts which are more in accord with the motivational demands and social position of lower-status individuals can be defined as immature, aggressive, or criminal. This means that the upper-status individual through critical evaluation, snobbery, "righteous indignation," and manipulation of sanctions can express toward the lower classes more or less legitimately, certain attitudes which are the psychological equivalents of illegitimate aggressive acts. These are also often the psychological equivalents of aggression for the person receiving them. The lower-status individual, however, cannot safely return aggression, nor does he have at hand as many incidences in which evaluations may act as equivalents of aggression, except in the family and among his peers. He can criticize the child and he can respond to the child with righteous indignation.

Resources for Socialization

Another condition which leads to greater control of emotions and introjection of hostility at the higher levels is the process of socialization itself. The thinking here is that individuals in higher status (that is, those receiving more esteem, power, and material comforts) are able to give their children more positive sanctions of an emotional nature, as well as greater rewards of social position and material comforts. They receive more from society (and, most likely, from their own family experiences) and can, without the economy· or equilibrium of their own psyches' suffering, give to the children more positive sanctions and fewer negative sanctions in the process of child training. A stronger emotional bond develops between the parent and the child, and across this stronger emotional bridge pass the parental ideals and expectations for the child. Under these conditions the child is better able to introject the parental image and norms. He develops a stronger superego and a more consistent and organized "generalized-other." His behavior is more adult and less ruled by impulsive needs. This is brought out clearly in Table 6, which is based on interviews with approximately 350 mothers of kindergarten-aged children. Children who are warmly accepted have stronger consciences than have rejected children.

The parent at the lower level receives less from society in the way of esteem, security, and material comforts. In addition, he probably receives more hostility from his peers and society in general. The absence of resources and receipt of aggression result in a

---

passed off as "pride" or indication of a "crotchety" nature when the actor has status but as "plain meanness" if the actor lacks status. It is better to be a big dictator than a little dictator.

"poverty" of positive affect. The economy of the psyche can be maintained only by dispelling this hostility to more vulnerable targets (e.g., the child).

Table 6
High Conscience: Relationship to Child Dependency and Maternal Acceptance-Rejection

ACCEPTANCE-REJECTION OF CHILD	PERCENTAGE OF CHILDREN RATED AS HAVING HIGH CONSCIENCE			
	Less Dependent		More Dependent	
Boys				
Rejected	10	(30)[a]	15	(26)
Accepted	21	(58)	33	(55)
Girls				
Rejected	18	(17)	31	(27)
Accepted	36	(60)	37	(46)

a. Figure in parentheses are number of cases.
Source: R. Sears, E. Maccoby, and H. Levin, *Patterns of Child Rearing* (New York: Harper & Row, Publishers, 1957), p. 383.

The poverty of positive rewards from society makes it difficult for the parent to "find" love to direct to the child. This weakens the emotional bond between parent and child, making more difficult the process of socialization. If the emotional bridge is weaker, then there will be less internalization of parental expectations, and love and its withdrawal cannot be used so effectively to bring about the desired social behavior. The parent resorts to physical punishment, to hostile deprivation, as the means of bringing about control *and* as a means of displacing hostility in order to maintain his personality and enhance his own status. Aggression and hostility may enhance status, for status is to some degree a relative matter: the expression of negative sanctions toward those about the individual tends to decrease their status and, relative to others (e.g., the child), to increase his own.

In response, the child withdraws from the parental ideal, internalizes the parent's expectations to a lesser degree, "flees" the home situation, and fails to develop a strong superego. This allows for more impulsive expression of affect (both positive and negative). And this continues the cycle, for as an adult and as a parent greater aggression is expressed externally because of the weaker superego.

External Restraint

Thus far we have said that there are more frustrations at the lower-class levels and hence that there is more aggression to express.

Further, we have said that certain norms already exist at different social levels which either constrain or free aggressive impulses. We have also said that the power structure (the control of sanctions) results in aggression's trickling down from the top to the bottom, and that for the individual in the lower levels a safe outlet for hostile impulses is the family, particularly the child.

And finally, we have said that the absence in the lower levels of resources (positive sanctions) for the socialization of the child leads to development of a personality which has not internalized certain adult standards and is thus more impulsive. By contrast, the upper-status parent's resources and socialization approach lead to development of a stronger superego in the child and a directing of whatever aggression there is toward the self.[7]

In what further way can the status system (the distribution of rewards, power, etc.) be understood to inhibit or encourage the expression of aggression externally?[8] The theoretical views and concepts of Henry and Short in *Suicide and Homicide* (1954) seem very helpful here. In their view and as was stated in the present work, aggression may be directed toward others or it may be turned against the self. The expression of aggression is facilitated if the aggression is both legitimate (in some sense) in the mind of the aggressor and if it is directed toward persons or institutions that are to some degree vulnerable. According to Henry and Short, a strong external restraint system offers a psychological legitimacy for aggression *against others*. The absence of a system of external restraint, they theorize, turns hostility toward the self. It seems advisable to go into some detail concerning their theoretical statements.

7. We would say the various prestige statuses a parent holds (not just his achieved social status) would have the same effect. Thus within a given socio-economic stratum, Caucasian parents would be less severe toward their children than would Negro parents. We would also expect that fathers within a general class who held high status in the work situation would be less severe than other fathers.

8. The way he handles aggression is conventionally and probably more importantly regarded as a function of personality. We need a measure not only of social variables (our main interest here) but also some measure of the functioning of the father's personality—e.g., the extent to which he uses displacement, etc. This would require a different research design. Our purpose is to explain social conditions which produce different kinds of personalities. A thorough study of family structure and the expression of aggression is presented in Daniel H. Funkenstein, Stanley H. King, and Margaret E. Drolette, *The Mastery of Stress* (Cambridge: Harvard University Press, 1957). This study shows that in an experimental situation those who express aggression outwardly tend to blame others for problems, tend to depend on authority as a solution to problems, and report the father as a dominant and severe person. This study, by Funkenstein, et al., its findings, and some of the questions and measures developed in it were the basis for many of the ideas and questions used for the present study.

Henry and Short define "external restraint" as "the degree to which behavior is required to conform to the demands and expectations of others in the external world" (p. 120). These expectations originate from those with whom one is closely involved ("the relational system") and from those of higher status. This means that those who are married, have children, are of Catholic faith, and live in stable urban or rural areas have strong relational systems. They are closely involved with groups and persons whose expectations they must meet. Likewise, individuals of low social status and little power are required to conform to the expectations of those of greater status.

By contrast, those who are single or divorced, are childless, Protestant, of high social status, and live in a casual urban setting have possibly the weakest external restraint systems. They may be acting in conformity with society's expectations more than the members of the former group, but the locus of control is different—it is internalized. The person *is* autonomous but is certainly not free to act in *any* way he pleases.

By reinterpretation of some of Durkheim's theory and work, and a detailed presentation of data on suicide and homicide in the United States, Henry and Short show that those groups with *low* external restraint systems have *high suicide* rates and *low homicide* rates. They also show that those groups mentioned above with strong external restraint systems tend to have low suicide rates and high homicide rates.

They interpret the findings in this way: Homicide is an act of aggression directed outward. If the individual's behavior is subjected to a system of strong external restraint in the form either of intimate social relations or of subordinate status, this aggression is legitimate, for it is possible and relatively easy to hold others responsible when frustrations occur. In contrast, those individuals of high status and little involvement with others are likely to interpret their problems and frustrations as consequences of their own free decisions and behavior. Such interpretation would lead to aggression being directed toward the self, or suicide.

With more moderate motivations, similar structures or situations would lead in the first case to the expression of aggression outward in the form of physical attack or verbal aggression; in the second case to the direction of feelings toward the self, resulting in guilt or depression.

The decreased individualism and increased external restraint in the lower strata also lead to a heightened expression of whatever positive affect (love) is at hand. Perhaps this is true because, again, *others* are more closely involved in one's life and therefore judged responsible for the satisfactions of life. Because of these conditions and this judgment, the others are loved more freely. This heightened and freer expression of both positive and negative affect is perhaps only another way of saying that the lower classes are more "emotional"—a common conclusion among those of higher statuses. Our approach, however, does point to structural conditions outside the personality which lead to this greater emotionality.

How can we apply the concept of external restraint to conditions of class and state their hypothesized effect on the parent-child relationship? Here it is sufficient to say that individuals of high social status tend to be in positions of control and power in occupational, community, church, political, and even informal social activities. Likewise, individuals of lower social status are controlled to a considerable extent by those of higher status, either by having subordinate roles in common activity or by not participating in decision-making activities. This again tends to result in those of the lower-status groups' viewing those of higher status as controlling their lives to a large degree—a condition that fosters the external expression of aggression. Nevertheless, these individuals when they experience anxiety or felings of frustration and deprivation, due to their power position, cannot aggress against those of higher status in any direct way without suffering the negative sanctions. In this situation the child, especially the male child, becomes a legitimate focus of hostility and aggression in the form of punitive child-rearing methods. He is not capable of effective retaliation, and the parent is supported in his disciplinary aggression by some concepts of the proper parental role. The strict parent is a good parent. Here we see certain parental traditions arising as rationalizations of the psychological impulses of dissatisfied and socially restrained parents.

Later we will be particularly interested in the operation of this external restraint system in one behavior system, the occupation. We will hypothesize that the degree of aggressive socializing techniques used by the father *within* a given social stratum will be associated with the degree of autonomy (absence of *external* restraint or control) in the work situation.

CONCLUSION

In this chapter we have briefly discussed social sanctions and the individual's psychological sensitivity to these sanctions, which enable society to bring about social order and cultural ideals. These processes also have certain manifest consequences dysfunctional for the implementation of the dominant goals. These consequences are aggression and deviant subcultures. The way in which aggression is handled at different levels of society and how it relates to certain roles in the family were also discussed.

We are now in a somewhat better position to attempt to explain a number of characteristic modes of dealing with several family functions that appear at different class levels. We will turn to this in the next chapters as we introduce the research methods and interpret several findings.

CHAPTER 5

The Nature of the Data

We now turn to a central interest of this work and the focus of our empirical research. How and *why* do the methods of socialization vary from class to class? Everyday conceptions and research had repeatedly stated that mothers (occasionally research was done on fathers) were more severe with their children at the lower levels of society. Also, research has shown that certain kinds of personalities (e.g., the authoritarian personality) result and seem to thrive much more in the lower strata than at the upper levels. Though these findings were discussed and critically reviewed, few individuals seemed to give a systematic social explanation of why this pattern prevailed in different social strata. Yet one of the variables, class (and here we have largely defined it as the independent or causal variable), is a social variable, and it seems reasonable that the explanation should draw on sociological concepts and should analyze the social conditions of class that would produce these results.

Our thinking led us to focus on occupation as the central factor defining social status or class. This, in turn, led us to view the father's role as crucial, for the father determines the family's status through his work and is most explicitly ranked in the society. Thus the interpersonal and emotional content of his experience in his class-associated occupation is communicated into the family through him and the way in which he plays the father role. To analyze this sequence with greater control the writer carried out certain research to obtain new data.

Facts and data are not absolute: they are relative to the researcher's procedures and framework of thought. The terms used even in speech and especially in a research work like this do not have absolute meaning either. It is the purpose of this chapter to spell out in some detail the sources of the data, the processes by which the data were obtained, and the operational meaning of some of our more important terms and variables. This is done for those individuals who want to know rather exactly what is meant by a table which shows that greater "authority" in the family is held by "middle-class" fathers than is held by lower-class fathers.

We try to not to do any great violence to the English language or to the accepted procedures and terminology of the human sciences. Therefore those individuals who are less interested in the exact steps of research procedures may find it advisable to proceed to the next chapter and refer back to this chapter only as it becomes necessary in understanding later tables and interpretations.

SOURCES OF DATA

The three major sources of data and the method of obtaining the relevant variables were as follows:

1. Sixteen interviews, lasting one to three hours, were conducted with fathers of 13 to 19-year-old sons. These interviews were partially structured and partially unstructured. The subjects were obtained from census listings, boys' club membership lists, and personal contact. The interviews determined their occupations, the social structures of their work situations, the emotional climates of the work situations, and their attitudes toward the work. Information was also obtained on parental attitudes toward the sons, degrees of affection, general family structures, and dominant disciplinary techniques. Where structured responses were obtained these were tabulated. Where the interview flowed more freely ratings were developed on relevant variables.

2. Certain data obtained from approximately 360 mothers of kindergarten-age children were reanalyzed in terms of the interests here. Variables were developed from information originally gathered by other researchers for other purposes. In the original study the mothers were contacted through suburban Boston kindergartens.[1] The interviews lasted about two or three hours and consisted of fairly detailed but largely open-ended questions.

3. Questionnaires were obtained from approximately 260 eleventh- and twelfth-grade boys in three high schools in and near

1. This was a study conducted at the Laboratory of Human Development, Harvard University. The study forms the basis for and is reported in R. Sears, E. Maccoby, and H. Levin, *Patterns of Child Rearing* (New York: Harper & Row, Publishers, 1957). I am indebted to E. Maccoby for permission to use the original data in my reanalysis.

Boston. The questionnaires were administered by the writer and an assistant to groups of 30 to 40 boys. A representative of the school introduced the researcher and the purpose of the study. The explained purpose tended to emphasize the influence of family and father's occupation on the son's vocational choice.

The questionnaire had been pretested and revised for ease in comprehension and usefulness in obtaining the desired information. In obtaining the data from the interviews with fathers, the possibility of getting data on family structures and fathers' occupations from sons by questionnaire was explored. The fathers' reports in interviews and the sons' reports from questionnaires revealed promising agreement. With experience gained in this small pretest a second questionnaire form was developed. This general form was given to a group of approximately ten sons and another group of fifteen sons. After administration to the groups each member was interviewed for 10 to 30 minutes to see if written reports and verbal reports communicated the same and the intended information, especially on certain troublesome questions. This led to further revisions and a fourth final form.

The questionnaire (Appendix) took approximately 50 to 60 minutes to answer and asked the son to answer general background questions on himself and his parents, and questions on the behavior of different family members, his work plans, and on his father's work situation. Some questions were open-ended and others were structured with stated alternative answers.

All three sources of data yielded information from urban and suburban Caucasians where the family was intact. In the two latter sources there was a fairly broad range of social class among the subjects. However, of the 16 fathers interviewed, all except one were in Class III or Class IV as measured by Hollingshead's index of social status.

Throughout this work, in presenting data gathered by this writer, Hollingshead's measure is used in the class placement of subjects. It gives a score to the head of the household based on occupation and education. The occupational scale of this index is a modification of the system developed by Alba Edwards and used by the United States Census Bureau. The educational scale of Hollingshead's index is divided into seven levels, from those with graduate professional training to those who have not finished grade school. In the development of the final score and placement of each family into one of the five social classes, occupation is given a greater weighting (seven) than education (four). A modification of Warner's class index was used in data gathered by Sears, Maccoby, and Levin.

Catholics, Protestants, and Jews are represented in all three sources. When the cases are divided into three classes as in Table 7, we find that the Roman Catholics are concentrated somewhat in the lower class (upper class: 28 per cent, middle class: 30 per cent, lower class: 42 per cent), the Jews are highly concentrated in the middle class (upper: 30 per cent, middle: 60 per cent, lower: 10 per cent) and the Protestants rather evenly divided among the classes (upper: 31 per cent, middle: 32.8 per cent, lower: 36.1 per cent).[2]

Of the total sample of high school boys, approximately 58 per cent were from Roman Catholic families, 13 per cent were from Jewish families, 26 per cent were from Protestant families, and the remaining 3 per cent were from families with no, undetermined, or other religious affiliation. This is certainly not typical of American society or even of urban America, but it is very near the pattern to be expected in these areas in metropolitan Boston.

The three sources of data are not *systematic* samples from a *specified* universe. When one is required to gain information on such personal matters as these with limted resources, cases must be gotten where cooperation can be obtained. Three school systems were contacted which were considered ideal in terms of size and social class composition. Only one of these three accepted, and approximately five other school systems had to be contacted before the additional cases were obtained. This resulted in what is probably a more culturally homogeneous group than was desired. Thus, about 235 of the 260 cases are from *suburban* communities that are *above* the average level for metropolitan Boston in terms of income and

2. Certain associations exist between family variables and religious affiliation. Protestant fathers have the greatest authority in the family, Roman Catholic families come next, and Jewish families tend to be somewhat matriarchal, holding class constant. Roman Catholic fathers tend to be the source of emotional support more frequently than Protestant and Jewish fathers. They also tend to be somewhat more severe socializers than Protestants (the least severe in this sample) and Jews when social class is held constant. The writer hesitates, however, to begin a voyage into this area, primarily because it seems difficult to present the data and interpret it properly with only statements of the correlations between variables. For example, do these associations reveal themselves because of the values implicit in the religion or because of the variable status a religion's affiliates hold as an ethnic group (even though social class as usually defined is held constant)? These cannot be answered properly at this point. Secondly, the associations between these variables (religion and family behavior) seem less clear-cut. This may be the case objectively or may result from the author's lack of theoretical preparation. "Clear-cutness" and meaningfulness in data often emerge only with a theoretical set that leads to predicted and understandable patterns. The reader is referred to G. Lenski, *The Religious Factor*, for a discussion of the meaning of religion and an interpretation of its influence on the family.

occupational level. Though the communities were above the average, we were able to get cases from all class levels.

It is possible, however, that Class V individuals in a middle-class (Class III) or upper-middle-class (Class II) community are, in terms of values and styles of life, more "middle class" than are their parallels in the central areas of the city.[3] If this is true, then the patterns and associations that emerge are, to a certain degree, reduced.

Three other selective factors may be operating in some significant way. First, these were public school students on a senior high school level. The more religiously oriented families would have some children in nearby parochial schools.

Second, certain families of the upper and occasionally middle class may send their children to private preparatory schools. Third, this is a senior high school, and certain individuals largely at the lower social class levels may have withdrawn from school on reaching the minimum age for release from compulsory attendance.

These factors again would tend to eliminate the more diverse elements in a metropolitan community. If they had composed part of the sample the results might have been somewhat different, though again we feel that the difference would have been in the direction of sharper and more explicit patterns than were found. Whatever may be the case, it is a caution that should be kept in mind.

Sons of *senior high school age* were selected as subjects because it was felt they were still involved in the family and could report on it accurately, yet were old enough to exercise some objectivity about it. Sons were chosen as being more crucially affected by social class than daughters and capable of providing more meaningful and valuable data on occupational choice. Moreover, it was felt the father-son relationship was particularly influenced by social class and by the father's experience in society and in work. The child's response rather than the parent's was sought, partly because of the economy of effort; however, another consideration was very important. That is, much of our interest was in a comparison of the role played by the mother and father. We decided that a report by either parent alone would not have given the balanced picture of both parents reported by the child.

The information from the senior high school boys is our major source of data. Though all five social classes are represented (as

3. Some indirect evidence for this is seen in "Class Segregation and Aspirations of Youth," by Alan B. Wilson (*American Sociological Review*, December, 1959), pp. 836-845.

shown in Table 7), the data (with several exceptions) are condensed into three classes: "upper class" (Classes I and II), "middle class" (Class III), and "lower class" (Classes IV and V). It should be recognized that our "lower class" includes individuals of considerably higher status than are usually grouped within that term. Also, our "upper class" is rather "middle class." It is hoped this deviation from customary terminology is justified by the increased simplicity of phrases.

Table 7
Class Distribution of Subjects

Class Level (Hollingshead)	Typical Occupations	Number of Cases	Term of Reference
I	Major professionals (e.g., doctor), major executives and owners	22	Upper class Total = 73
II	Minor professionals (e.g., dentists) and some semiprofessionals, lesser executives and owners	51	
III	Proprietors of small stores, salesmen, clerical and lower white-collar workers	94	Middle class Total = 94
IV	Skilled and semiskilled workers	78	Lower class Total = 96
V	Unskilled and semiskilled workers	18	

Several pages were added to the son's questionnaire which the researcher did not expect everyone to complete. They were added to keep the faster workers occupied. For this reason some tables have 20–30 fewer cases than Table 7 would indicate.

METHODS OF ANALYSIS

In order that the presentation of data related to our ideas or hypotheses and its interpretation may proceed as meaningfully as possible, methodological problems and definitions of different concepts are dealt with at this point. Occasionally, however, special methodological considerations will be discussed at the time that data is being presented. It should be recalled that most of the procedural statements here apply only to the treatment of data gathered by this researcher or of data as reanalyzed by him.

The general rule we have followed in presentation of the data is to divide the total number of cases as near the midpoint as possible. This rule was followed to prevent the ego-involved researcher from moving the dividing line to a point which would support the hypotheses to a more dramatic degree or give slight support in cases where there was perhaps no "real" support.

The percentage of cases on one side of the dividing line at each class level is then given. No measures of correlation are given, for most of these make assumptions about the distribution and cardinality of the data which we cannot make. Nor are tests of significance given for these data. Like any data which are not *systematically* drawn from a specified universe, they cannot be generalized with a calculable error.

The dividing point creates two categories of cases (e.g., one group of severe mothers, the other group of mild mothers). Occasionally the dividing point places together cases which are somewhat different (e.g., hostile and average mothers in one group and mild mothers in the other group), but in relative terms they are categorized together for purposes of simplicity.

BASIC DEFINITIONS OF THE STUDY

Severity of Socialization

The son was asked to answer this lead statement in two places (once for father and once for mother):

Below is a list of things a *father* (*mother*) might do when a boy about *10* or *12* years old had done something the father (mother) regarded as *definitely* bad or wrong. Read the list, and thinking about your punishment during that period, decide which three things in the list describe best what your father (mother) was likely to do when you had done something he (she) regarded as *definitely* bad or wrong.

This was followed by a list of ten different methods from "reason with you calmly" to "spank or hit or shake you."

The subject was then asked to go back and rank the three chosen from the most commonly to the third most commonly used. This question and the techniques of socialization listed may be seen on page 277 in the Appendix. This question and list was a modification of a form used by Daniel R. Miller, Guy Swanson, and other workers for research at the University of Michigan (1960, p. 412-413).

The subject was asked to answer with regard to what had happened when he was "10 or 12" years of age for two reasons. First, he would be less reluctant to report what the parents had done in the past. Second, at his present age (for most boys, 16-17 years) his parents would make relatively little use of the more severe physical techniques of socialization.

To establish the scale of severity of socialization technique, eight adults were asked to rate the techniques in terms of the amount of "hostility," "aggressiveness," or "meanness" each technique would indicate. These adults were two psychiatrists, one psychologist, two anthropologists, one sociologist, and two nonprofessionals (a clerical worker and a driver-salesman). A composite of their ratings, the writer's, and those of 34 boys (see p. 283 in the Appendix) resulted in the following ranking (in order of increasing severity):

1. Reason with you calmly.
2. Not punish you directly, but act hurt or disappointed in you.
3. Warn you not to ever do it again and tell you what would happen if you did.
4. Ask you to apologize or show that you are sorry.
5. Not punish you directly, but ignore you and act angry.
6. Not really raise his (her) voice, but talk to you in a way that made you feel terrible.
7. Spank or hit or shake you but only as a last resort.
8. Punish you in some definite way like not letting you go to the movies, making you stay in the house, or not giving you any spending money.
9. Yell at you or scold you or really bawl you out.
10. Spank or hit or shake you.

In general, the adults and the 34 subjects agreed closely on the ranking of the methods except for number eight above. Possibly as a consequence of their peer-orientedness, deprivation of privileges and freedom was rated, on the average, approximately ninth by adolescents but only about sixth by adults. A compromise favoring the sentiments of the subjects was made.

The more psychologically oriented adult raters expressed some concern about their ratings of such techniques as "Not punish you directly, but act hurt or disappointed." Though they resolved their ambivalence by making ratings very similar to those of the others, it was only after some thinking through and talking to the researcher.

There was very close agreement between boys of different class levels regarding the ranking of the different socialization techniques.

The total severity of socialization score was determined in this manner:

    Rank of severity of first-chosen technique $\times$ 3
    Rank of second-chosen technique $\times$ 2
    Rank of third-chosen technique $\times$ 1

These were then summed. The minimum score could be as low as 10 ($3 \times 1 + 2 \times 2 + 1 \times 3$) or as high as 56 ($3 \times 10 + 2 \times 9 + 1 \times 8$).

A Measure of Father's Hostility

The severity-of-socialization question asked what would be done if the child had done something considered bad.

Four questions (66, 68, 71, and 74, pages 281-282) asked about the father's general behavior (e.g., when this son was a child, this father would often spank his son—sometimes, it seemed, for sort of unimportant things). These questions were combined to form a measure of general hostility. This was not given a great deal of pretest and is not used extensively in the presentation of data.

Source of Emotional Support

This is based on four questions and determines which parent is the major source of affection and support (see questions 40, 42, 43, 44 and 45). These questions are:

- In your family when both your parents are around who do you usually talk over your worries with?
- Some parents show their warmth and affection openly while other parents are quite reserved in showing that they like someone. Would you say your *mother* (*father*) is: (alternatives designating varying degrees of affection followed).
- If something nice happened to you (you get a good grade, you get into a club or sport you wanted, etc.) and both your parents are around, who do you usually talk it over with the most?
- Who do you enjoy spending the most time with?

The scores could vary from the arithmetic sum of the answers (See Appendix) of the subject who chose his mother in three and listed his mother as very affectionate to the other extreme where the father was chosen in all and rated as very affectionate. The reader should keep in mind that this score is largely a relative one.

That is, it does not measure the absolute emotional support given by the parents but the relative importance of the father and mother.

Source of Authority

This score or measure is based on these questions (41, 46, and 49):

- Who is the main source of authority regarding most matters in the family?
- In your family, when both your parents are around, who usually exercises discipline over you?
- In the last 3 or 4 years, who in your family has generally had the final say in what you should do (how often you should go out, and where, how much homework you should do, etc.)?

Again, the various scores for authority are relative. That is, the son may respond "father, mostly" for all three questions, or at the other extreme he may respond "mother, mostly" for all three.

We also discuss the "power" relationships and "authoritarianism" in the family, but these are somewhat different from authority as we view and define it. We shall discuss authoritarianism later.

We now turn to the presentation of data, gathered by others and by this researcher, which reveal the relationship between socialization techniques, their severity, parent-child relationships, and social class. This review and presentation of data will show how the function of socialization is associated with social class. We will try to give insight to this association within the theoretical orientation already discussed.

CHAPTER 6

Family Norms as Traditions
of Adjustment to Status

"My oldest son is eleven," she remarked, completely reassured. ". . . his father struck him once and the boy was ill for a whole week, even though it was only a gentle blow."

"How different from me!" thought Julien. "Only yesterday my father beat me. How lucky these rich people are!"

—Stendhal

Our basic interest is in explaining the patterns of behavior that are characteristic of families in various strata of society. Our central area of concern within this interest is the methods of socialization of the child that arise at these various strata and how the parents' position in society might be a primary "cause" in the choice of techniques. This is not a new concern, for a century ago Stendhal's introspective and observant hero, Julien, found evidence for class variation in the familial fortunes of young and not so young children.

We begin the chapter by pointing out the basic psychological responses to cultural evaluation. We discuss in a somewhat speculative way how this evaluation and the response to it by the father feed into the family and bring about special emotional climates and typical roles for wife and children, particularly the son.

A second major section discusses how the structurally isolated kinship system *in industrial society* (unlike the functionally diffuse and embedded primitive kinship system in undifferentiated societies) combine with special patterns of resources for males and females in different statuses to produce unique conditions for familial adjustment.

Given certain amounts of resources (status) for males at different class levels, given particular relative amounts for males and females

73

at different class levels, and given the psychological responses to these, we then begin to explore the consequences for the family's functions. How do these conditions influence what the family does for the society and for the individual (and of course through him indirectly for the society again)?

We discuss these topics in each case by first presenting our ideas and then offering data from several sources (including research by this writer) that lend support to our interpretations.

AN INTERPRETIVE DISCUSSION OF THE INFLUENCE OF STATUS ON FAMILY ROLES AND PROCESSES

In previous chapters we have outlined the basic values or standards which create the ranking and strata in contemporary American society. It is a ranking that focuses on one's productive mastery of the external situation. This value system makes the occupational role and the husband-father's position in the occupational sphere crucial for the family's status. His daily exposure to the conditions of his work and to society's evaluation of him make the husband-father role a good point from which to begin our analysis. Again our analysis will, in the interest of simplicity, focus on the status of the lower-class father-husband.

Status in American Society and the Male's Response to Self

Social and residential segregation and the development of subcultural norms tend to limit one's reference group and the standards by which one reacts to associates and self. This segregation is not complete. There is, in the various segments of a society (particularly in American society) a realization of the general norms by which one is being evaluated. In America the themes that each individual is responsible for his lot in life, that each individual has considerable opportunity to achieve success if he applies himself, and that achievement is of the greatest importance, lead to a sensitivity about status coupled with a concern about personal responsibility for relative success or failure (Kornhauser, 1938).[1]

1. Further evidence of varying strength supporting these points is provided by a cross-cultural review of public opinion data by Inkeles (1960). That the evidence is as variable as it is may result from the different forms of the questions, the varying degree of industrialization and focus on achievement in the different societies, and the fact that respondents were both male and female. The importance of this latter factor will be elaborated upon.

Whatever may be his personal norms, the individual in the lower levels in American society may feel certain inadequacies, resentments, dissatisfactions, and feelings of lowered self-esteem; in some instances this effect may be more pronounced when they are not his personal norms. He realizes that his accent, mannerisms, dress, attitudes, occupation, and ethnic background are often disesteemed. We would expect these responses to be greater among the "urban proletariat"—those who in their daily activities are frequently exposed (more so than rural dwellers) to the opinions held toward them and their disadvantaged position (Beers, 1953). These expectations and assumptions are, in part, supported by data given in Tables 8 and 11, which show a nearly consistent increase in dissatisfactions (frustrations) as one moves from the higher to the lower social levels. This dissatisfaction is considerably reduced among rural workers but is quite marked among urban manual workers regarding their life and *work situation* (Table 8).

Table 8
Satisfaction with Work and Lives of Men in Different Social Categories and Levels

	Farmers	Urban Manual Workers	Urban Professionals
Percentage satisfied with their lot in life	84	71	88
Percentage who would choose the same work if beginning again	70	46	70

Source: Selected columns from Howard W. Beers, "Rural Urban Differences: Some Evidence from Public Opinion Polls," *Rural Sociology,* vol. 18, no. 1, 1953, p. 10.

This dissatisfaction and stress seem reasonable in a society such as our own where the main area of social activity of the adult male, other than his family, is his occupation. His occupation is quite important emotionally, for it is not only one of his main roles but is the dominant behavior by which *he and his family* are judged and placed in a certain stratum in society.

Ascriptive Role Compensation in Response to Frustration in Achieved Roles

A hypothesized response on the part of the lower level male to this dissatisfaction or frustration in his achieved role (occupation and class) is a focus on certain ascriptive roles in order to gain alternate satisfaction and status. This is one of his problem-solving responses.[2] One of the important ascriptive roles through which the lower-level worker attempts to gain status, a role particularly involved in family behavior, is the male role as it is traditionally defined. The traditional definition seems to emphasize high sexual activity, physical power, and control over others, with a relatively free expression of aggression.

It appears, however, that there are particular problems for the male in using the ascriptive husband-father role "adequately" as a compensating role for his felt frustrations in the occupational sphere. This is true for several basic reasons: first, the emphasis on the sexual role (maleness and sexual activity) in part is in conflict with the familial and *domestic* roles of the husband-father; second, another response, aggression, when coupled with certain definitions of maleness (e.g., unrestrained sexuality, arrogant patriarchy), leads the father to relate to his wife and children in a way which creates emotional problems and distance. He is likely to play his family roles in a manner that creates problems of identification with the husband-father role for the son.

Other role compensations of an ascriptive nature involve the emphases on patriotism, peer-group conformity and loyalty, and kinship roles. These will be discussed in Chap. 9 where we will attempt to show that these compensatory emphases are partial origins of the subcultural themes that exist at various levels of society. Here we shall attempt to explain how aggression and compensation in the traditionally defined male role interact with the husband-father role to produce varying family patterns.

Evidence that there are these emphases on "maleness," "femaleness," and sexual activity at the lower levels can be found in several sources. The work by Kinsey and his associates (1948) shows that sexual activity of a social nature is considerably greater in the lower levels, especially for the male. Table 9 shows this to be the case, as do several tables presented in Chapters 8 and 9. Here we have supporting evidence for our interpretation that low achieved status (occupation and education) leads to an emphasis on an ascriptive quality, sexuality—especially sexuality expressed interpersonally. Data from a study in Puerto Rico of the lower class perhaps give a detailed definition of "traditional" maleness and the sexual role in this stratum. Subjects were asked: "Speaking of being

2. In certain ways I am indebted to a statement by Kahl (1952, p. 304) for this general view of the matter.

Table 9
Sexual Behavior in the American Male (Single, 16-20 Years of Age) at Different Educational Levels

Years of Education	Mean Orgasms per Week	Per Cent of Total Outlet Social in Nature	Per Cent of Total Outlet Solitary in Nature
13 or over	2.7	18	82
9-12	3.5	55	44[a]
0-8	3.2	65	34[a]

Source: Selected columns from Alfred Kinsey, Wardell Pomeroy, and Clyde Martin, *Sexual Behavior in the Human Male* (Philadelphia: W. B. Saunders Company, 1948), pp. 336, 378.
a. Approximately 1 per cent of the total outlets are animal contacts and are not tabulated at these class levels.

a 'complete man': How does a man show it? How does he prove it?" (Stycos, 1955, p. 310). Table 10 shows the various responses of the subjects. Here we see the importance of the themes of sexuality, physical aggression, and power.

Rates of physical assault and homicide at various social levels are perhaps further evidence of the norms of adjustive responses made by males who have low achieved status.

It seems also that individuals in the lower-status groups view

Table 10
Evidences of Machismo (Distribution of Responses to Question on the Definition of Maleness)[a]

	Per Cent
By conquering women sexually	16.8
By dominating women	8.4
By sexual potency	8.4
By begetting children	5.6
Through courage	11.2
Through honor and chivalry	14.0
Through honesty and reliability	18.2
By being a good neighbor	9.3
Through civic virtues (working hard, carrying out duties at work and at home, gaining community respect, etc.)	14.0
Through abusiveness (picking fights, boasting, gambling, drinking, etc.)	15.4
In other ways (charity work, acting like a male, etc.)	7.0
Number of respondents (72)	
Total responses (92)	

Source: J. Mayone Stycos, *Family and Fertility in Puerto Rico* (New York: Columbia University Press, 1955), p. 34.
a. Percentages are based on the number of respondents. Since most respondents cited more than one characteristic, percentages total more than 100.

sexual categories and sexual roles as defining a much broader and
more significant area of their lives than do higher-status individuals.
We are not speaking exclusively of sexual behavior but are talking
to an important degree about the extent to which sex groups are
the significant reference groups for the individual in defining what
he should and should not do, what his aspirations are, and how he
should relate to people. This interpretation is supported not only by
the general impression of the greater focus on sexuality and on
"maleness" and "femaleness" at the lower levels but also by studies
of "typical" interests among men and women (as measured by the
Strong Interest Inventory and the Kuder Preference Record) at
different occupational levels (Roe, 1956, pp. 160-161).

We have stated that role compensation is an attempt to gain
status and satisfaction in ascribed roles when the individual is unsuccessful in achieved roles. A closer look at the occupationally
frustrated members of the lower class indicates that they pursue
status in various ascribed roles (Americanism, the sexual role, and
peer-group attachments) with a kind of striving typical of middle-
class Americans in their pursuit of occupational success.[3] It may
be that this attempt to *achieve* success—in what were traditionally
considered ascribed roles that "just came naturally"—is what gives
them their characteristically "exaggerated" quality in industrial
society.

Aggression, in Response to Frustration,
Reinforces the Traditional Male Role

Table 10 shows that dissatisfaction (or frustration) in various
areas of life increases in the lower levels of society. This dissatisfaction finds an outlet and reinforces the traditional male role in
the lower classes by the familiar psychological mechanism in which
frustration (here regarding esteem, occupation, material comforts) leads to aggression. The focus on this role solves two problems: (1) gaining status in some alternate behavior system when
status in the social and occupational sphere is low, and (2) releasing certain accumulated hostilities and frustrations as a consequence
of his lower status and greater dissatisfaction generally.

These conditions and responses, it is hypothesized, partially
explain the observed tendency for parents (particularly the father),
in the lower social classes, to use techniques of socialization that
are generally considered more hostile and severe, and to relate to

---

3. I am indebted to Winston White for this particular perspective.

Table 11

Responses to Various Questions About Their Lives Among Men at Different Social Class Levels
(Based on Median Rental of Area of Residence)

	"Wealthy" Class	"Upper Middle" Class	"Middle" Class	"Working" a Class
		PER CENT RESPONDING "YES"		
1. Do working people in general get fair treatment and fair play?	91	72	49	45
		PER CENT RESPONDING "NO" (DISSATISFACTION)		
2. Do you feel your children (or those of your friends and neighbors) have as much opportunity as they should have?	0	30	37	47
3. Do you like the kind of work you do?	0	3	11	22
4. Do you feel that your pay is fair?	0	8	38	35
5. Would you say you are treated fairly by people you work for?	0	1	5	15
6. Do you feel your work is steady and that there is no danger of losing your job?	15	21	28	48
7. Do you feel that you have as much opportunity to enjoy life as you should have?	8	17	43	48
		PER CENT WITH "VERY STRONG" OR "RATHER STRONG" DESIRE		
8. Would you like to have things more settled and safe in your life so that there would be nothing to worry about or be afraid of as you look ahead?	38	64	75	71
9. Do you feel that you want greater personal freedom than you have? Would you like to live your life more as you please and do things of your own free will without feeling forced to act this way or that?	21	29	52	45
10. Do you especially want people to think highly of you, to feel that you are a "somebody"?	71	64	56	40

Source: Selected columns from Arthur Kornhauser, "Attitudes of Economic Groups," *Public Opinion Quarterly*, April, 1938, pp. 262-263.

a. In this study the "working class" was not the lowest economic group interviewed. However, the "lower class" subjects were not asked any of the questions presented in the table.

the child in a way that is less warm and supportive. It seems (as we shall elaborate later) that the associations between social status and parent-child relationships would be less for the mother than the father. This, it is hypothesized, would be the case for two reasons: the mother is less exposed to the differential evaluation of society (the sanctions received are less variable from class to class) and therefore her frustration and aggression would be less associated with social status, and the frustration experienced at the lower levels does not reinforce her role as a loving female and mother but rather is in conflict with it.

Returning to the male-father-husband role, it should be recognized that the role compensation we are speaking of can work in two directions. That is, individuals who have high motivation to gain status in *achieved* roles may do so because of certain difficulties in obtaining status and satisfaction in such *ascribed* roles as membership in ethnic group, neighborhood, peer group, sex or family group. Individuals who succeed in occupational activities in our society require motivation and skills which emphasize rationality, technical competence, and a deemphasis of particularistic ties to ascriptive groups.

Evelyn Ellis in a study of unmarried career women concludes:

. . . upward social mobility is likely to be an out-growth of basically neurotic drives resulting from unsatisfactory early primary group relations, and . . . mobility leads to a continuation of superficial, impermanent primary group relations and other overt manifestations of emotional maladjustment. (Ellis, 1952.)

It seems that the factors involved would not be quite the same for men for upward mobility in one's occupation is a more expected pattern of behavior. Nevertheless, a study of 350 college undergraduates showed that a high level of occupational aspiration was associated with feelings of rejection by parents and of "not being wanted" by fathers (Dynes, Clarke, and Dinitz, 1956).

Social Class and Severity of Socialization

Our view is that individuals who hold low social status in society (or in any behavior system), particularly in an urban and industrial society, experience greater *external* restraint, greater frustration in material comfort and in feelings of self-esteem. This frustration and lower status lead to certain responses, especially for the father-husband; displaced and externally expressed aggression, withdrawal from the family, and what we have called *role compensation.* The aggression is displaced from the system in which it is received (where his power and status are relatively low—e.g., the work situation or society in general) to a system where he is less vulnerable because of his position of power (the family or the parent-child relationship).

Certain norms seem to be rationalizations of this need to express displaced aggression. The stern parent is the good parent and the good child is the obedient child (Duvall, 1946). The child is naturally naughty and must be broken with severe punishment. This latter dictum was central in the Puritan morality of colonial America (Winch, 1952, pp. 232-238).

If our analysis is accurate, then nonhostile and relatively permissive child-rearing practices would not become accepted practice for low-status parents without some change in the over-all structure of social rewards.[4]

It was felt that the son in the family was likely to be an object of this hostility. Certain norms make the parent role (and particularly the *father* role vis-à-vis the *son*) an acceptable place for the release of hostility in the process of socialization. Fathers should be stern and more severe as parents, sons are just "naturally meaner," "bound to get in trouble," and must be dealt with firmly or even harshly to control them. Does the association between socialization techniques chosen and status support our explanation? Do the more frustrated (in terms of material comfort and in feelings of self-esteem) and the more externally controlled express and release their frustration by using the more aggressive and punitive techniques? Our perspective predicts that this will be so. Let us turn to the data to see if they give support to this interpretation.

A thorough and systematic review of the studies of parent-child relationships was made by Bronfenbrenner (in Maccoby, Newcomb, and Hartley, 1958, pp. 400-425), and we depend heavily on this. Table 12 presents the techniques of discipline most characteristic of the different class levels found in eight different studies in various

---

4. It should also be recognized that those social levels toward which this suasion is often directed in our society are most recently from rural and peasant cultures in which kinship units were as much economic organizations as emotional havens and socializing groups. As economic groups they were dealing with the pressing problem of keeping alive. This activity in a subsistence economy requires the exercise of authority and cautious control over the child. In some sense there was not sufficient time and "emotional capital" to think of "producing" an improved personality (the child as a *product*). Like Topsy, the child just grew, or was used emotionally (*"consumed"*) while the family focused its attentions on the pressing problems of nature, the crops, the community gossip, love, and the "basic" needs of life.

Table 12
Techniques of Discipline

Sample	Approximate Date of Practice	Number of Cases Reporting	Age	DIRECTION OF RELATIONSHIP*				Nature of Love-oriented Technique	Other Significant Trends for Middle Class
				Physical Punishment	Reasoning	Isolation	Love-oriented Technique		
National II	1932	1947	1-5	—†					Infractions more often ignored†
National III	1932	839	6-12		++†	++†			More children deprived of pleasure as punishment
National IV	1932	3130	1-12						
Chicago I	1943	100	5	+		—	++†	Praise for good behavior.	Soiling child more often ignored† rather than spanked† or shown disgust
Detroit I	1950	115	12-14	—†	++†		++†	Mother expresses disappointment or appeals to guilt	
Detroit II	1950	222	0-19	—			+	Mother uses symbolic rather than direct rewards and punishments	
Eugene	1950	206	0-18	—	0	++†	0		
Boston	1951-52	372	5	—†	+	+	0	No difference in over-all use of praise or withdrawal of love	Less use of ridicule,† deprivation of privileges** or praise for no trouble at the table†

* Plus sign indicates practice was more common in middle class than in working class.

† Denotes difference between classes significant at 5 per cent level or better.

** The difference between percentages is not significant but the difference between mean ratings is significant at the 5 per cent level or better.

Source: Urie Bronfenbrenner, "Socialization and Social Class through Time and Space," in E. Maccoby, T. Newcomb, and E. Hartley (Eds.), Readings in Social Psychology (New York: Holt, Rinehart & Winston, Inc., 1958), p. 418.

parts of the United States between 1932 and 1952. All studies except one (Chicago I, 1943) show the working class (the more deprived class) using physical punishment to a greater extent than the middle class. The middle class tends to resort to reasoning with the child, isolation, and love-oriented techniques more frequently. According to our own judgment, the judgments of our adult raters, and of 34 adolescent sons in our sample, these latter techniques (except perhaps isolation) are viewed as less hostile and as having less aggressive content.

The responses of adolescent sons gathered by this researcher show the same trend for both fathers and mothers. Tables 13 and 14 show that a higher percentage of lower-status mothers and fathers are severe socializers (see pp. 70-71 for an explanation of this variable and the nature of the questions). This trend is more pronounced for the fathers than the mothers. That is, the difference between the lower class and the upper class for the fathers is 49 per cent versus 33 per cent, while the difference for the mothers is only 47 per cent versus 40 per cent.

Evidently there is a tendency for lower-class parents in their socializing interaction with the child to use techniques of discipline which are judged by sons (and our judges) as more hostile and which release and express more aggression toward the child. The last column in Table 12 gives additional areas of behavior in which the middle-class seems less aggressively punitive and more permissive. Thus there is "less use of ridicule" and infractions are more often ignored.

Middle-class parents, however, do make more demands concerning educational achievement and self care. They "convey in a variety of ways on the one hand, the kind of behavior that is expected of the child; on the other, the realization that transgression means the interruption of a mutually valued relationship" (Bronfenbrenner, 1958, p. 419). The middle-class parent reasons with the child or draws on the child's sense of guilt, a sense of guilt which the harshly socialized lower-class child may have only weakly.

Table 13
Percentage of Fathers Using Relatively Severe Techniques of Discipline at Each Social Class Level

	Number Using Relatively Mild Techniques	Number Using Relatively Severe Techniques	Per Cent Using Severe Techniques
Upper class	48	24	33
Middle class	52	40	43
Lower class	47	45	49

In general, working- and lower-class families are more likely to punish for offenses, more likely to punish with ridicule or by inflicting physical pain. If our interpretation is correct, the lower-class parent, especially the lower-class father, with his paucity of positive sanctions received from society, has few to direct to the child in the socialization process. Indeed, he uses this interpersonal situation to release certain negative sanctions. If this condition develops, then the parent-child relationship may not be "mutually valued." Its interruption, rather than being a loss to be avoided by acting in accord with parental desires and ideals (identification), may actually be sought to some degree. It is sought because it provides the child with an excuse to flee the family situation. It may indicate why the higher-level parent can "choose" withdrawal-of-love techniques while the lower-level parent must "choose" the more severe techniques. The latter cannot use effectively the threatened withdrawal of a warm relationship.

Table 14
Percentage of Mothers Using Relatively Severe Techniques of Discipline at Each Social Class Level

	Number Using Relatively Mild Techniques	Number Using Relatively Severe Techniques	Per Cent Using Severe Techniques
Upper class	43	29	40
Middle class	58	35	38
Lower class	49	43	47

With only this data showing simple association we cannot be certain the association is correctly interpreted. Perhaps it is not the conditions spelled out which produce the predicted choice of techniques. They may only be the consequence of inherited social class traditions. If, however, they are inherited norms, it remains necessary to explain why different norms developed originally and why they are sustained through generations. Our theoretical perspective seems to provide some light on this matter as do the data already presented and to be presented (especially Tables 31 and 38).[5]

The writer feels that the correlation is more than simple associa-

5. One could also reasonably argue that these specific social norms of child-rearing are neither *self*-sustaining social traditions specifically about child rearing, nor, as the approach here has proposed, norms developed as modes of adjustment to differential evaluation and *social* status in an achievement-oriented society. The different norms are instead the parental manifestation of different subcultures or broad modes of life. Thus the greater use of physical punishment in the lower levels should not be considered significant because of its aggressive content but because

tion. Previously we discussed and gave data (Tables 8 and 11) which showed that the lower-status individual was truly more dissatisfied with his life, opportunities, security, and work. It is this anxiety, dissatisfaction, or frustration which acts as the intervening psychological variable between the social ranking and its parental-role consequences —severity of socialization techniques.

We will give added support for our interpretation when we look at specific conditions of the fathers' life situations within *each* social class and show their relationship to the variation in severity of disciplinary methods. In Chap. 7 we will show how the degree of work satisfaction, of subjection to rigid control in work, and type of work all influence the fathers' choice in predictable ways which give support to our approach.

It also appears that data collected by others and by this researcher lend strength to the idea that the aggressive content of the method of discipline is a significant key to the family's general emotional structure. Other measures indicate that the method of discipline and its degree of hostility only manifests one aspect of the general quality of the parent-child relationship. These data will be reviewed in the section entitled "Over-all Warmth of Parent-Child Relationship."

Social Class and Type of Socialization Technique Used

In terms of certain theories of socialization and of identification, the *type* of technique used may be considered more significant than its degree of severity or the degree of warmth it suggests. Thus Sears, et al. (1957, pp. 368-93) find only slight association between the general degree of warmth or acceptance and the development of conscience (taken by them as one basic measure of identification). They did find (p. 386), however, that praise, withdrawal of love when coupled with high love, and isolation are much more effective in producing a strong conscience than are physical punishment or deprivation of privileges.

Table 15 shows the distribution in our data of the most commonly used techniques by fathers and mothers at each social class level. We see that the upper-class parent, more than other parents, uses "emotional" control of the child; the middle-class parent tends to use

---

it reflects the more physically active or motoric orientation of the working classes (Miller and Swanson, 1960, pp. 34-142). But again, it seems necessary to explain the original development of such general subcultural themes. And if subcultures are associated with a *social* variable (class), it seems important to give some *social* explanation for their development.

direct verbal communication of sanctions or control; and the lower-class parent tends to use physically expressed sanctions. This difference in the use of physical sanctions between the middle-class white-collar father (21 per cent) and the lower-class manual worker (39 per cent) is rather sharp, and again the association between paternal behavior and class is greater than is the association for maternal behavior. The white-collar worker is more likely (63 per cent) to use verbal communication of sanctions than the manual worker (49 per cent). Here we see each father playing his parental role with the same skills or characteristic modes of action used in his occupation. One is again reminded of the findings by Miller and Swanson that working-class individuals as early as adolescence seem to excel in motoric skills and higher-status youths to excel in symbolic behavior.

Also, the differences shown in these tables are, as one might expect, in terms of the mean rank of the severity of the techniques in each category. The methods in the "Love-Withdrawal" column of Table 15 have a ranking of severity of 2, 4, and 5 with a mean of 3.67. The

Table 15
Per Cent of Fathers and Mothers Choosing Each Type of Discipline Technique at Each Social Class Level (First Choice)

	Total Number of Sons Reporting	Love-Withdrawal and Communication (Often Non-verbal) of Emotional Attitudes,[a]		Verbal Communication of Sanction,[a]		Physical Control or Physically Expressed Sanctions,[a]	
		Per Cent		Per Cent		Per Cent	
		Fathers	Mothers	Fathers	Mothers	Fathers	Mothers
Upper class	72	19	33	52	44	29	23
Middle class	91	16	29	63	46	21	25
Lower class	90	12	25	49	48	39	27

a. In terms of the list of socialization techniques given (above, p. 70), column one in this table is composed of numbers 2, 4, and 5; column two in this table is composed of numbers 1, 3, 6, and 9 of that list; and column 3 of this table is composed of numbers 7, 8, and 10 of that list.

methods in the next column (direct verbal communication) have a ranking of 1, 3, 6, and 9 with a mean of 4.75, and those in the last column (physically expressed sanctions) include techniques ranked 7, 8, and 10 with a mean of 8.33. These techniques, as one moves from the first column to the last column, seem not only increasingly severe but increasingly direct, manipulative, and lacking in subtlety. This factor as well as the degree of severity itself may have significant consequences for the socialization process.

We shall try to give some interpretation of the significance of these kinds of techniques in a later chapter in our discussion of identification. We would only make one brief comment here. What slight trends can be observed indicate that the type of technique chosen by the *mother* seems more highly associated with the process of identification with the *father* than the techniques chosen by the father himself. If she chooses emotional control and verbal expression of sanctions, identification with the father is somewhat greater.

Over-all Warmth of Parent-Child Relationship

Perhaps all parent-child interaction is to some degree socializing. Nevertheless we recognize that certain interaction is relatively free from the explicit rewarding, directing, and disciplining that we have just been discussing. What is the over-all character of the parent-child relationship outside these authoritative situations? Do we again find greater hostility and less warmth at the lower levels of society and greater warmth in the higher levels? Our general position would be to expect coolness, excessive control, and aggression to pervade the entire relationship at the lower levels. Table 17, which brings together thirteen studies, shows this to be the case. Though there are some limited exceptions, this table shows that the working-class parent is more "irritable," is more rejecting, introduces "more prohibitive discipline beyond risk of danger or injury" and is less "warm."

Table 16 presents data which show that the relationship between the father and child, outside specific discipline and authority situations, varies in different classes. A quality of paternal coolness and hostility is a more common observation in the lower class. These data are based on the responses of the Boston and suburban high school sons to questions 66, 68, 71, and 74 in the Appendix. These questions asked if the father seemed unnecessarily or unpredictably distant, rejecting, or aggressive in several ways. Here we see that two-thirds of the lower-class fathers are judged relatively more rejecting. For the middle-class fathers, the figure falls to 56 per cent;

Table 16
Relationship Between a Measure of Hostility Toward the Son and Social Class Level of Father

	Relatively Hostile	Not Hostile	Per Cent Not Hostile
Upper class	34	34	50
Middle class	44	34	44
Lower class	51	25	33

for the upper class it is only one-half. This provides further evidence for our position, looking at a somewhat different dimension of parent-child relationships.

Anxiety—an Additional Response to Low Status

Other responses to frustration are generally observed in clinical and experimental studies in psychology. These are regression and anxiety. It is felt that these also help explain the type of parental role generally at the lower level and especially characteristic of the lower-class father. His anxiety is a consequence of his marginal position economically; of his weaker position in the power and prestige structure of society (as well as in the family, as we shall see); of his greater vulnerability to negative sanctions vis-à-vis the power structure as represented by the police, courts, and employers. He is more vulnerable to negative sanctions because of his marginal conformity to norms and his marginal achievement. This vulnerability, and its resulting anxiety, lead the father (or parent or any authority figure) to demand rigid conformity from the child (or any subordinate), partially as a release from the felt anxiety. This demand for rigid conformity from the child, it is hoped, will also protect the father from negative sanctions from a society which looks less tolerantly on the deviant behavior of the child of the lower-status parent. Numerous phrases in Table 17 which characterize the parental role of the working class seem to connote anxiety ("excessive contact," "intrusive" [in two studies], "more prohibitive discipline beyond risk of danger or injury," "father demands instant obedience," "emphasis on neatness, cleanliness, and order"), but no phrases which characterize the middle class communicate anxiety in the parental role.

This picture of an anxious (and hostile) parent demanding obedience and conformity seems an apt definition of the authoritarian personality acting in his parental role. Again, empirical evidence indicates that this type of personality and these family roles are more common in the lower socioeconomic groups and among particular types of occupations (E. Frenkel-Brunswik in R. Christie and M. Jahoda, eds., 1954, pp. 232-234; Lipset, 1960, pp. 97-130; Stouffer, 1955; Levinson and Huffman, 1955).

This parent-child relationship possibly explains in another way why the aggressive authoritarian parent is able to make a reasonable adjustment to the power system and to his controlled and frustrated position. He adjusts by acting out the submitting component of the parent-child relationship which he learned in childhood and which now proves suitable in the work situation or in society as a whole. The heightened demand to be controlled may be a residue from his experiences as a child of anxiously controlling parents.

Another finding fits in with these conditions and the general position we have been taking regarding the compensatory responses in ascribed roles. One of the more universal aspects of authoritarianism is the tendency toward rigid dichotomization of male and female sex roles. "Masculinity and femininity are conceived of as opposites, with no overlapping traits" (Levinson and Huffman, 1955, p. 255).

The view taken here is that these two aspects of the authoritarian personality, rigid demands to control or be controlled and dichotomization of sex roles, arise not from any necessary process internal to the personality but as responses to the individual's position in the social structure. His low achieved status produces both an emphasis on ascribed sexual roles and a feeling of anxious vulnerability. His anxious feelings are soothed by rigidly defined social relationships.

Thus the lower-class parent experiences anxiety and his relatively less advantaged position leads him to attempt to solve problems that arise or are anticipated through "exaggerated" control or "exaggerated" demands to be controlled. This orientation suggests a social structural explanation of why the authoritarian response occurs in the lower classes. It seems one could generalize this orientation so that it would help explain authoritarian and rigid behavior in other social settings as a consequence of a low status in those settings.

Regression as a Response to Status Deprivation

We have said that regression is an attempt to move back into previous behavior systems which provided and seem to offer the individual greater status or rewards than does the present system. Again, we would expect certain fathers who are receiving fewer rewards in their occupations to seek satisfaction in alternative areas of behavior through which they have already passed. This regressive behavior is motivated by an expectation that greater status will be obtained in previously experienced systems of behavior. In terms of our society's norms this would be behavior freer of social control and dominated more by the impulses of the id.

Regressive motivations in the familial role would seem to lead to greater libidinal and sexual activity with the spouse and to greater impulsive gratification outside the marital relationship.

This regressive response would also influence the parental role. The child would be viewed as an emotional object, there would be greater inconsistency in treatment, and there would be freer expression of positive and negative affect. This means that the child would be treated more in accordance with the parent's emotions at the time and less in accordance with the "objective" characteristics of the child's behavior.

These patterns again seem to be characteristic of child treatment at the lower-status levels; this is supported by the research of Kohn (1959, p. 366). Speaking of the orientation of the working class toward punishment, he says, ". . . it provides a positive rationale for punishing the child in precisely those circumstances when one might most like to do so." By contrast, middle-class parents attempted more frequently to determine the child's intent. They would then punish or not punish in terms of this psychic state of the child and in terms of certain developmental goals rather than in terms of the consequences of the child's acts and their (the parents) emotional responses to those acts. One could also assume that working-class parents are more likely to express affection on personal impulse, whereas middle-class parents are more likely to use affection to reward good behavior, and its withdrawal to punish bad behavior. With characteristic middle-class foresight and as a consequence of culturally determined postponement of gratification in the interests of future productivity, interpersonal affection, as a resource, is not consumed in impulse-pleasure vis-à-vis the child. Rather, it is withheld or expended in the interests of productive control of the child for future achievement.

Response to Father's Status by Other Family Members

Thus far we have talked mostly about the parents' (especially the fathers') general familial response to extrafamilial or societal evaluation (class position). There are also intrafamilial evaluations of public status and family competence which determine the esteem enjoyed in the family and further modify family roles.

It appears that the wife withdraws some respect and begins to exercise more authority over the family and more autonomy in her own behavior in response to the father's low status. For example, one study (Sears, Maccoby, and Levin, 1957, p. 533) found a

Table 17
Over-all Character of Parent-Child Relationship

Sample	Approx. Date of Practice	No. of Cases Reported	Age	Middle-class Trend	Working-class Trend
Berkeley I	1928-32	31	1-3	Grants autonomy / Cooperative / Equalitarian	Expresses affection / Excessive contact / Intrusive / Irritable / Punitive / Ignores child
National I	1932	494	0-1		Baby picked up when cries†
National IV	1932	3239	1-12	Higher percentage of children punished†	Nothing done to allay child's fears†
Yellow Springs, Ohio	1940	124	3-12	Acceptant-democratic	Indulgent / Active-rejectant
Berkeley II	1939-41	31	9-11	Grants autonomy / Cooperative / Equalitarian / Expresses affection	Excessive-contact / Intrusive / Irritable / Punitive / Ignores child
Chicago I	1943	100	5		Father plays with child more†
Chicago II	1943-44	433	1-5	"Developmental" conception of "good mother" and "good child."†	"Traditional" conception of "good mother" and "good child."†
New Haven I	1949-50	219	1	More necessary discipline to prevent injury or danger.†	More prohibitive discipline beyond risk of danger or injury.
Boston	1951-52	372	5	Mother warmer toward child† / Father warmer toward child* / Father exercises more authority* / Mother has higher esteem for father† / Mother delighted about pregnancy† / Both parents more often share authority*	Father demands instant obedience† / Child ridiculed† / Greater rejection of child† / Emphasis on neatness, cleanliness, and order† / Parents disagree more on child-rearing policy*
New Haven II	1951-53	48	14-17	Fathers have more power in family decisions† / Parents agree in value orientations†	
Palo Alto	1953	73	2½-5½	Baby picked up when cries†	Mother carries through demands rather than dropping the subject†
Eugene	1955-56	206	0-18	Better relationship between father and child†	
Washington, D.C.	1956-57	400	10-11	Desirable qualities are happiness,* considerateness,* curiosity,* self-control*	Desirable qualities are neatness-cleanliness,* obedience*

* Trend significant at 5 per cent level or better.
† The difference between percentages is not significant but the difference between mean ratings is significant at the 5 per cent level or better.
Source: Urie Bronfenbrenner, "Socialization and Social Class through Time and Space," in *Readings in Social Psychology*, E. Maccoby, T. Newcomb, and E. Hartley (Eds.) (New York: Holt, Rinehart & Winston, Inc., 1958), p. 421.

correlation of — .24 between social status and the mother's evaluation of the father. Also, Table 3 summarizes other research which shows the increase in the mother's power and authority in the lower strata of society.[6] These changes and responses occur because she considers the father less adequate, and is in addition more likely to be working and contributing relatively more to the family income than is the case for the higher-status wife. The latter, by contrast, has much status to gain and maintain by adjusting her own needs to the emotional and occupational demands of her husband's position and by providing him with a rehabilitating emotional retreat.

These motivations for adaptive flexibility on the part of the higher-status wife may be partially reflected in the lower divorce and desertion rates, and in reports of greater happiness in marriage at higher social levels.

Son's Response to Father's Status

It is hypothesized that the son's response is somewhat similar. Less respect and affection are felt for the lower-class father, partially because of the mother's attitude but also because the father fails to give the son advantages (prestige in society, material comfort, and protection from the evaluation and, to some degree, exploitation by more advantaged elements in society).

Table 42 in Chap. 8 shows how our adolescent sons' admiration and their judgment that they have modeled their behavior after their fathers' decline with declining status of their fathers and families.

Perhaps a more important and direct reason for the lessened affection is the hostility directed toward the son by the low-status father. This hostility is directed into the family and toward the son as a consequence of the father's position in society, and in an attempt to maintain his personality.

Let us continue on a rather general level. When acting as an agent of authority, the father responds to his position and his wife's and son's attitudes with further attempts to control both wife and child with aggression and rigidity. This is true for two reasons. First, he is, relative to the higher-status father, "poorer" in resources or access to positive sanctions to bring about control. Second, this fact makes it more difficult for him to build up an emotional tie with

---

6. Again we should point out that we are ignoring the special personality factors that might lead individuals to behave quite differently from our predictions. Our attempt is to discuss the general factors which impinge on persons occupying social categories and gain some understanding of how this leads to general tendencies of action in those categories.

the other members of the family such that love and the possibility of withdrawal of love can operate effectively to control behavior.

If this general line of reasoning is correct, then we would expect him to withdraw somewhat from an active position in the family and participate in other groups in order to escape his weaker and disesteemed position in the family. We will see later in this chapter how the father's authority in the family and emotional involvement in the son's life (which we consider to be indicators of involvement in the family) decline as we move to the lower levels of society.

The father's hostility and withdrawal from the family lead to two responses by the son. The lower-status son (in comparison with the upper-status son) turns more to the mother than to the father for emotional support and identification. This is true even though, in an absolute sense, the mother may provide less emotional support for the son than does the upper-status mother. Second, he feels social pressures to mature and he attempts to find other male-role models outside the family which will assist him in this process. This condition and his response perhaps explain the extreme importance of same-sex peer groups at this class level.[7]

The close identification with the mother, the absence of an adequate father image, the pressure to achieve masculine adulthood, seem to combine to form the basis of the delinquent response on the part of the lower-status male youth, especially the Negro. This delinquent response is an attempt to define himself and his behavior as masculine by rebelling against the dominant standards of society presented by the feminine figure, the mother.[8]

Support for a Continuing Cycle

Problems in identification with an adult "socialized" and "responsible" male lead to aggressive rebellion against the socially conforming mother. Here is perhaps the beginning of the cycle again in the working-class subculture. As a consequence certain values,

7. For example, it appears that teen-age males in the lower social classes attempt to obtain heterosexual expression more frequently in the company of peers than is true for upper-status youths. This may be a manifestation of dependence on them for a definition of and support in the masculine role.

8. This process is discussed in great and clarifying detail by Albert Cohen in *Delinquent Boys, The Culture of the Gang* (New York: The Free Press of Glencoe, 1955) and by Talcott Parsons in "Certain Primary Sources . . . ," 1954, pp. 299-314. In fact, a number of our ideas in this section and throughout the book are special modifications of their insightful statements. Here the reader is referred to the discussion and presentation of data on the process of identification in the first sections of Chap. 8.

modes of behavior, levels of school achievement, and dress are learned and accepted which are disesteemed by general society. This results in further feelings of disesteem and frustration, aggression and aggressive rejection of dominant norms of behavior, and withdrawal (or isolation) from "adult" standards (the mother's and the school's). The peer-group activities, and the validation of the traditional ascriptive male role in terms of cars, sports, "hanging" (lounging and loafing), sexual activity, and hostilely tinged masculine initiative, become a major concern. The son has thus rebelled against the "feminine" standards of society and turned to his peers for assistance in a definition of and socialization toward adult masculinity. These processes seem to help explain the power and structure of youth groups in our society at different class levels and for the two sexes. They seem to explain (1) why peer groups or gangs seem relatively more important and demanding at lower class levels, (2) why peer groups or gangs are more important to boys than to girls, and (3) why the lower-level male peer groups take on their hostile cast.

They may also assist greatly in explaining the rapid drop in the male crime rate in their late twenties. Presumably by this time the individual has gained increased confidence in his family and sexual role (especially with marriage). In addition he now has a marital family in which he can express not only love but hostility (toward the wife and children), hostility which was previously directed toward society. In this sense "getting married and settling down" provides an emotional outlet which the single individual does not have. We would hypothesize that those who remain single (especially in the lower classes) do not show this drop in crime rate in the late twenties. Some data (Gillin, 1946) suggest this to be the case, but unfortunately the control of certain variables (age, sex, class level, type of crime, etc.) is not carried out in a way which allows a test of this idea. (See pp. 115, 199 for further discussion on this point.)

Other Areas of Parent-Child Relations and Socialization

Before moving to the next major division of this chapter, where new data and interpretations will be given, it seems necessary to introduce results concerning other aspects of parental roles. These are areas in which certain patterns of association with social class have been found by various researchers, and again, they have been summarized by Bronfenbrenner. These findings are given here because they offer additional support to our perspective. They again show the lower classes to be more severe, more restrictive, and more punitive. However, in certain areas of behavior, the upper levels of society are more demanding of the child, though these demands seem to be communicated with less overt harshness. Nevertheless, the reader should be aware that in some areas the parent's will is as much imposed on the child in the middle class as is the case in other areas for the lower-class parent and child.

Using the orientation developed by Bronfenbrenner we find three additional areas of interest: (1) the development of control of impulse expression (oral behavior, elimination, sexuality, and aggression), (2) control of movement and freedom, (3) training for autonomy and achievement.

A review of a number of studies of parent-child relations reveals that the middle class seems less severe and more permissive with regard to such acts as thumb-sucking, eating with fingers, toilet accidents, sexual behavior, and aggression toward peers and parents.

With regard to the control of movement and freedom, we find a pattern or shift through time from the early 1930s to the early 1950s. The middle class begins this period somewhat more restrictively but later becomes considerably less controlling—giving the child autonomy. There is some problem in interpreting these results and the shift. Some of the earlier studies tended to ask questions in which "autonomy" might really be neglect of the child. That is, "freedom" to move about may sometimes indicate disinterest in the child or a desire to get him out of the way.

With regard to this area of parent-child relations, Bronfenbrenner says in summary: "Thus far, the trends that have appeared point predominantly in one direction—increasing leniency on the part of middle-class parents" (1958, p. 414).

The previous discussion in this book has been concerned largely with the quality of the responses of the parent to the child. What is the nature of the demands made of the child by the parent and how do these vary in the different social strata?

Bronfenbrenner's work categorizes this area of interest into four subareas: (1) response to the child's needs for dependency, (2) the child's progress in taking care of himself and assuming responsibility, (3) demands and expectations for the child in general, and (4) academic aspirations and expectations for the child.

In response to the child's need for dependency the higher-status mothers again appear somewhat more tolerant of these needs of the child. Is this because childhood dependency occurs in greater degree in the lower levels of society, or is it because the ideal in the lower levels is much greater independence than in the middle classes, thus requiring more severe treatment of dependency when it appears? The studies do not really provide an answer to these questions. Or, finally, is it merely that parents in the lower levels use incidences of dependency as occasions for the expression of hostility felt toward the child and hostility displaced from other objects in society? Though our orientation would lead us to expect this as at least a partial answer, we have no analysis that would support this.

There seems to be no trend or association regarding the expectations for self-care. However, in other areas (helping with housework, expressions of value placed on child's autonomy and mastery of tasks), there seems to be a clear trend: the middle-class mothers and fathers "require" more of their children than do urban working-class parents (Bronfenbrenner, 1958, p. 424). This requirement by middle-class parents may be more of a teaching device than an interest in getting immediate assistance. The working-class mothers and fathers, by contrast, may find it more effort than aid to attempt to secure assistance from younger children. This would be particularly true if the parent-child relationship is somewhat more strained and negative than in the middle-class family.

Academic Aspirations and
Expectations for the Child

Various studies cited by Bronfenbrenner also show that these middle-class parents make greater demands for school achievement and length of attendance. Thus we observe this relationship: greater permissiveness among middle-class parents than among working-class parents regarding the satisfaction of the child's desires and needs but a generally higher demand for performance, especially in the mastery of tasks and school. What general meaning might these have and what general consequences might result in the different social classes? One interpretation seems meaningful. The lower-class parent is communicating to the child inaction and "don'ts." The child is punished severely for making errors and is not particularly encouraged to perform. By contrast, the middle-class parent seems to be communicating action and performance, even if it is occasionally bad action or in error. The former seems to be the typical atmosphere of a traditional and stable (or rigid) society. The latter attitude is typical of the dominant values of the trial-and-error, bustling, achieving American society.[9]

9. This difference in children reminds the writer of the differences "observed"

THE INFLUENCE OF THE DISTRIBUTION OF SANCTIONS ON THE MALE AND FEMALE IN COMPLEX SOCIETIES

Much of what we have said regarding status influences both male and female, both husband-father and wife-mother. It is felt, however, that the amount of rewards received and resources held covers a much broader range for men than for women in a complex society. Women are less highly praised and less highly condemned. They are seldom heads of state or sentenced to death. We would predict that this difference in range would result in a much greater variability in the amount of stresses felt and much greater variation in behavior at different status levels for men than for women.[10] This might be expected, for it is the highly specialized occupational activity (and the corresponding extreme range of sanctions) occupied by males that is characteristic of modern society. In this sense, the female role is more traditional and more primitive, less specialized, and less subject to the extremes of high and low evaluation according to the society-wide system of sanctions. In some sense, less "achievement" is expected of her; perhaps this leads to fewer strains.

Somewhat greater strains in some areas (relative to those felt by women at the lower level) may be experienced by women at the upper levels. They may have particular difficulty (after passing through the school system where achievement is expected) playing their ascribed female roles in the family (Parsons, 1954, pp. 307-309). These roles require a certain amount of emotional and physical submission to the husband rather than competition on "equal" grounds.

The Female Role and the Kinship System

Not only is the woman's role less differentiated, but what variability does exist is often less apparent as a consequence of the

in rats by American and German psychologists as reported by Bertrand Russell. Curiously, German rats seemed to move cautiously with well-thought-out cognitive maps. Meanwhile, American rats, displaying a certain projective similarity to their observers, seemed to be moving toward success through bustling trial and error.

10. This is shown in the rates of mental illness among men and among women at different statuses (A. Hollingshead and F. Redlich, 1958, pp. 408-410). The rate of mental illness for women in the upper levels during adulthood is only slightly below their percentage in the total population. The percentage for men at this level is considerably below general rates. By contrast at the lower levels, the rate for women is only twice as great as its expected percentage but the rate for men is three times their percentage in the population as a whole. See Table 26 in this chapter.

segregation of the classes. The female, at whatever social level, is embedded to a greater extent in her kin and her class-segregated neighborhood, which become her reference groups for self-evaluation. This leads, at the lower levels, to fewer feelings of deprivation, fewer experiences of disesteeming evaluations relative to her husband (especially if she does not work). At the upper levels, it may also lead to fewer *positive* evaluations and sanctions for the wife relative to her husband. This does not ignore the fact, however, that the husband and wife occupy in some sense the same general status. Wives receive particular statuses as a consequence of their husbands' positions in society, and in many respects they share the same life chances as their husbands.

This greater exposure of the husband to the differential evaluation and power is most noticeable (at least in the urban industrial society) in his occupational role and whatever community roles he may have.

The Variable Influence of Status on the Two Parental Roles

Our prediction is that certain aspects of (1) the parental role (the ability to exercise authority, to provide emotional support, and to express hostility toward the child) and (2) social status will be more highly associated in the father role. Mothers, on the contrary, will play their roles in a less differentiated fashion at different class levels. This is felt to be the case because certain other factors of a more intimate nature than general social status (status in neighborhood, physical appearance, natal family experiences) might be relatively more important for the mother in providing her satisfaction in life and her ability to play her familial role.[11]

This general approach indicates that the mother in the lower classes, relative to the father, should provide greater emotional support, perhaps exercise more confident authority, and express less hostility toward the child. At the upper levels the mother's position in these areas will be less prominent and the father's more prominent. In terms of absolute level both she and her husband may, however, provide greater emotional support, greater control or guidance, and express less hostility toward the child than is true at the lower levels. We see again certain conditions operating to

11. The reduced variability of women compared with men is seen in a number of areas: intellectual scores, mental illness rates (from class to class), and years of education (from class to class).

decrease the importance of the father in the family in the lower levels. This creates problems for the son in terms of what his own adult male role shall be. The "big brother" movement seems to be an attempt to solve this problem by providing an "adequate" adult male (usually with middle-class values) as a model for the lower-class child. This may "keep him out of trouble" by, most probably, weakening the hold of his peer group and its values.

Though the mother's role in the lower class seems less impeded by her social position than the role of the father, she is still disesteemed by society. Our expectation is that this disesteem makes it difficult for her to express the positive emotions necessary for "adequate" socialization.[12] Her response, like that of the lower-class male, will be to compensate for her low social-class status by resorting to excellence in her ascribed role of femaleness as traditionally defined. This will mean a focus on sexual desirability, emotional attentiveness, and docility. There is some conflict, for her sexual role, unlike the male's, is not reinforced by the motivations (dissatisfaction and aggression) which arise from the evaluation received from society.[13] Perhaps the role that would emerge would be a combination of neglect and solicitous control mixed with hostile demands for obedience and conformity (see Table 17).

Relative Severity of Mother and Father at Different Status Levels

Let us investigate data regarding the relative severity of father and mother at each class level. Oddly enough, a review of the literature reveals that this has not been of specific concern to most researchers. However, if the degree of severity relates to the development of the superego, to the process of identification, and if the two parents as male parent or female parent have special involvements with girls and boys, then consistent patterns of relative severity

12. We place "adequate" in quotes because the individual with a less inhibiting superego and a spontaneous expression of emotion may be admired more in certain groups and may achieve better adjustment with his peers.

13. It appears that at the very lowest social levels aggressive need and its association with masculinity lead some teen-age girls to a special definition of the female role. Much of the traditional role of feminine docility is overwhelmed and they become behaviorally and verbally aggressive, begin to wear leather jackets, loaf, and run in gangs. This masculine-aggressive definition does not seem to interfere with sexual accessibility. This impression was obtained from reading the daily professional diary kept by a social worker (attached to the Special Youth Project of Boston, Walter B. Miller, director) during two years of work with a group of lower-class Negro girls.

at different class levels can help us explain much. They can help explain family structure, "problems" within the family, and sex-role development typical at different class levels.

We have already seen (Tables 13 and 14) that the degree of severity varies more for fathers than mothers. The father's severity appears to be more responsive to the differences in conditions at the various levels of society. Table 18 shows that this pattern also prevails when the data is handled somewhat differently. That is, the first and third most commonly used methods of discipline show the father's choice to be more highly associated with his status. Why should this be so? Earlier we offered the hypothesis that the father is more exposed to the evaluations of society than is the mother. Not only is the father more exposed to the differential evaluations of society in daily life and work but the family's class position is judged by himself and others to be more directly a consequence of his actions and position in society. It is his responsibility. We would reason that at the lower levels of society he will feel more acutely the frustration, and the resulting severity of his techniques is thus more highly associated with his status than is that of the mother's techniques. By contrast, the father at the upper levels, again feeling greater responsibility for the family's status and greater exposure to society's positive evaluation of him, will feel greater satisfaction. This reduces his motivations for aggressive family behavior and increases his positive resources to a greater degree than is true for his upper-level wife as mother.

The lower-class father, as a consequence of his greater involvement in general society, may also feel more strongly the external control which society exercises over the lower-class individual (see the discussion of external restraint in Chap. 4). Wives at various levels of society will experience much less variation in this degree of "external restraint" than is the case for their husbands. Thus,

Table 18

Percentage of Parents at Each Social Class Level Using Relatively Severe Discipline Techniques for Their Three Most Commonly Used Methods
(Total Cases in All Three Classes = 253)

	TOTAL CASES	FIRST CHOICE Father	FIRST CHOICE Mother	SECOND CHOICE Father	SECOND CHOICE Mother	THIRD CHOICE Father	THIRD CHOICE Mother
Upper class	72	37	37	10	10	57	56
Middle class	91	35	35	21	20	71	56
Lower class	90	52	41	19	19	70	57

according to our data, the mother at the upper levels of society is possibly somewhat more likely than the father to be severe in dealing with her son, but as one moves down the strata of society the father becomes increasingly severe.[14]

If our view is correct we would expect the Oedipal problem to be more intense among *lower* class *boys*, especially those who develop some problem in interacting with their peers. This is true because the father is relatively more distant and severe. We would predict that the Electra complex would appear more frequently among *upper* class *girls* where the forceful prestige of the father might lead the girl to great admiration or love and identification with the father.[15] It may be that some process such as this results in these trends: the tendency for the percentage of unmarried among upper-class women and lower-class men to be higher than among their sisters and brothers at other class levels, the tendency for homosexuality to be higher among lower-class men and higher-statused (college-educated) women who have strongly identified with a prestigeful father; and the tendency for men to marry down the social ladder.

Marrying down might be viewed as an "exchange" between strata of society. The upper classes occasionally "allow" their adequately identified males to marry the more adequately identified females of somewhat lower levels. This leaves those less adequate in familial roles, the upper-class female and the lower-class male, somewhat outside the marriage exchange and the family. Perhaps they turn their efforts to compensating activities in occupational roles, particularly the upwardly mobile ascriptively maladjusted lower-status male, or to more "regressive" libidinal roles (the *Skid Row* habitant or the procurer).

14. There is some danger, if only Tables 13 and 14 are studied, in viewing the greater association between class and father's role as really a function of the relatively greater hostility of the mother at the upper level rather than the increased severity of the father at the lower level. Table 18 and additional manners of analyzing this data which look at the specific relative severity of a given father and mother indicate strongly that the father's variation is greater and is a function of increasing severity of the lower-class father. This is true not so much because the *median* severity of the lower-class father is greater but because a sizable minority of this class are *much more* severe than is the case in the other classes.

15. It seems that the heroines portrayed by the actress Katherine Hepburn in the 1930s and 1940s were particularly plagued with this problem. Writers also seem to find the Electra theme a more common choice when dealing with the higher-statused family, and a reasonable facsimile of the Oedipal theme when dealing with the lower class (e.g., the estrangement between the coal-miner father and son and the son's close tie to the mother in D. H. Lawrence's *Sons and Lovers*).

It appears to this writer that the number of individuals of a single status who are criminally deviant or who have contributed to the achievement-oriented and innovating culture of the West is disproportionate to their number in the population. Perhaps several roles can be placed on a continuum. This continuum is the degree of emergence from the ascriptive *undifferentiated* biosocial base of human society. In this view the married female role is still largely based in this familial biosocial past and its undifferentiated status leads to less variation in sanctions received and status held. The married male role is defined moderately independently of the biosocial norms of the family and man's social past, though compared to the single male he is less frequently "subnormal" or "supernormal." The single individual or the familially marginal (e.g., childless, divorced, or maritally maladjusted) person, particularly the male, is most cut off from or liberated from the family and the conservative cultural climate it tends to perpetuate. This position may lead to great variation in his behavior as a person or a social group, from the most condemned to the most esteemed.

PRESENTATION OF DATA ON THE STRUCTURE OF FAMILY ROLES

Social Status and the Structure of Authority in the Family

It might be thought that the father in the lower class, if he wishes to express hostility, would maintain his position of control over the child and family in order that aggression could be expressed through his power position. In fact, this tends to be the "natural" line of thinking, given the individualistic slant of certain theoretical orientations which use the concept of "authoritarianism." This theoretical approach, with its individualistic heritage and traditional hostility to control, tends to view rigid hostility as an inevitable component of authority.

Our position leads us to predict the opposite. In the lower classes, the hold of extrafamilial statuses and rewards (the peer group and the sexual role), the father's feelings of familial and social inadequacy, and the greater likelihood of the wife's working all operate to reduce his involvement in the family and his exercise of authority without noticeably blocking the opportunities for aggression in the family. Here our expectation is supported. Table 19 shows that a general measure of authority results in a distribution where almost two-thirds of the fathers at the upper-class level clearly exercise most

authority. At the lower-class level slightly less than one-hal̸
fathers are clearly the major source of authority in the fam̸

Table 19
The Main Source of Authority in the Family
at Each Social Class Level

	Generally Father[a] (Number)	Generally Mother (Number)	Father (Per Cent)
Upper class	46	26	64
Middle class	57	36	61
Lower class	44	47	48

a. The figures in this column do not include cases where boy reported father was slightly more likely to be the source of authority. If they are included the relative picture at each class does not change.

This pattern has been found by a number of researchers and was reported in Chap. 2, Table 3. The pattern should also have some influence on the child's conception of family and sex roles, his identification, and, in terms of Strodtbeck's findings (1958), consequences for the boy's upward mobility from lower status. These will be discussed in Chap. 8.

Though the father generally exercises greater authority at the upper-class levels, he does so with greater "permissiveness" and with less rigidly tinged aggressiveness. These two generalizations are drawn from the figures presented in Tables 20 and 21. These tables show that the father in the upper classes is the general authority in the family, the main authority over the son, the main disciplinarian of the son; they show that he exercises "devoted" concern and control, and explains the requirements he makes of the son more frequently than the father in the lower classes.

Though we do not have parallel questions for the mother on all of these questions (Table 21), the general picture is the reverse except for two questions. Upper-class mothers are also more likely to explain their reasons for requiring the son to do something, but the difference between upper-class mothers and lower-class mothers (6 per cent) is much less than the difference between upper-class fathers and lower-class fathers (16 per cent) on this question. This can be seen in the first column of percentage figures in Table 21.

16. Approximately one-half of our questions in the sphere of authority and emotional support are worded in a way which probably reduces the class differences in *paternal* roles. These questions ask the subject which parent carries out a certain function "when both parents are around." Not only does the lower class father function less when he is there but he is around a little less frequently than the upper-class father (question 52, Appendix).

This perhaps shows again that the parental role of the father is more likely to vary at different class levels than is the role of the mother.

Though it is dangerous to depend too heavily on one question, the column entitled "Per Cent Who Usually Discuss Family Matters with Sons" in Table 21 presents an interesting distribution. The fathers at different class levels do not reveal any particular pattern on this, but the mother at the lower-class level is more likely (58 per cent) to discuss matters with her son than the mother at the upper-class level (46 per cent). Perhaps the mother and son in the upper-class level have less need to do this because the father is in control. The mother and son in the lower class may form a kind of decision-making coalition which excludes the father, causing, or as a consequence of, the father's withdrawal from the family. This line of thinking suggests the importance of bringing together findings concerning status in the family at different class levels, typical forms of behavior within small groups (their status structure or who communicates with whom), and theories of identification.

For example, a study of the literature on identification indicates that not only do certain kinds of socializing techniques increase the likelihood of identification, but also that the control of sanctions over the child itself increases identification with the controlling figure. The relatively adequate and powerful mother figure in the lower classes and the relatively more adequate and powerful father figure in the upper classes of society may help explain many of the characteristic patterns of identification. They help explain not only the family at that time but the way in which the next generation plays out family and other life roles which are sex-linked or involved with authority. Thus there may be a certain incompatibility in the lower class between one's conception of oneself as adult male (free from the controlling mother) and the acceptance of *any* authority. Acceptance of the authority here has more connotations of child-like acceptance of feminine control.

I believe that these questions, which were developed originally to measure authoritarianism, and the related results give further evidence of the intellectual confusion that can result from erroneous or unanalyzed use of concepts such as authoritarianism. It is a line of thought which suggests the equation of the two elements of this syndrome—authority and rigid hostility—and then expects to find one where it finds the other; or worse, after long familiarity with the syndrome, fails to distinguish the two at all. If these two elements are clearly distinguished, then there is no particular reason to expect that those higher-statused fathers who deal kindly and permissively with their sons and who explain their requirements will feel the need to discuss family matters with the son if they are the confident decision makers in the family (see Table 21). The con-

Table 20
Structure of Authority in the Family
at Different Social Class Levels

Class	Approximate Total Cases	Main Authority in Family (Per Cent of Fathers)	Main Authority over Son (Per Cent of Fathers)	Main Disciplinarian When Both Parents Present (Per Cent of Fathers)
Upper	70	64	54	59
Middle	90	61	43	59
Lower	90	48	45	36

Table 21
Amount and Type of Authority Exercised Over Son
by Father and Mother

Class	Approximate Total Cases	Per Cent Exercising Devoted and Close Control[a] Fathers	Per Cent Who Deal with Son Permissively Fathers
Upper	70	55	55
Middle	90	35	54
Lower	90	51	49

		Per Cent Who Usually Explain Requirements		Per Cent Who Usually Discuss Family Matters with Son	
		Fathers	Mothers	Fathers	Mothers
Upper	70	62	61	27	46
Middle	90	54	51	24	47
Lower	90	46	55	29	58

a. These figures based on responses to question 50 in Appendix.

trolling father is not necessarily the "bad" father. His strong control may be kind and devoted.[17] In analyzing the parent-child relation-

17. Table 21 shows that *our* middle-level fathers exercise the least devoted and close control over their sons. There was a certain weakness in the wording of the descriptive paragraphs of this question. It was possible for the son to respond in terms of the theme of devotedness *or* the theme of control. It may be that the upper-class sons replied in terms of one or both, the lower-class boys in terms of the other (strong, maybe harsh, control). This could explain the similarity in frequencies for these two groups while maintaining a "real" difference consistent with the pictures revealed by better and other questions. It might also help explain the

ship it seems wise to clearly distinguish three dimensions often encompassed in such terms. They are: (1) the dimension of high emotional and behavioral involvement to lack of involvement and indifference, (2) the dimension of positive (love) to negative (hostility) feelings, and (3) the degree of control exercised.

Instrumental and Expressive Authority in Parental Roles

My mother, an excellent woman, devoutly religious and devoted to her household, took care of our education, both physical and religious. My father did not concern himself with it, absorbed as he was with the work in his occupation. (Thibaudeau, 1875, pp. 52-53; as quoted in Barber, 1955, p. 49.)

In Talcott Parsons' general theory of action, the social system is differentiated along two basic axes: the instrumental-consummatory axis and the internal-external (to the system) axis. These have been defined earlier (Chap. 1). The family and its role structure are taken by Parsons et al. (1955) as a special case of system differentiation. In this theory the father is taken as the instrumental leader of the family and the mother as the expressive (consummatory) specialist.

Zelditch, in a chapter in *Family, Socialization, and Interaction Process* (Parsons and Bales, 1955, pp. 307-351), subjects this propositon to a cross-cultural test using ethnographic data from 56 societies. The terms are defined, as regards the family, by Zelditch in these ways:

Ego, therefore, will be considered *instrumental* leader of the nuclear family if the ethnographer's report offers statements of the form:

1. Ego is boss-manager of the farm; leader of the hunt, etc. Ego is the final court of appeals, final judge and executor of punishment, discipline, and control over the children of the family.

Ego will be considered *expressive* leader of the nuclear family if the ethnographer's report offers statements of the form:

2. Ego is the mediator, conciliator, of the family; ego soothes over disputes, resolves hostilities in the family. Ego is affectionate, solicitous, warm, emotional to the children of the family; ego is the "comforter," the "consoler," is relatively indulgent, relatively unpunishing. (p. 318.)

---

low percentage of middle-level fathers by contrast. Perhaps they are neither particularly controlling nor devoted but epitomize certain American family virtues of "freedom" for the child and self-reliance (letting him solve his own problems). We do not, however, have a great deal of faith in this rather complex interpretation and it might be well to let the figures stand in their naked unimportance.

A study of the societies reveals that most (46) bear out the Parsons-Bales proposition. Most of the remainder seem to lend themselves to some kind of explanation which renders them into cases in partial support of the proposition.

Two questions were introduced into the schedule to determine the degree to which the family role structure in the different classes would agree with this cross-cultural picture. These questions were about instrumental and expressive behavior which would not be universally recognized as unquestionably masculine or feminine in nature. The first question asked about decision making in an instrumental area (the use of money, question 47, the Appendix) and the second in an expressive area (recreation plans, question 48). These results are given in Table 22.

Table 22
Percentage of Parents Generally Making Decisions in Two Areas at Each Social Class Level

Class	Total Cases	Per Cent Making Instrumental Decisions			Per Cent Making Expressive Decisions		
		Father	Equal	Mother	Father	Equal	Mother
Upper	65	42	39	19	26	47	27
Middle	80	44	36	20	25	34	41
Lower	86	41	34	25	29	37	34

We see the father more frequently making instrumental decisions at all class levels, though the balance shifts a bit toward the mother in the lower class. In the expressive sphere the mother is somewhat more likely to make decisions at all class levels, and again, this occurs with greater frequency at the lower-class level than at the upper-class level. It occurs most frequently at the middle-class level, however.[18]

The general pattern is probably what would be expected in terms of the theoretical statements of Bales and Parsons, and of Zelditch's cross-cultural research. This is not clearly the case, however, for our questions ask who *makes decisions* (an instrumental function by Zelditch's definition) in two areas. One area, recreation, we considered consummatory or expressive. The other area, handling expenditures, was considered instrumental. Our data suggest that who is going to exercise power (action of an *instrumental* nature) is deter-

18. There is also some increase in the percentage of parents who *share* decisions equally in these two areas in the higher strata. A more detailed analysis of the responses to other questions on authority shows this also occurring rather frequently there.

mined not solely by the sex of the parent but by the *area of decision making*.

Another point makes it difficult to evaluate the meaning of this bit of data. There has been some lack of stability in the meaning of the terms "instrumental" and "expressive" (or consummatory) as the general theory of action has been developed or used by different writers. Thus, in terms of certain statements by Parsons, the matter of making decisions about what is to be done (a social system's goals or general policy) is consummatory and part of the *polity*. This seems somewhat contrary to Zelditch's definition, though there are problems about the precise system of reference in his definition.

We had anticipated an increase in the expressive decision-making power of the father at the lower levels.[19] This was expected because of results obtained from data gathered by Henry Wechsler (1958) which were kindly made available to and reanalyzed by this writer. These data, unlike most later found by the writer, showed the father to act increasingly as the source of affection among Harvard College undergraduates as one moves down the social-class scale. This pattern seems to tell us about the role structure in the stable upper-class and in lower-middle-class (or middle-class) families that produce upwardly mobile boys (Harvard graduates). It does not seem to tell us about the role structure of average families at different class levels. For this reason we will present these findings in the discussion of social mobility.

Social Status and Emotional Support
Received from Each Parent

Our theoretical focus on status leads us to reason in certain ways and make certain predictions. Because of the father's motivation to express hostility in the family situation, perhaps because of his greater tendency to view the son as a competitor for his wife's affection, and because of the father's ties to his peers and his withdrawal from the family as a consequence of feelings of social and familial inadequacy, the father in the lower class will tend to be the major source of affection less frequently.[20] In the father's absence the

19. There is the very slightest suggestion that something like this is operating. The data in Table 22 can be analyzed in a way which shows that though the lower-class father loses both kinds of authority, he loses less authority in the expressive realm than in the instrumental realm.

20. Preliminary interpretations of the family experiences of boys in lower-class leather-jacketed gangs indicate much rejection by the father as a consequence of the father's anxiety about showing affection toward the son. It appears that affec-

mother becomes very important as a source of affection and confidence. This perhaps creates further strains between the father and son. It also may lead to a close identification with the mother and rebellious adolescent attempts to escape this control and identification with the mother. As we discussed earlier, this may be the source of motivation for delinquency and adolescent aggressive pranks.

Table 23
Percentage of Sons Gaining Emotional Support from Their Fathers More Than Their Mothers

	Number Predominately from Mother	Number Predominately from Father[a]	Per Cent Predominately from Father[a]
Upper class	28	37	57
Middle class	39	41	51
Lower class	50	27	35

a. The figures in these columns include those who receive equally from each parent. This amounts to about ten cases at each class level. The mothers' percentage is the complement of these figures.

Table 24
Percentage of Fathers Who Play Dominant Role in Various Activities of Emotional Support

	Total Cases	Sons Talk Over Worries with Fathers Generally (Per Cent)[a]	Sons Talk Over Successes with Fathers Generally (Per Cent)[a]	Sons Prefer to Spend More Time with Fathers than with Mothers (Per Cent)[a]
Upper class	65	38	54	62
Middle class	80	31	37	59
Lower class	77	24	38	48

a. Per cents of sons who generally talk with mothers or prefer mothers are the complements of the figures in the table.

Tables 23 and 24 support this picture to a rather striking degree. Mothers in the lower class are nearly twice as frequently the source of emotional support as the father. In the upper class the situation is markedly the opposite (Table 23). Table 24 shows that this pattern repeats itself for three of the questions which make up the emotional support score of Table 23. This reveals that when the

tion toward the son arouses repressed erotic motivations which are controlled by hostile rejection. This would be in accord with our earlier discussion of the hold of the same-sex peer group over the father after marriage. This interpretation was provided by Dr. Eleanor E. Maccoby.

lower-class son must choose which parent is *more* supportive he chooses his mother.

This measure of emotional support received may give further support to our prediction about the probable class distribution of Oedipus and Electra complexes and their consequent influence on family roles of adults of the next generation.

Table 23 shows the combined responses to the three questions in Table 24 and a fourth question which is not presented there. This fourth question asked the son to indicate how open his mother and father were in expressing their affection. It asked for an absolute rating of each rather than asking him to compare his two parents. Here one would expect the upper-class mother to be warmer than the lower-class mother. Actually, no real difference is observed. After dichotomizing the cases, we find 58 per cent of the upper-class mothers to be open in the expression of their affection and 60 per cent of the lower-class mothers. This may be a weakness of the question, or again may indicate that there is much less association between general status and the mother's behavior in the family. A later analysis will give us some possible understanding of why the upper-class, *nonworking* housewife and mother may be less warm. That is, in *this* group the lower warmth may be real.

AN INTERPRETIVE REVIEW OF THE INFLUENCE OF STATUS ON PARTICULAR FUNCTIONS OF THE FAMILY

We have looked at some of the influences of status on socialization and interacting roles in the family. Another important way of analyzing the family is to discuss in detail its functions—that is, to classify and analyze the things it contributes to society and the individual. In the simplest societies the family or kinship system "does" almost everything (political activities, reproduction, religious functions, etc.), for "society" and "kin" are intertwining and nearly coterminous. In an industrial society the kinship system becomes greatly simplified and gives up much of its functionality to other institutions. Nevertheless, it carries out several functions which are of interest to us here. The functions are points for further elaboration of our approach; we see that the influence of status on the socialization function is not simple and direct but gets greatly complicated and obfuscated as the family carries out other functions: reproduction, maintenance of the adult's and child's personality (once socialized), and placement. Much of our analysis so far has looked at the influence on the socialization function as the family carries out its personality-maintenance functions at various status levels. We have proposed that it is probably because the personality-maintenance problems are so taxing in the deprived levels of society that the "undesirable" familial responses emerge in these levels. For an analysis of other responses and their influence on another function, let us see how reproduction is influenced by status.

Social Status and the Reproductive Function

A pattern long prevailing in Western industrial society is the inverse relationship between social status and the birth rate; Table 25 shows this relationship. The pattern may show some signs of disappearing in highly urbanized areas and in the United States (even though it is still revealed clearly in the number of siblings of our subjects in different classes).

It has not been well established how permanent and common this shift really is. Edin and Hutchinson (1935) found in Stockholm that the upper economic groups are somewhat more fertile than the lower income groups. This possible shift in the relationship between birth rate and status is often explained by the assumption that knowledge and skills in contraceptive techniques have trickled down to the lower-status groups.

A study by Stycos (1955) indicates, however, that having children or not, using contraceptives or not, depends on much more than the accessibility and knowledge of contraceptive devices. Motivations regarding one's status and sex role, not surprisingly, enter the picture.

Table 25
Mean Number of Children Per Family
at Different Class Levels
New Haven, 1950

Class	Number of Children
I	1.6
II	1.7
III	3.4
IV	4.0
V	4.7 (estimate)

Source: Compiled from data given in A. Hollingshead and F. Redlich, *Social Class and Mental Illness* (New York: John Wiley & Sons, Inc., 1958), pp. 69-134.

The higher birth rate in the lower levels of Puerto Rican society seems to result from several factors and needs: the greater importance of kin as sources of emotional support and economic security, the importance placed on femininity and forceful masculinity (*machismo*). Masculinity and femininity are manifested, in part, in sexuality and by having many children (see Table 10). Drawing on our approach, we would interpret this as a greater need to validate one's ascribed role, female or male, given the relatively low status in the achieved roles, occupation or class. Though the official culture of Puerto Rico is greatly influenced by Protestant United States possession, it is probably not dominated by that ethic and for this reason the motivations may be somewhat different.

It would also seem that the impulsive demands for unfettered and immediate erotic gratification (perhaps a rather anxious and regressive response to frustration) lead to somewhat greater sexual activity and less planned contraception.

And, relative to the authority-exercising higher strata, there is a greater need to have children (who occupy a lower power position) over whom they can exercise authority, toward whom they can express aggression with relative immunity, in whose eyes they may appear esteemed, and with whom they can unguardedly, and in security, regress.

One need only watch analytically the behavior of, say, traditionally minded whites toward most Negroes ("They're just like children") to see how those of higher status "use" those of lower status for similar relaxation and regression at a time and in a manner somewhat of their own choosing. So, perhaps, parents at the bottom without such socially defined adult "children" require to a greater degree numerous members of an unskilled new generation with whom these same regressive needs and roles can be acted out daily. And children are not without their regressive opposites—pets.

The effects of status feed through the reproductive function to again influence socialization and placement. Just as the poor seem to have more mouths to feed and fewer economic resources with which to do it, so they also have a greater number of hearts and minds to develop and fewer positive emotional resources with which to do it. In this way social status and the birth rate influence socialization. Some indirect evidence for this view is found in Sears et al. (1957, pp. 57, 409).

Social Status and the Personality-maintenance Function

We said earlier that one of the important functions of the family in complex societies was the personality-maintenance function. That is, the family provides ascriptive security, a situation in which a person may be himself. It is an arena in which love and hostility can be exchanged more intimately and more freely.

The family maintains the personality of the adult because, to an important extent, somatic needs, infantile and childhood needs and situations in the family first created the personality and the structure of its present needs. It still requires the family situation to satisfy these hidden and overt needs of the adult in adult ways. One cannot act with the rather impersonal, controlled, and changing standards of general society at all times without suffering considerable tension, anxiety, and possibly feelings of rejection.

A thread of ideas which is basic to our interests is this: the experiences of individuals in different classes are quite different at work and in daily life. Individuals at the bottom, though they may have more personality problems to begin with and may drift into the lower strata, continue as adults to have many more societal experiences which create great problems of interpersonal adjustment. These problems are then reflected in familial roles, particularly in the way in which the parent socializes the child.

However the relevant data may be interpreted, there can be little doubt that (1) those occupying lower levels in our society think and act in ways which get them classified as severely maladjusted, and that (2) marital status relates to mental health, especially among males in the lower levels of society. These are shown strikingly in Tables 26 and 27.

Table 26
Social Class, Marital Status, and Mental Disorder

Social Class Level (Approximate)	Total Population Married	Total Population Single	RATE OF ALL MENTAL DISORDERS PER 100,000 Married (Age 20-49)		Single (Age 20-49)	
			Male	Female	Male	Female
I & II (Upper and upper middle)	488	2044	510	719	3336	1728
III (Lower middle)	389	2273	300	528	1829	2306
IV (Working)	495	2590	480	432	2346	1503
V (Lower)	1095	5598	1010	1029	6502	1756

Source: Data compiled by author from several tables in appendix 4, pp. 408-423, in A. Hollingshead and F. Redlich, *Social Class and Mental Illness* (New York: John Wiley and Sons, Inc., 1958).

This suggests from our perspective that the distribution of esteem and power (status or class) is reflected in the strains felt and the rate of psychological casualties in the different classes. It also suggests, since the rate of mental illness among single males (those without the family arena) at the lower levels is particularly high, that the familial situation is "used" to sustain the personality of the individual, especially the married male, at the lower levels.

Table 27
Social Class, Marital Stability, and Mental Disorder

Social Class Level (Approximate)	Divorce and Separation Rate[a]	Median Per Cent Marriages Rated Happy[b]	Per Cent Children Under 17 Living in Broken Homes[c]	Per Cent Unmarried[c]	Rate of Psychosis per 100,000[c]
Upper and upper middle	7.6	67	4	8	200
Middle	10.4	60	10	8	291
Working	12.5	58	18	9	518
Lower	23.0	52	41	12	1504

a. Data in this column obtained from reports of high school students in Spokane, Washington. Source: "Differential Divorce Rates by Occupations," in H. Ashley Weeks, Social Forces, Vol. 21 (March, 1943), pp. 334-337.

b. Data in this column obtained by asking acquaintances of couples to rate happiness of marriage. From Richard O. Lang, "The Rating of Happiness in Marriage" (unpublished Master's thesis, University of Chicago, 1932). Reproduced as graph in Meyer Nimkoff, Marriage and the Family, p. 200. Blood and Wolfe (1960, pp. 171 and 228) give similar evidence.

c. Data in these columns from A. Hollingshead and F. Redlich, Social Class and Mental Illness (New York: John Wiley and Sons, Inc., 1958).

The greater strains and problems of adjustment seem to intrude into the family's life and affect its general happiness and stability (Table 27). The divorce and separation rates are three times higher in the lower levels than in the upper levels, and even those who remain married at the lower levels seem less happily married.

These conditions are reflected further in the large per cent of children in broken homes and the problem the socialized child has in developing sufficient motivations to enter into marriage (i.e., the larger per cent of unmarried at the lower levels of society). The parent-child strains result in inadequate internalization of the adult family roles.

These interpretations must be regarded with considerable caution, for there are, no doubt, selective factors related to mental health operating to determine who marries and who remains single. These figures are not presented to prove the line of thought but rather to give some feel of the magnitude of differences and the reasonableness of the approach being taken here.

The Displacement of Aggression
by the Married and Unmarried

If unmarried and a minor, the male's lower status (and its consequences) in work or in school is reinforced by his lower status in the family situation as well. With this added position of low status he directs his accumulated hostility not so much into the family (though siblings may be vulnerable), but toward society in general, in youthful pranks or in crime. And as we have maintained in our discussion of the personality maintenance function of the family, if married he may direct it to other family members.

We would hypothesize that the intimate and emotional nature of the family, as a group which absorbs hostility, may explain the rather sharp drop in crime rates in the late twenties among males in our society. Aggression which in adolescence and the early twenties was directed toward the society is now expressed in the family— an "arena of emotions."

Crime rates among the married and unmarried are summarized by Sutherland in this way:

> Married males have a lower commitment rate than single males in all age groups except fifteen to nineteen; the rate is only slightly lower in the age twenty to twenty-four, but is significantly lower in later ages.[21]

This aggression expressed in the family also impedes a satisfactory marital relationship unless the wife is sufficiently masochistic. The traditional and Freudian view that women are in some way more disposed toward masochism may rest somewhat on physiology. This does not seem necessarily invalid, even from our sociological perspective. Much of this disposition, however, may be a normative development to rationalize the greater needs for males to impulsively regress within the husband-wife relationship. This need arises from the Oedipal problem and resolution, and from the demand that the adult male in his extrafamilial roles act with greater emotional control and with independence away from the security of the "hearth." Once the norm develops out of social need and behavior, the girl through socialization and identification with her mother finds this norm somewhat more consistent with her own motivations.

21. Edwin H. Sutherland and Donald R. Cressey, *Principles of Criminology* (Philadelphia: J. B. Lippincott Company, 1955), p. 186. The higher rate among the 15-19 age group is probably largely a function of the class distribution of crime and the class distribution of early marriages. In both cases the rates are high in the lower levels of society.

Though we would guess that suffering seems to be enjoyed somewhat more among lower-level women (particularly lower-middle-class women) than among other segments of the population, this preference does not seem sufficient to absorb the hostility expressed by the husband. Conflict, desertions, divorces, wife-beating, and the arrival of police to solve family problems form a pattern progressively more common as one moves down the class levels in the urban situation. The wife is less willing to adapt her emotions to the needs of the husband because she has less to gain in terms of prestige, material comforts, and security. This inflexibility may result in conflict and the husband's or wife's withdrawal from the marital relationship.

SUMMARY

From the various tables and sources of data a general picture emerges regarding parental roles and social status.

1. Parents tend to be more severe and hostile socializers at the lower levels of society.

2. Fathers at the lower levels, and possibly mothers at the upper levels, tend to be somewhat more severe than their spouses.

3. These two factors are explained as a consequence of the distribution of rewards in the society by class and by sex (of parent) within classes. It is reasoned that variation in rewards (esteem, power, etc.) results in variation in satisfaction with life and with the kinds of sanctions that can be used in the parental role. Psychological responses are used as intervening variables to explain the way in which this variation in satisfaction associated with status results in the variation in the adjustive norms of parental roles at different class levels.

4. The greater variation in status and esteem in society is again reflected most strongly in the father-role in other areas of family life. He, relative to the mother, acts as a more important source of authority, emotional involvement, and warmth in the upper strata of society. He is less important in all these areas at the lower levels.

The variation by class and parent in these family role conditions: severity of socialization, degree of hostility, locus of authority, and locus of emotional support, give some support to our discussion in this chapter of the family and class genesis of identification and patterns of sexual behavior in the different classes. They will be used later (Chap. 8) to analyze further the process of identification and to provide additional evidence of their influence on adult sex roles and occupational choice.

From the tables here and from other studies reviewed by Bronenbrenner we observe these patterns: those parents occupying higher status seem to be more permissive of *certain* "undesirable" behavior (such as the expression of impulse, aggression, and sexuality) but present the child with higher expectations and demands in other areas, particularly in the areas of mastery of skills and academic achievement. These expectations are implemented with less "severe" socialization techniques while, or perhaps because, the overall relationship is more affectionate.

Further investigation in this work will attempt to look more carefully at the father's role than most studies have thus far done, to look particularly at this role as it influences the postadolescent male, and to look more analytically at the defining components of social class—especially those experiences related to the father's work experience. We also want to develop a statement which will form a basis for our discussions of emerging subcultures.

In the next chapter we investigate further aspects of the influence of status on family roles. We attempt to determine if our perspective on the general influence of status can be used meaningfully to investigate the influence the father's specific position in the structure of work has on his family action. There we proceed to investigate more thoroughly the influence of autonomy and external restraint —conditions we have thus far neglected.

CHAPTER 7

Work and the Family

THE ECONOMIC SYSTEM AND THE
FAMILY—A REVIEW

In a broad and indirect sense this entire book is concerned with the influence of work on the family. This is true because the individual's occupation seems crucial in determining his placement in the status system of our society. It then has many of the consequences we have tried to outline. In this chapter, however, we wish to look at the direct influence of specific aspects of work on the nature of behavior in the family. This problem is not new or an unexplored field.

Murdock (1949), in his broad study of the structure of kinship behavior, points out and substantiates the central significance of economic factors and the allocation of economic roles in the determination of kinship rules. This process is sometimes placed in dramatic relief. For example, in the study of the Tanala-Betsileo (Linton and Kardiner, 1947), we see changes occurring rapidly within a generation or two. Changes in the method of cultivation and the size and location of fields of rice brought about great changes in the residence of family groups, particularly newly married ones. These in turn influenced the emotional attitudes between generations and the functioning of the kinship system in the political and religious systems. That is, the use of smaller and sometimes isolated fields resulted in an emphasis on the nuclear family and a reduction of the involvement of kinship systems in the political and religious institutions.

This is a pattern frequently observed in what one might incautiously call the evolution of society. The segregation of family behavior is especially helpful in explaining the kinship system of Western industrial societies. These societies have an economic system which places a premium on mobility of the population, geographically and socially. This tends to diminish greatly the emotional and functional significance of kin beyond the nuclear family. It reduces the possibility of the kin group itself operating as a political group or as an economic organization. The economic system of industrial societies not only emphasizes the nuclear family at the expense of more extended kin ties, it also changes the structure of emotions within the nuclear family. Just as several centuries ago it greatly weakened the obligations and emotional ties between members of an extended family (e.g., between aunt and niece), now through the socializing influence of peers, teachers, school, and welfare organizations, it may tend to greatly weaken the ties between members of the immediate nuclear family.

The economic system also has other indirect influences on the roles of the nuclear family. It has been found that during the depression (Bakke, 1940) and among the chronically unemployed (Frazier, 1939) the father-husband loses authority. And Elizabeth Bott's study (1957, pp. 106-113) shows that in a society which is already relatively mobile, the more mobile elements take on certain characteristics (e.g., equality of husband and wife) that are considered ideal in contemporary eyes. In her intensive interviews of twenty families in urban England she found certain patterns of family behavior emerging which, though they associated with social class, associated even more with the degree to which the couple had moved (usually in response to new economic opportunities) and had become isolated from past associations. If husband and wife were still located (socially and geographically) where they had grown up they continued to maintain those past ties of kin, friends, and peers. In this situation they also shared fewer social activities, interests, and household tasks. There was less sharing of emotional needs and less "togetherness." By contrast, if they had "moved" and were now isolated from their past social involvements they tended to turn toward one another and begin to share with one another certain needs, tasks, and leisure activities.

As stated, we want to look at the specific conditions of work and their influence on particular roles in the family. A study done in the Detroit area by the University of Michigan (Miller and Swanson, 1958) attempted to relate methods of child-rearing not only to "class" as a somewhat undefined variable but also to the particular type of occupation of the father. The basic division of occupations was between those which demanded initiative, individual action, and risk-taking; and those of a bureaucratic nature where ideal behavior would be conformity to established practices and the decisions of superiors.

That research chose to look in detail at occupation for some of the same reasons we have. The importance of occupation for family behavior—it was felt—rests not simply on its significance in placing the family in some prestige position. Certain types of occupations draw certain types of husbands and wives and in turn are instrumental in creating certain attitudes and philosophies.[1] These philosophies are then reflected in family behavior.

This theory was borne out in general. Parents in those cases where the father held an entrepreneurial type of occupation tended to expect and foster internalization of norms in the child at a somewhat earlier age and in a greater number of areas than was the case for bureaucratically employed fathers. Also, the mothers of the entrepreneurial group, compared with the bureaucratic group, had a more active and controlling approach toward their family situation and life.

Hammond (in Oeser and Hammond, 1954, pp. 238-248) reports on various activity and authority patterns in the family and shows their relationship to the father's work position. The important patterns which he found were:

1. Autonomic   (husband acts and decides in a number of areas, wife acts and decides independently in a number of areas)
2. Syncratic   (husband and wife tend to act and decide in a number of areas together)
3. Husband autocratic (husband decides and acts or has wife act in a number of areas)
4. Wife autocratic   (wife decides and acts or has husband act in a number of areas)

In general he found that the employers and self-employed almost all have autonomic family patterns, and that two-thirds of the skilled workers have the syncratic pattern. There was some tendency for the "husband autocratic" type to predominate in the semiskilled group.

Hammond brought forth four factors which he felt helped to explain these findings:

1. For another example of this process see Robert K. Merton, "Bureaucratic Structure and Personality," *Social Theory and Social Structure* (New York: The Free Press of Glencoe, 1949), pp. 151-160.

1. Ideological factors. In general, members of the two upper economic groups support a political ideology of laissez-faire. Thus each spouse should have an area of personal sovereignty.

2. Educational and 3. Cultural lag. The family is a conservative institution and it seems likely that the less alert or involved members of society may retain traditional patterns after they have become inappropriate for the urban industrial setting (e.g., the "husband autocratic" pattern).

4. Reciprocal satisfactions in work and family situations. If the father "derives satisfactions from his role in one situation, then he will not be forced to seek it in the other." This evidently refers primarily to the satisfaction obtained in exercising authority. If authority is exercised and activity is high in the work then he is apt to let his wife take control of the family. This interpretation is in some conflict with our general findings and approach.

Evidence of the interaction of work satisfaction and family behavior was also obtained. A correlation of 0.51 was found between the husband's dissatisfaction with his work and the general level of tension between family members in the home. This is a finding in agreement with our approach and findings (Table 38).

STATUS, SANCTIONS, AND WORK

Given our interest in status, let us see if we can look at the work situation and define it in terms of many or few rewards. Perhaps we can then trace the influence on the family of this wealth or poverty of sanctions in work, using some of our previous concepts and introducing a new emphasis. This is not to deny the influence of the family on other areas of life and on work, itself. Later we will deal with this direction of influence in our discussion of the son's occupational choice. Work also has a more immediate day-to-day influence on the husband-father's behavior outside the family.

The new emphasis or concept which we want to introduce here is autonomy in the social organization of work. We want to trace its consequences for the motivations of the husband-father.[2]

It is outside our scope to try to tie together for our purposes the body of literature of such writers as Blau (1946), Gouldner (1959a), Barnard (1938), Firth (1939), and Homans (1950,

2. The manner in which these two systems (social structure and the personality) can be integrated for purposes of theoretical development and research is dealt with in a rewarding and insightful way by Alex Inkeles, "Personality and Social Structure," in Robert K. Merton, Leonard Broom, Leonard S. Cottrell, Jr., eds., *Sociology Today* (New York: Basic Books, Inc., 1959), pp. 249-276.

especially pp. 48-130, 369-440). These writers deal with the structure, functioning, and integration of work as a social system. Our limited approach has certain dangers, for the problems of primary-group structure, reference groups, the meaning of authority, and specialization may not be sufficiently within our focus of attention and errors may be committed as a consequence. Nevertheless, recognizing these limits, we will attempt to offer an analysis of *certain* variables which are a definition of status and which we believe influence the motivational structure of the worker sufficiently for him to carry this affect into the family system.

Types of Statuses

A person's status consists of inherited and accumulated sanctions, positive and negative. Now, since our interest is in status, it might be appropriate for us to try to make some analysis of the kinds of statuses people have in general *and* in a work situation. There are some problems in doing this, for in a concrete sense there are as many statuses as there are normative systems and concrete groups. On an analytical level a statement of what kinds of statuses there are would require a definitive statement of the over-all organization of society or social systems and their significant subsystems.

Weber, in his discussion of this problem, proposes the three broad types: wealth, honor, and power (1946, pp. 180-195). Very simply stated, these three refer to the individual's resources in the economic institution, the approval and honor he receives as a consequence of certain ascriptive memberships and styles of life, and the control or influence he has in political and communal activities.

Parsons (1954, pp. 386-439) gives a more detailed and systematic statement on the problem of status and stratification. Again simply stated, the position is that evaluations and statuses can be analytically distinguished in each of the functionally specialized systems in society. Statuses also appear in each specialized subsystem at various levels of social organization.

It seems wise for our purposes to bypass this important problem and instead propose a rather simple paradigm which has value in our discussion of the relationship between general social status, status and experiences in the work setting, and the family. It is a statement which is developed for this purpose but which we hope might have general application to status and social control in society generally. We will talk about the broad *kinds of sanctions* (rather than kinds of statuses) or resources that can be given or taken away, that can be exchanged to obtain a particular status in a given interaction system. And we will talk about the broad pattern or *structure of this exchange* of sanctions. That is, we will talk about the basic choices available to social actors in distributing sanctions.

Analytical Types of Sanctions

For the purpose of analysis, we can distinguish between various types of sanctions. Basically, they seem to be: (1) *interpersonal* approval or disapproval, (2) material possessions, (3) control over others (authority or power), and (4) control over self (autonomy). Let us discuss and define these four and explain why we use them.

Interpersonal Approval and Disapproval. Behavior or qualities in accord with expectations lead to approval, and behavior or qualities which disappoint or frustrate expectations lead to disapproval. Approval or disapproval may be of various forms and strength. It may be intimate physical contact, a smile, a vote a "yes," a "no," or even attempts to slay. One of the examples, a vote, indicates organized and indirect. Also, such examples as a smile or a "no" indicate that the value of the sanction depends on the psychological importance of the individual sanctioning.

Material Comforts and Possessions. A second type of sanction consists of objects possessed, physical comforts obtained, and perhaps money. However, money is such a general mechanism of sanctioning that it may indicate approval, power, or mere shrewdness, and may in turn be used to obtain certain desired resources.

Control over Others. A third type is authority, responsibility, and power. That is, control over the behavior of others. If the control is normative it comes about not necessarily because of some manipulation of approval and disapproval nor of material products but because the individual occupies a certain position vis-à-vis another person or group (the bureaucratic chief) or has a certain "hold" over others which brings forth commitment to him (the charismatic leader). The individual has control over others not because he must bargain with or coerce those under his command by giving or taking away great approval and material comforts, but because he is supported by certain commitments to legitimate norms in the one case and to the person in the other.

If the authority or control becomes nonnormative (naked power), then the wielder of power is operating in quite another dimension. No longer does the powerful individual occupy a position through legitimate support and commitment. He now must use coercion. He must manipulate various kinds of sanctions.

Control over Self. A fourth type of sanction is autonomy. The analyses of power, status, and authority have generally tended to focus more on how much control is being exercised by someone *over someone.* We must also study the socially controlled distribution of autonomy (power and authority to control oneself) and perhaps freedom (permission to "achieve" or conform in excess of norms or permission to fall short of norms). This autonomy or freedom is something that is desired in varying degrees and which a society may give or take away. Not only is it a desirable state in itself but it may be used in a way to obtain further positive sanctions or avoid certain negative sanctions. It is this somewhat neglected source of status which we will study in terms of its effect on the worker and upon his family roles.

Autonomy is also a type of status and social variable which ties in with the concept of "external restraint," a concept which was a basic tool in Henry and Short's discussion (1954) of the relationship between status and the handling of aggression. Our own treatment and predictions of the influence of autonomy on family behavior follow many of their basic lines of thought as presented in their own work and as was discussed in Chap. 4.

Of the four types of sanctions which may provide an individual status within the specific conditions of the work situation, autonomy is the only one we will analyze in detail. We do not have data which might provide food for thought about the influence of varying degrees of approval or possessions *within* the work situation. Our whole study of social class, of course, attempts to look at the influence of these two types of sanctions and the variations of status they provide the father *outside* the work situation.

How Sanctions Are Used

In discussing power and authority the distinction between authority (legitimate power) and "naked power" (illegitimate power) is usually made. We feel that this distinction should not be limited to power. There is normative and nonnormative access to sanctions and behavior in other areas. Thus approval can be legitimate (a vote) or illegitimate (seduction), economic resources and status can be used legitimately (a purchase) or illegitimately (a bribe, gambling profits), and autonomy may be legitimate (individual responsibility) or illegitimate (excessive withdrawal). Let us turn to the problem of the social control of social control (sanctioning) and relate it to autonomy.

The individual applying or receiving sanctions may (with varying degrees of freedom as a consequence of the degree and detail
of normative control) use these sanctions in ways determined by two
basic conditions. *First,* he may use them or have them used for relatively immediate gratification (consummatory) or he may not consume them or not allow the sanctions received to be expended
except for some more distant goal. This latter choice would be using
the sanctions instrumentally. *Second,* the sanctions are consumed
or put into use for oneself (or the unit of reference) or are put into
use or expended on someone else or another unit of society. Perhaps
the following diagram will assist communication.

Chart 1
Choice of Use of Sanctions
(Rewards and Punishments)

	Instrumental (Reality Principle)	Consummatory (Pleasure Principle)
Public Use	Public Investment or Exchange A	Public Celebrations or Pleasure B
Private Use	Private Savings and Investment C	Private Gratification D

In terms of money these choices are easily understood. One
spends freely for one's own pleasure (cell D) or for another's
pleasure (cell B). Or one saves and invests for future private gain
(cell C) or is taxed or gives or invests for future public gain (cell A).[3]
In terms of approval or disapproval it may be less clear. As an
example, one might ask, "Does a supervisor express criticism and
approval of a subordinate only in a way to gratify certain immediate
needs to express hostility or affection (cell D), or does he express

---

3. *Private* and *public* refer not just to the person and society. They are relative
terms, *private* referring to the smaller and more immediate unit and *public* to some
more inclusive unit of society. In this sense they are like Homans' and Parsons' *internal* and *external* systems.

disapproval or approval in a way that may require control of impulse but will in the long run make the worker a more effective producer for society (cell A)?"

Similarly, the well-loved husband may "consume" this love in order to maintain or increase his own gratificational balance or he may use this receipt of positive affect for patient and loving socialization of the child (cell A) or higher occupational achievement (cell A).[4]

Defining Components of Autonomy

The individual or group, however, is not free to choose freely in what way he will use the sanctions. Certain norms are recognized, and countersanctions are used to enforce the proper use of sanctions. The detail and degree of specification of use, however, vary in different situations. If a person wishes to buy a coat the price given is a very specific statement of the use of sanctions. The countersanctions if the coat is stolen, though somewhat less specific, are well known. If, however, one is placed in charge of a class of problem students the general instructions may be to "use your best judgment." There is, of course, a body of more detailed but implicitly understood instructions. Nevertheless, a large area of behavior (social control and expenditure of sanctions) is to be determined as circumstances and the judgment of the teacher dictate.

Let us relate the above points to our interest in this chapter. As one moves from the highest level of symbolic control (culture) to the rules in particular social situations, the statements regarding the approved behavior become more specific and detailed. Some of these statements are the rules determining how (or in what cells of Chart 1) sanctions will be expended. Likewise, we feel that as one moves from positions of high status to low status in most systems and in the work situation, the norms for the use of sanctions attached to the individual's role become more detailed and specific. This is true just as in the body as a system, the central nervous system (as a subsystem), which is in "control," seems to determine policy whereas the circulatory system must play its role in a more specific way. Thus not only are norms more specific at the lower levels but the use of sanctions to enforce those norms is more specific and detailed.

It is this variation in specification and detail of expected behavior

---

4. That the personality as a system or any social system operates something like a bank account may be a dangerous assumption. That is, that it can give out certain sanctions only if certain sanctions are received. How valid or helpful it is can only be determined by using it.

and use of sanctions *and* the locus of control over the individual
which we believe define the variable of autonomy. Perhaps Chart 2
clarifies our points. In this chart the policy maker or artist has the
greatest autonomy. The assembly-line worker has the least.

Chart 2
Levels and Categories of Autonomy

Locus of Control

		Other Individuals (as Sanctioning Agent)	The Self (Internalized Norms and Their Sanctions)
Degree of Specification of Norms of Behavior and Use of Sanctions	Low	Administrator Policy Advisor	Policy Maker Creative Artist
	High	Assembly-Line Worker	Technical Specialist

Autonomy and the Individual

Generally, one who has access to a large supply of positive sanctions (status) is expected to have, and is granted, the right to control
himself and determine the use he will make of his access to these
sanctions. This grant and expectation is in itself, for most individuals,
a further reward.

Why is the individual with access to many sanctions given further
positive sanctions (autonomy)? We feel that his skills, his personality, and his knowledge (all of which are sanctions he can give or
take away) place him in a position to bargain for a work role more
in accord with his own motivational needs. We do not maintain
that such a bargaining process goes on explicitly when each incum-
bent enters a position. Rather, these factors produce traditions which
are generally accepted so long as they continue to work on the implicit
or explicit level.

Autonomy is advantageous (generally) not only to the high-status
individual or subgroup, but to the system as a whole. It allows the
individual a certain flexibility as to when he may use sanctions instrumentally and for the public good and when he may use them for
personal gratification. This flexibility allows him to maintain a
gratificational balance and motivational level higher than would be
possible with high specification. It also allows him to use his own

judgment in creating independent and insightful solutions to system problems.

There is, of course, the possibility that he will abuse his autonomy. Only an ideally "public-spirited" individual would be completely guiltless of this "abuse."[5] Several things seem to be operating here, however: (1) Freedom to abuse this position maintains his motivational level so that his over-all contribution to the activity is satisfactory to other members of the system and is probably even greater than it would otherwise be. (2) His status and autonomy (access to flexible use of sanctions) allow him legitimately to siphon off certain of these positive sanctions into other areas of his personal life. In the family this allows him to be a better economic provider, to be a more loving and patient father and husband, and to take a vacation or a "breather" determined more by his needs than is possible at the lower levels. (3) The "abuse" has normative limitations—a person cannot embezzle to provide an education for his son—but the individual's recognized ability to act within these limits is part of occupational socialization and is one of the requirements (e.g., responsibility, honesty, etc.) for elevation to high status.

Finally, this approach does not imply that individuals of high status in the work situation (at least in an achievement-oriented society) are free to produce or not to produce, to conform or not to conform. In the work situation they must generally conform, produce, and contribute more. But these individuals have, to a greater extent, internalized the norms of the referent interactive system, or, possibly, norms of even greater excellence. They are in a sense more complete systems; they control themselves and thus have autonomy.

Though rigid control safeguards against inefficiency or abuse of sanctions in the short run, it makes resource allocation (in terms of (1) the particular situation faced and, (2) the individual's motivational level) inefficient in the long run. With regard to the second point, inefficiency results because certain deprivations cause resentment to build up in the individual and reduce his motivations for work. With regard to the first point, sanctions or resources must be expended according to short-run demands for conformity to the existing protective norms and not according to the most effective allocation for long-range goals.

The position of the autonomous person (or group) allows him greater freedom in determining exactly when and how much to

5. "Public-spirited" is used here in the sense that there is perfect accord between his own norms and society's expectations and between his own needs and behavior and society's needs and expectations.

produce and when and how many sanctions may be consumed in the work situation to sustain his gratificational balance and motivational level.[6] Autonomy is perhaps greatest for the creative artist, somewhat less for the business entrepreneur, and perhaps least for a closely supervised electrician's helper or bus driver who must make his trips on schedule.

From this perspective, the individual who has little autonomy generally must follow detailed specifications of how he will use sanctions (time, his energy, and his interest), and these specifications are made by others. Generally, unless he is a person who enjoys subjecting himself to such control, he experiences greater deprivation and frustration. These are discharged in the work situation to a certain degree, but his weaker and controlled position makes this difficult (unless he is a low-level supervisor).[7] It is our hypothesis that the aggression developed by frustration finds outlets in other areas of his life. Criminal behavior, revolutionary activity, and hostile control in the family are responses to these conditions of work.

A Basic Hypothesis

Within a particular social class or general occupational stratum, those individuals who enjoy great autonomy in their work will tend to show less hostility in their families and toward their children in the socialization process. Those individuals who experience more detailed normative and interpersonal control will express greater hostility in the family situation.

Our theoretical explanation for this would be somewhat similar to our theoretical explanation for the relationship between status in general and society. First, the individual with little autonomy experiences greater deprivation because of his inability to use sanctions or resources flexibly. He is an instrument of the goals chosen

6. For a discussion of what happens when there are specific controls (high specification of the use of sanctions by external agents) in the work situation see Chris Argyris, *Personality and Organization* (New York: Harper & Brothers, 1957), pp. 54-79 and 118-119. Though Argyris and this writer provide evidence and I believe acceptable theory to support our views, future sociologists of knowledge may view these as intellectual attempts to support the prevailing cultural dogma—individualism and freedom.

7. It is interesting that Elizabeth Cohen (1958) finds that upward educational mobility begins to appear strongly for the first time (as one moves up the occupational strata) among the sons of foremen. This has a significance for our data in two ways. These fathers may gain more satisfaction in work and also may discharge more aggression to subordinates. As our data show, nonhostile fathers are likely to have upwardly mobile sons.

by those with higher status. Second, he is controlled by pressures external to himself legitimizing outwardly expressed aggression.

By contrast, the individual with high autonomy is controlled by more general norms and by himself (the superego or internalized norms). This personal locus of control produces less frustration because he can make individual adjustments to sustain his motivations—he is in a position of self-control and can allocate rewards and punishment in terms of the choices of uses of sanctions given in Chart 1 (p. 125). If he was unable to exercise this choice, greater dissatisfaction would result.

High-status individuals do feel stresses and do express aggression, but evidence indicates they actually have less aggression. And further, the aggression that is aroused is less apt to be directed toward others. This is true because there is less legitimacy for the development of a general predisposition to attack others. Instead, aggression is more likely to be directed toward the self, for the self is in control.

WORK AUTONOMY AND FAMILY BEHAVIOR

We now turn to several sources of data as a test of this basic hypothesis. First, let us discuss some of the research procedures in this area.

Methodological Discussion

Earlier in our discussion we said autonomy consisted of the degree of specification of behavior (norms and use of resources or sanctions) and the degree of control by self or by others. No precise operational formula can be provided which defines this variable or its components. Almost every question (Appendix) asked the son about the father's work was used in making a final rating of the father's autonomy. Let us be as detailed as possible, however, about the procedure used in analyzing the data obtained with the use of the questionnaire.

All cases were first placed in one of five social classes according to Hollingshead's Two-Factor Index. The cases were then divided into a self-employed and an other-employed group.

Each case was then rated in terms of the general level of autonomy for that particular class level and employment group. Thus, the measure of autonomy is a relative one within the class level.

Though more refined rankings had been made earlier, finally each employment group was dichotomized into those with relatively high and relatively low autonomy. This created four basic categories of autonomy (see Table 31).

For some analyses the number of categories in the self-employed, low autonomy group was rather small (e.g.—when class was held constant). For this reason we sometimes condensed the two self-employed groups into one group (Table 30) and at other times (Table 29) we ignored the employment type altogether.[8]

The rating of the autonomy of the work was done in three steps: (1) all the information about the work was read and a general rating was determined. (2) if other-employed, a quantitative score was derived from questions 26, 27, 28, 33, and 34 (Appendix). If self-employed, the description and question 34 were used for a score. (3) If there was agreement between (1) and (2) the case was set aside as coded. If (1) and (2) disagreed, the case was studied more thoroughly and a decision made or the case was eliminated if no decision could be reached.

If what has been said regarding the importance of status and external restraint in providing motivation for the external expression of hostility is true, then holding general social status constant, fathers who are self-employed should express less hostility toward sons in socialization than do those employed by others. Of the latter, those most closely controlled or supervised should express the greatest aggression in socialization. Our hypothesis is tested by three sources of data. These are interviews or reports obtained from the father, the mother, and the son.

Father's Report

Questions similar to those asked of sons in the questionnaire were also asked of an unrelated group of fathers in interviews. Notes were taken during each interview, and as complete a reproduction of the interview as possible was created from these notes and from memory soon after the interview. The sections on work were separated from the sections on the father role, and the information

---

8. As we had originally thought of the problem we felt that any self-employed individual would probably have more autonomy than any other-employed individual. This was not true for approximately 25 per cent of the self-employed individuals. Though self-employed, they often had to meet tight deadlines (e.g., contractors), deal with demanding clientele (self-employed salesmen), or repeat the same detailed work (private accountants). No real decision could be made as to whether they were as a group the same, more, or less autonomous than the more autonomous other-employed individuals. This led to the various ways of treatment depending on the special circumstances.

was coded in terms of the father's satisfaction with work, the degree of autonomy, the degree of aggression expressed toward the son ("He's a real lazy one, alright."), and the degree of rejection of the son.[9]

Table 28 shows that relationship between aggressiveness expressed toward the son and the *autonomy* of the work situation. The relationship shown is in accord with our expectation, for more aggressive statements are made by fathers in highly controlled work situations. The cases include individuals from three of Hollingshead's class levels (II, III, and IV), and this relationship might be thought to be a consequence of class, because the entire group was ranked as a whole without distinctions between strata. An analysis indicated, however, that there was no association between absolute level of autonomy and social class in this group of fathers. For that reason it is not possible that class was the hidden factor determining the father's relationship to the son.

Table 28
Degree of Aggressiveness Expressed Toward Son and Father's Autonomy

	Considerable Aggression (No. of Fathers)	Some Aggression (No. of Fathers)	No Aggression (No. of Fathers)
High-autonomy work	0	2	4
Low-autonomy work	5	1	2

Though the interviews were from one to three hours long, there were few of them. Let us look at additional material to see if we can gain further evidence on this hypothesis.

Mother's Report

The data to be presented in this section were derived from approximately 360 interviews with mothers conducted by the Laboratory of Human Development at Harvard University. There was usually little material on occupation, but for approximately one-third of the cases there were sufficient data for this writer to be able to make a rating of the level of autonomy of the father's work. Again,

9. The relationship between rejection and autonomy is essentially the same as the relationship between aggressive statements and autonomy, which will be presented in Table 28.

The relationship between severity of socialization and satisfaction with work is negative and is discussed later in this chapter.

Table 29
Father's Role in Various Areas (by Mother's Report) and Autonomy in the Work Situation

Class	Autonomy Level[a]	Approximate Number of Cases	Per Cent of Mothers Expressing Dissatisfaction with Father's Treatment of Child (e.g., "Too Rough")	Per Cent of Fathers Who Spank Frequently	Per Cent of Fathers Who Make Higher Demand for Obedience Than Mothers	Per Cent of Fathers Who Make High Demand for Immediate Obedience	Per Cent of Fathers Who Are More Strict Than Mother	Per Cent of Parents Who Use Physical Punishment Frequently
Upper[b]	High	8	37.5	37.5	50.0	12.5	12.5	44.4
	Low	19	42.2	47.3	88.3	55.5	50.0	47.4
Middle	High	38	62.5	42.0	62.5	48.7	32.3	43.3
	Low	16	56.3	50.0	75.0	43.8	33.3	35.3
Low	High	15	38.5	40.0	77.7	33.3	28.6	37.5
	Low	21	42.2	38.1	60.0	52.4	20.0	61.9

a. This is a relative measure at each class level.

b. These data were analyzed in two other ways. In one way the distribution was studied at each of eight social class levels (instead of the three into which the cases are condensed here). This again showed the greater number of cases falling in the predicted cells for about two-thirds of the distributions. A second way of analyzing the data distinguished three levels of autonomy: self-employed, high autonomy (other-employed), and low autonomy (other-employed). The predicted relationship was found in the distribution of cases for the two categories of the other-employed. However, the relationship between the high-autonomy (other-employed) and the self-employed was not consistent. Sometimes one was the less severe and demanding parent and sometimes the other.

our expectation was that fathers in the more autonomous jobs would be less severe, less likely to use physical punishment, etc. Table 29 is a summary table of six measures of the father's behavior in the family that were developed previously by coders and made available to the author. Our hypothesis would lead us to expect a lower percentage of fathers in high-autonomy work than of those in low-autonomy work behaving in the manner reported (in the column heading). A study of the table shows this to be true in two out of the three classes under each question. Also, the average percentage differences (7.7 per cent) in instances which disagree with the expectations are much smaller than the average percentage differences (17 per cent) in instances which agree. Thus, these cases give some additional evidence for the influence of autonomy on the father's family behavior. The influence seems particularly evident in the upper-class level.

Son's Report

The final and perhaps most important source of data for a test of the influence of the work experience is given by the responses of approximately 250 sons.

Table 30 gives the available evidence from this source. Looking at those who are *employed by others* we see in all three classes that those in the high-autonomy groups are less likely to use severe socialization techniques. The differences range from approximately 9 to 15 per cent. Though these are not great, they are consistently in the direction predicted.

The results for the self-employed are less clear and should be discussed. In the original rating of the autonomy level of *some* self-employed, certain problems arose. They seemed rather highly controlled by the demands of customers or business associates, and yet it was recognized that they were *self*-employed. Though we felt that a sizable minority (perhaps 25 per cent) was less autonomous than the members of the high-autonomy self-employed group, a further dichotomization would have resulted in very small numbers of cases in some categories. For this reason we placed all the self-employed in one group, with a slight expectation that they would as a group be less severe. As the data is presented (Table 30), this does not seem to be the case. Perhaps the inclusion of the less autonomous workers in this group obscures the expected ordering.

It also may be that the entrepreneurial groups are somewhat more traditional and severe in their socialization techniques than their autonomy and general social status would indicate. This may be particularly true for the self-employed lower-class person. At least, this interpretation might fit in with other data we analyzed (see footnote, Table 29) and with the general findings and theoretical approach presented in *The Changing American Parent* (1958).[10]

Table 30
The Relationship Between Techniques of Discipline Used by Father and Autonomy of Father's Job at Each Social Class Level

Class	Level of Autonomy	Number of Fathers Using Relatively Mild Techniques	Number of Fathers Using Relatively Severe Techniques	Per Cent Using More Severe Techniques
	Self-employed	20	10	33.3
Upper	High (other-employed)	9	5	35.7
	Low (other-employed)	10	8	44.4
	Self-employed	17	12	41.4
Middle	High (other-employed)	12	7	36.8
	Low (other-employed)	16	17	51.5
	Self-employed	3	5[a]	62.5
Lower	High (other-employed)	23	18	43.9
	Low (other-employed)	16	18	53.0

a. All are technological jobs; this has a significance, as will be shown.

Perhaps we can condense all the cases, ignoring class, thus providing a sufficient number of cases in the self-employed group to again dichotomize that group into those with high and low autonomy. This seems quite a reasonable procedure, for it should be recalled that autonomy was measured relative to a particular class level in the initial ratings, and therefore class is already held constant. It also allows an investigation of the effect of both the category of employment and the level of autonomy.

This analysis gives the ordering of per cent of severe fathers that

10. Additional responses were analyzed regarding the authoritarianism (non-democratic but not necessarily hostile control) of the father in his dealings with the son, the structure of authority, and the degree to which the son was consulted on matters. A fairly consistent pattern emerges. In comparison with the high autonomy other-employed father, the self-employed father seems to behave in a more "authoritarian" manner with the son, explains fewer requirements, consults with him less, but exercises less actual authority over the son and over the family generally. The reduced authority may be a consequence of a more demanding occupation as a self-employed individual. This involvement in work may also explain his less frequent role as the major source of affection. The difference between the self-employed and the high-autonomy other-employed in this role is marked (45 versus 86 per cent) in the upper class.

we anticipated and is shown in Table 31. There we see that the highly autonomous self-employed are least severe, the less autonomous self-employed and the highly autonomous other-employed fathers are intermediate, and the less autonomous other-employed are most severe. The differences between neighboring categories are rather small and should be viewed with caution, especially since the predicted order was reached after some manipulation of the data.

Table 31
The Relationship Between Techniques of Discipline Used by Father and Autonomy of Father's Job

LEVEL OF AUTONOMY

Employment Status	Autonomy Level	Number of Fathers Using Relatively Mild Techniques	Number of Fathers Using Relatively Severe Techniques	Per Cent Using Severe Techniques
Self-Employed[a]	High	26	14	35.0
	Low	11	8	42.1
Other-Employed	High	44	30	40.5
	Low	42	43	50.6

a. The eight cases in the lower class are omitted, for no general standard of autonomy for such a small group could be developed at that social class level.

Our findings seem, however, to fairly consistently support the expected greater severity of those employed by others in low autonomy positions. Also, when all three independent sources of data are reviewed, there is a general picture of support.

Though we have focused on autonomy, we have not done so with the expectation of explaining "all" in the family. Our interest was more in an application of a general theory concerning the handling of aggression to a specific area—the degree of control in the work situation and the severity of socialization techniques. Our findings give some additional support to the general theory proposed by Henry and Short.

AUTONOMY, TYPE OF WORK, AND FAMILY BEHAVIOR

The previous discussion and data dealing with autonomy and its meaning led to further considerations and analysis. In developing a statement regarding the meaning of autonomy the picture of the assembly-line worker and the alienated manual worker developed by Marx often came to mind. This picture did not seem to apply so dramatically, however, to such occupations as postal worker or barber. After some experience in ranking the autonomy of workers, it appeared that technological occupations (engineering, factory work, cement pouring) were less autonomous than other types of work. This, then, became a major concern in the ranking process, for the researcher wanted the autonomy ranking to reflect the objective situation and not biases from an academic perspective.

Nevertheless, it appears even after this precaution that technological jobs are objectively less autonomous than organization jobs. That is, the sons "agree" with the general and abstracted ranking of autonomy made by the writer. Of the five questions asked the sons (questions 26, 27, 28, 33, and 34 of the Appendix) which required the selection of a specific alternative (and thus would allow for no interpretive bias on the part of the researcher), sons disproportionately selected specific answers indicating autonomy in those cases which the writer had rated as autonomous. This was true to a marked degree on three of the five questions, true to only a slight degree on a fourth, and showed no relation on the fifth. The last question dealt with meeting tight deadlines and schedules and this condition, though restrictive in quality, may be a more important factor in jobs that are otherwise generally autonomous.

Why should technical occupations be less autonomous than organizational and other types of work? We will try to give our theoretical explanation for this, but let us first define these terms and present the data.

Types of Work

Our initial attempt was to use some form of Parsons' four basic functional specializations of a social system for a classification of work. Individuals would be placed first in one of the four categories in terms of the basic focus of the general enterprise (a hospital, a factory) and then categorized in terms of *their* special roles in the enterprise (e.g., perhaps personnel work or the integrative specialization). Though this seems a feasible approach theoretically, it did create several practical problems. Particular occupations did not neatly categorize themselves into one of the four divisions at each level. This only reinforces what we know and what Parsons has said himself—that concrete institutions or roles are not pure cases of these analytically derived functional specializations. Perhaps a rating in terms of the basic dimensions by which the social system is differentiated (instrumental-expressive and internal-external dimensions) would have been a wiser start. These dimensions, however, do not seem sufficiently well defined for use in such concrete matters as this. (See pp. 11-12—especially the footnote—for further discussion.)

It was decided that the work of Anne Roe (1956, pp. 135-250) provided a simple but sophisticated set of categories of work. There is a tendency, however, for the categories to rest more on personality differences of the incumbents rather than on the social functions of the occupation. This set of categories, the names used, and their meanings are:

Service	The occupations in this category cater to the personal tastes, needs, and welfare of others (barbers or psychiatric social workers).
Business contacts	This category consists of salesmen and dealers who deal directly with clients and have as a major goal persuasion or sales (auctioneers or public relation experts).
Organization	This "group is concerned primarily with the *organization* and *efficient* functioning of *governmental* and *commercial* enterprises" (e.g., postal clerks, executives).
Technology	This group includes all the modern industrial occupations except the managerial, clerical, and sales occupation. Technological occupations deal with the *production, maintenance,* and *transportation* of *commodities* and *utilities.*
Outdoor	These are the largely rural occupations such as fisherman, farmer, or nurseryman.
Science	These are the research scientists and applied scientists (doctors, weather observers, etc.) in nonindustrial settings.
General cultural	These occupations are concerned with "the preservation and development of the general cultural heritage" (scholars, lawyers, the clergy, librarians, editors, etc.).
Arts and entertainment	These occupations use special skills in the creative arts (drama, music, etc.) and entertainment (athletic performers).

The number of cases in all except two categories was not sufficiently large for them to be dealt with in a meaningful and satisfying way. Our focus will be on the two: organization and technology.

Autonomy and Type of Work: Data

Table 32 shows the relationship between class, autonomy, and type of work. Looking only at organization and technology, we see that in the two higher classes almost all self-employed individuals are in organization jobs. In the lower class, all self-employed (save one) are in technological occupations. Thus, even within the type of employment, *kind* of occupation is related to general social class. This is not an irrelevant factor in explaining the association between class and famliy behavior, and our theoretical discussion below will attempt an explication.

The significance of the qualitative type of occupation is again emphasized when we observe the relationship between qualitative type and autonomy level. Among the other-employed workers we observe that about 70 per cent of the organization workers are found in highly autonomous work. In the technological group, by contrast, slightly less than 50 per cent fall in that group.

The ratings were based on rather detailed *descriptive* material provided by sons. What factors about the different types of work on a more abstract and theoretical level also lead the writer to consider this difference in ranking objectively valid? It appears that two qualities distinguish these two types of work: the degree of interaction with people, and the energy level and control level of the work. This latter factor will be discussed first.

Autonomy and Type of Work: Theory

Culture is a system of symbolic control which tends to guide the behavior of many people in many situations. It is on the level of symbols and communication, and as such is what might be called a low-energy but high-control system of behavior. Now, certain occupations tend to participate in this activity much more than other occupations. The clergy, the literati, scientists, politicians, live daily in this realm, and, indeed, one of our categories is entitled "General Cultural."

Several reasons preclude our discussing this cultural category. One is that the number of cases in the category is small; a second, most important, reason is that the special position of members of

Table 32
Class Level, Autonomy Level, and Occupational Type

Social Class	Autonomy Level	Service	Business Contacts	Organization	Technology	Outdoor	Science	General Cultural	Arts and Entertainment
Upper	Self-employed		2	15	1		8	5	
	High	1	2	14	8			2	
	Low		1	4	7				
Middle	Self-employed	2	7	22	1		2		
	High	1	12	16	8		1		3
	Low		1	5	9				1
Lower	Self-employed	1		1	8				
	High	10	1	4	30	3			
	Low	3			31	1			

the category in *American* society may place strains on them as a group and may be reflected in their family behavior. Their marginal acceptance (as esteemed but feared) may be a consequence of our individualistic heritage and its fear of civilized control on a social level. Organizational occupations, though less culturally involved, still participate in this realm, have low energy and high control levels, and have conventional acceptance in our society.

By contrast, other occupations are concerned with high energy but low control systems of behavior. The technological realm seems the best example here, for it deals with "the production, maintenance and transportation of commodities and utilities." This means great effort must be expended (in terms of actual physical involvement and man hours) to bring about changes toward the desired goal.

How do these differences relate to a concept like autonomy? It would appear that the development of society (and perhaps life as a system of behavior) begins from a point where ascribed (inherited) behavior is the response to the conditions of the immediate situation. With the development of symbols the individual is freed from these ascribed reactions, and responses to conditions of a broader range (the past, the future, conditions in other parts of the environment) are possible. Symbols make possible more autonomous responses on the part of the individual involved and allow for more flexible, less routinized, and less ascribed behavior and use of resources. We would predict then that those occupations which are more involved in this symbolic control system (and are not so controlled by immediate conditions) will present the same patterns of family behavior observed among the more autonomous groups as shown in Table 31 (page 136).

It is recognized that higher-level technological occupations (e.g., engineering) are involved in the cultural realm (science and its symbols), but we hypothesize that within a particular occupational level they will be, relative to organizational and general cultural occupations, less involved in this realm and thus less autonomous.

Certain occupations are not only more cultural (in the sense of being involved in the cultural system and its symbolic norms), they are also more social. That is, they are concerned with other people, with the exchange of information and sentiments, and with establishing some organization for the relationships between people. By their nature, specification of the use of resources must be fairly low (one of our components of autonomy). The individual dealing with people must be given more latitude, for he cannot predict how the others will respond. By contrast, the individual dealing with things can be expected to deal with them in rather specific and detailed ways, for he and society have control over them.[11]

Let us compare the two types of occupations which the previous table shows do differ in autonomy according to the writer's ranking *and* the sons' responses. And further, the previous discussion offers a theoretical rationale that suggests that they would differ in autonomy. The two occupational groups—organization and technology— also seem to be conventional occupations with few problems of acceptability and with enough cases for study.

Type of Work and Family Behavior

We would predict that, within a given social class, fathers engaged in organizational occupations would be less severe in their socialization techniques and would have warmer relationships with their children. This would be true because in a rather abstract way —which we have attempted to outline—the father is more autonomous.

Table 33
Degree of Affection of Fathers in Different Types of Occupations (as Reported by Mothers of Kindergarten-aged Sons and Daughters)

Class Level	Type of Occupation	Fathers Warm (Number)	Fathers Cool (Number)	Per Cent Fathers Warm
Upper	Organization	21	16	56.8
	Technology	10	10	50.0
Middle	Organization	36	29	55.4
	Technology	12	19	38.7
Lower	Organization	7	1	87.5
	Technology	38	38	50.0

Tables 33 (based on a reanalysis of the Sears, Maccoby, and Levin data), 34, and 35 give support for this prediction and interpretation. In all tables and nearly all classes organizational fathers are less severe and warmer. This seems to be true when both sons and daughters are the objects of the fathers' behavior (Table 33) and at different age levels (kindergarten children in Table 33 and high-school-age sons in Tables 34 and 35).

11. It is these distinctive problems for society which David Riesman in *The Lonely Crowd* (New Haven: Yale University Press, 1950) feels create some of the differences between contemporary other-directed society, which must deal with the problems of social organization, and nineteenth-century inner-directed society, which had the basic problem of controlling the physical environment.

Though the data support the explanatory development, the writer does not consider the point proven. There again is the problem of what kinds of personalities choose these different types of occupations. Individuals who feel comfortable with others and are drawn toward people (their children included) probably choose the organizational occupations. Possibly individuals with greater needs to present themselves as, or who are, more forceful and "masculine," choose technological occupations. Roe finds at all occupational levels that the technological workers score highest for masculinity on the Strong Vocational Interest Blank.

Table 34
Emotional Support by Father and Type
of Occupation Held by Father
(as Reported by High-School-aged Sons)

Class Level	Type of Occupation	Low Emotional Support (Number)	High Emotional Support (Number)	High Emotional Support (Per Cent)
Upper	Organization	12	18	60.0
	Technology	5	8	61.6
Middle	Organization	19	19	50.0
	Technology	7	6	46.2
Lower	Organization	2	2	50.0
	Technology	37	18	32.8

The needs and self-concepts then motivate the father to treat the child rather severely and coldly in order to validate a conception of himself as a particular kind of man.

An analysis of an additional category, service occupations, which

Table 35
Severity of Socialization Techniques and Type
of Job Held by Father
(as Reported by Sons)

Class Level	Type of Occupation	Low Severity	High Severity	Per Cent High Severity
Upper	Organization	18	15	45.5
	Technology	7	9	56.3
Middle	Organization	17	24	58.6
	Technology	4	13	76.5
Lower	Organization	0	4	100.0[a]
	Technology	22	46	67.7

a. Though in opposition to the hypothesis, it is much the smallest number of cases in any category and all had been rated low in autonomy as Table 32 shows.

uld also be quite social in nature and which is traditionally de-
ied as less masculine, shows that these fathers are more likely to
e the sources of authority and affection for their sons than fathers
in technological occupations. Perhaps fathers occupied in serving
others are more familial and domesticated in their general orientation.

These tables present patterns which should become the focus
of additional analysis and research. It appears that the increasing
percentage of technological workers at lower levels accounts for
much of the increase in severity and hostility as one moves down
the scale of social classes.

Is autonomy a variable that operates independent of social class
and type of occupation? To find out, the severity of the father's
socialization techniques and its relationship to autonomy within a
particular social class and within a particular occupational type was
analyzed. The analysis showed that autonomy was still operating
to produce more severe socializers: there was slight support for the
hypothesis when all three choices of socialization techniques were
combined, very marked and consistent support when first choice of
socialization technique was considered. For example, when first
choice of method of discipline was looked at, upper-class, high-
autonomy, organizationally employed fathers are seen to be severe
socializers in only 22 per cent of the cases. Lower-class, low-autonomy, technologically employed fathers are severe socializers in 53
per cent of the cases. The differences (31 per cent) is considerably
greater than the simple difference between upper-class and lower-
class fathers (16 per cent) shown previously.

Occupational level (and thus social class) and the qualitative
type of occupation are correlated. Organizational-type occupations
by their definition seem to be at a higher level than technological
ones, even though certain incumbents in each group may enjoy generally the same society-wide prestige. These statements are placed
in a broader theoretical system in Parson's statement in *Sociology
Today* (1959). Particularly relevant here is his distinction between
the managerial level and the technical level (pp. 4-13). Though
the terms are referring to somewhat different concepts than is the
case here, the general perspective has aided this development.

The findings presented in this section and the general study here
indicate that elements which have been lumped under the broad
term of "class" or "social-economic status" should be analyzed in
detail and that their influence on human behavior should be traced.
Perhaps a detailed analysis might resolve certain debates in the
literature regarding the character of parental behavior at different
levels of society. For example, the differences found between the

Chicago and Harvard studies regarding the severity and rigidity of parental control at various social levels may be a function of the questions asked (David and Havighurst, 1955). *Or* it may be a function of the type of people asked and their position, in the broadest sense, in society. Important in their social position would be not only their society-wide prestige or social class but also the kind of occupations held and the kind of subculture in which it would place the family.

POWER IN THE WORK SITUATION
AND FAMILY BEHAVIOR

Of the various kinds of sanctions that may contribute to status in work, we can look at a second type: power, or the degree of control an individual has over other individuals on a direct person-to-person or indirect basis. Point four in our summary of Hammond's work (p. 121) shows the interaction between power at work and behavior at home. We have only the most limited evidence of the power held by the father in his work situation: the number of individuals supervised. We make the quite simple prediction that the more power the individual wields in the work situation the greater the likelihood that his behavior as father and socializer will be less hostile. Why should this be our prediction? The answer to this is not so simple.

The husband-father in the higher levels of the occupational sphere not only receives less frustration-inducing experiences, but is also more likely to exhibit greater control over aggressive impulses (due to his class-linked socialization experiences and also selective work placement) and perhaps direct them toward himself or use them in attempts to master situations. When he does "choose" to express aggression in the work situation this can be done through an emotionally exploitative use of his authority. This is done from a protected position of status or power.

A second answer is possible. It could also be that the exercise of power leads to greater satisfaction and less aggression. The absence of power and its resultant dissatisfaction, which may be felt keenly, given the definition of the male role in our society, may lead to aggression.

What are the satisfactions which power provides, and what frustrations are felt with its lack? A partial answer is provided if we return to one of our earlier positions. We said that aggression, or its functional equivalent in the psychological balance of the individual, tended to trickle down the status system. The father who supervises others may not only have greater control over aggressive impulses but can sometimes express hostility or its psychological equivalents, if not its social equivalent, in the work situation. Certain supervisory activities (assumptions of superiority-inferiority, criticism, a show of impatience, unexpected administrative changes and resulting manipulation of subordinates through the crises) may be socially defined as quite legitimate, but on the personality level they release certain tensions and hostilities just as illegitimate aggression does. This may even be acted out in a relatively pleasant way, but it still releases certain dissatisfactions derived from experiences elsewhere—even the family. Whatever aggression is felt by the higher-status father can be released more completely in interaction with subordinates. The subordinate, by contrast, finds it necessary or at least more convenient to displace the aggression from the work situation into the family.

The work situation of the lower-status husband-father is not devoid of opportunities for expression of affect and aggression. Restriction of production, theft, and refusal to understand instructions may function as indirect aggression toward management. He may also direct it toward his work companions, but they are an ingroup and this can prove threatening. It is felt that the accumulation of hostility which cannot be expressed safely in the work situation is greater for the lower-status worker. In some way he must express this outside his work situation. We have discussed and given data on the familial consequences of this work position. (All low-status workers, however, are not married, and aggression of this sort is, as was discussed earlier, displaced differentially by the married and unmarried.)

Table 36
Severity of Father's Socialization Techniques
and Number of People Supervised

Class	Number Supervised	Low Severity (Number)	High Severity (Number)	High Severity (Per Cent)
Upper	One or more	22	22	50.0
	None	3	4	57.2
Middle	One or more	18	26	59.1
	None	13	19	59.4
Lower	One or more	12	14	53.8
	None	15	34	69.4

A study of Table 36 shows that fathers in the upper and lower classes who have subordinates are less severe with their children than those who have no subordinates in the work situation to absorb their negative sanctions and motivations to aggress. Without subordinates to act as recipients of aggression, they displace the aggression from the work situation to subordinates in the family situation.

Whatever the "real" explanation may be, the data in Table 36 support the prediction and theoretical view with which this section commenced. Here is a problem which requires much more thorough study before any conclusion can be made about the causal processes at work.

WORK SATISFACTION AND FAMILY BEHAVIOR

We have now talked about autonomy and power. We do not have precise data on two other types of sanctions which we have discussed—interpersonal approval and material possessions. We do have information on the father's general satisfaction with his work, and this might be taken as a kind of subjective interpretation by the father of his general well being, all types of sanctions considered, in the work. What result does variation in this have on his paternal role? As we cautioned earlier, we cannot be certain, given the data available, just what factors cause what results (of the observed associations) or if we should even use this terminology. Our line of thought, however, was that the father in the lower levels of society is aware of his evaluation, feels deprived in his achieved role, compensates for this by physically aggressive masculine behavior, receives aggression and control in the work situation, and redirects this hostility into the family situation. Let us look at our data with these factors in mind.

Table 37 shows a definite association between level of occupation and satisfaction. Over one-half of those at the top are reported

Table 37
Relationship Between Father's Satisfaction with Work
(By Son's Report) and Level of Occupation

Occupation Level (by Warner)	Likes Very Much		Likes		Likes Fairly Well or Dislikes		Total Number of Cases
	No.	Per Cent	No.	Per Cent	No.	Per Cent	
High (Level 1, 2)	34	50.8	19	28.2	14	20.9	67
Medium (Level 3, 4)	17	18.5	41	44.6	34	37.0	92
Low (Level 5, 6, 7)	11	14.7	30	40.0	34	45.4	75

to like their job "very much" or "extremely well." By contrast, nearly one-half of those in the lower level are reported to like their jobs only "fairly well" or to "hate it." Does this type of dissatisfaction independent of social class lead to hostile treatment of the child? It appears to be rather highly associated. Two measures of paternal hostility are presented in Table 38, and they show that within a particular social class the more dissatisfied fathers are the more severe socializers and the more hostile generally.

Table 38
Father's Satisfaction with Work, Severity of Socialization Techniques, and Degree of Hostility Expressed to Son

Class	Attitude Toward Work (Son's Report)	Total Cases in Each Category	Per Cent of Fathers Using Techniques of High Severity	Per Cent of Fathers Generally Hostile to Son
Upper	Likes very much	31	42.0	32.2
	Likes	21	62.0	38.7
	Likes fairly well or dislikes	14	64.4	50.0
Middle	Likes very much	17	47.2	37.5
	Likes	46	63.9	34.2
	Likes fairly well or dislikes	25	72.0	58.3
Lower	Likes very much	12	66.7	27.4
	Likes	26	61.6	47.6
	Likes fairly well or dislikes	39	71.9	47.4

Though it seems rather unlikely that the son would associate these two variables, it may be that the son tends generally to report bad things ("hates his work") about aggressive fathers. Independent data, however, suggest that this is not really the case. Eleven of the sixteen fathers interviewed personally were asked exactly the same questions about work satisfaction and severity of socialization techniques. Here the rank order correlation was — .25 and in the predicted direction. The rank order correlation between the interviewer's judgment of the father's satisfaction with work and severity of socialization techniques was — .39. This is again a figure that is, though small, in agreement with the prediction.

WORK AND THE MOTHER'S ROLE

Though a basic goal of this work is an investigation of the influence of achieved status on the father's family behavior, let us turn to a sparse harvest of data on work and the mother's role. We have said on a number of occasions that the mother's authority is greater in the lower classes because of the husband's reduced economic competence, and because she can often compete with him as an economic provider. We have already seen that mothers in the lower class are more likely to work (Tables 2 and 3), and we have also seen that lower-level mothers hold greater authority.

Our data also show that lower-class mothers are more likely to work (or to have recently worked), and this is shown in Table 39. We also see in Table 40, that there is a direct relationship between their working and the likelihood that they exercise authority.

Table 39
Per Cent of Mothers Working or Having Recently Worked at Each Class Level

Class Level	Total (Number)	Per Cent Working
I	21	23.8
II	47	23.4
III	86	43.0
IV	73	56.2
V	16	68.7

Table 40
Locus of Authority and Mother's Work Role

Work Status of Mother	Father Major Source of Authority (Per Cent)	Parents Equal in Authority (Per Cent)	Mother Major Source of Authority (Per Cent)	
Mother does not work	49.1	30.7	20.1	100% = 114
Mother works or has recently worked	39.0	27.0	34.0	100% = 82

If the mother works, it appears that she is not only more likely to hold authority but may also have a slight tendency to lose her function as a source of emotional support. This hint of a pattern can be seen in Table 41 (columns 1 and 2). Is this consequence or mere association? Again, without some measure of the mother's personality we cannot say whether she finds herself disinterested in the housewife-mother role and goes to work or having gone to work she loses some of her familial functions as traditionally defined. Whatever may be the causal relationship, the working mother is likely to be the powerful but emotionally distant mother.

When social class is held constant, the numbers become rather small in some categories and interpretation becomes difficult, but the same general pattern repeats itself in each class except one— mothers in our upper class who do not work are much *less* likely to be the major source of affection than are mothers in this class who work. Out of 50 mothers at this level who do not work, only 16 (32 per cent) are the major source of affection. This compares with eight working mothers who are the major source of affection out of a total of 13 working mothers at this level. Though this is a small number, it is 62 per cent of that total.

Table 41
Locus of Affection and Mother's Work Role

Work Status of Mother	Father Major Emotional Spport (Per Cent)	Parents Equal in Emotional Support (Per Cent)	Mother Major Emotional Support (Per Cent)	
Mother does not work	19.3	36.7	43.9	100% = 114
Mother works or has recently worked	25.6	29.3	45.1	100% = 82

Perhaps the nonworking mother in the achievement-oriented subculture of the upper class (as we are using the term) experiences greater strains in accepting her ascribed role as the giving mother. This would not be surprising if one looks at the expectations placed on the coeducationally socialized girl in this level of society. Through high school and college she is expected to compete and achieve. The rather marked shift in expectations with marriage and motherhood may produce real resentments which become quite strong if work is not a possible outlet.

Or the smaller amount of emotional support given by the non-working mother at this level may result from her attempting unsuccessfully to compete with her competent and prestigious husband for the confidence of the son. This may lead to certain strains in the female role in the upper strata of society just as the male role seems to involve special strains in the lower class.

We should be aware, of course, that our measure of social class is specifically a measure of the male's competence (occupation and education) in an achievement-oriented society. So the upper-class male and the lower-class male are deviating greatly from the societal mean for men. Perhaps the chances that a deviating male will marry an equally deviating wife (i.e., equally "competent" in the upper classes, equally "incompetent" in the lower classes) are less for both the upper-class and the lower-class husband. For this reason one might expect more competent fathers (relative to their wives) in the upper class and more competent mothers (relative to their husbands) in the lower class. This is reminiscent of the phenomenon revealed by Galton that the progeny of exceptional parents regress to the mean of the general population. Here, with the usual measure of social class, spouses and children of exceptional males regress both up and down to the general mean for the population of women and children. Is it surprising then that we find patriarchy at the upper levels of society, matriarchy at the lower levels, and egalitarianism at the middle levels?

CHAPTER 8

Status and the Socialized Son

In this chapter we will discuss certain ideas concerning the probable influence of status on the development of the child in the family and on his eventual adult behavior. We will try to support these ideas with known data from several sources and particularly with data gathered by the writer. The patterns observed will be analyzed not simply as characteristics of the socialized personality of the child at different class levels but as consequences of the structure of society, of the distribution of resources for socialization, and of the resulting parental roles.

THE FAMILY AND THE SOCIALIZATION PROCESS

We have evidence that parents at the lower levels of society are more severe, more likely to use physical modes of discipline, and less warm. We also have evidence that the relative severity of mothers and fathers varies from class to class. It appears that mothers are almost as severe or are even more severe than fathers at the higher levels of society, but that fathers become increasingly severe and cool to the child, relative to mothers, in the lower strata of society. It also appears that, at least in relation to sons, mothers are very central figures in lower-level families but become decreasingly significant in the higher levels. The complement to this is that fathers become less significant as one moves down the classes —they have less authority, play less significant parts in the emotional life of the family, and seem to be generally less involved in the family. What would be some expected consequences of these patterns and what data can we offer to support our expectations and hypotheses?

We have already outlined some consequences of this situation in Chapter 4 in the section entitled "Sociological Conditions Leading to External Expression of Aggression." There we pointed out that parents in those statuses with few positive sanctions for socialization resort to negative sanctions to train and control the child. Though negative sanctions are effective to some degree, they are less effective (in bringing about socialization and identification with the parental image) than the emotional closeness possible with positive sanctions. In Freudian perspective, if the parental image and ideals are not sufficiently internalized, the superego suffers atrophy. This suggests that impulses are subject to fewer controls and that individual initiative and personal responsibility operate at a lower level.

By contrast, the parent who receives esteem, security, and love from society can use these resources as positive sanctions for the more effective moulding of the child in the parental image. A more "adult" personality is the product: the superego is more highly developed and life is lived by the "reality principle" rather than by the "pleasure principle." This means that certain impulses (love and aggression) are held within and perhaps expressed in other areas or at other times in a more "realistic" fashion.

This view seems to provide a social structural or social status explanation of several forms of behavior which characteristically vary at different class levels. The reduced control of hostile impulses (as a consequence of status-determined patterns of socialization) at the lower levels of society is reflected in the higher rates of homicide, general crimes against persons, and wife-beating, and in the norm of being tough.

This reduced control of impulses may also have some objective advantages. Thus, positive affect is expressed more freely and without the self-conscious and inhibiting mechanisms of the superego. Perhaps the greater amount of sexual behavior, the patterns of jovial horseplay and joking, and the nearly constant tide of emotionally charged social involvement of many lower-class individuals are manifestations of this condition. The picture may be accurate even though some researchers find the number of highly isolated individuals (often defined by the middle-class criterion of frequency of "visits") to be larger at the lower levels.

Just as lack of control of impulses may have certain advantages as well as disadvantages, so also control and introjection of emotions may have certain disadvantages as well as the recognized advantages. For example, we observe that suicide rates seem to complement homicide rates as we move up and down the class ladder. The higher rate of suicide at the upper levels of society may be a consequence of the check on the external expression of aggression and a turning it in on the self: one commits the final act of self-aggression in suicide. And other, less extreme psychological phenomena seem to support this interpretation. We find guilt and depressive psychosis, relative to other psychoses, more common at the upper levels of society; and assaultive psychoses, e.g., paranoid schizophrenia, more frequent at the lower levels of the social system.

This picture is in agreement with an earlier statement about social interaction at different class levels in our society. The individualism of the upper levels of society is revealed in a person who seems to be more self-contained—he characteristically hates himself condemns himself, feels guilt (commits suicide), or loves himself (is proud and self-appreciative). By contrast, the lower-class individual seems more other-involved, directing both positive and negative affect more freely. His personality is less *self*-conscious and more permeable. It is a relatively open system of affective exchange with other affective systems (personalities or groups).

A Brief Review of Theories
of Identification

Let us talk about the process of socialization in a somewhat more limited but detailed way. In the process of socialization the child is taught by the parent, through explicit and implicit rewards and punishment, to behave in certain ways. Other processes are operating, however, besides this action by the parent. The child is trying to relate his own behavior to the parent's. As viewed by Winch (1962), he may try to fashion his behavior after that of the parent (similar identification) or he may try to model his behavior not to copy but to complement the parent's behavior (reciprocal identification). Finally, for various reasons he may strive to be quite the opposite of the parent (negative identification). However the processes take place, behaviorally, psychologically, or even unconsciously, Winch assumes that the parental model is of central significance.

Several theorists have taken social learning and identification as a basic focus in the analysis of human behavior. For example, George Mead's discussion (1934) of the importance of words or symbols in role taking and role playing gives added meaning to the process of identification with family roles, either as played by the child's particular parents or as defined in his community.

Freud saw perhaps three basic stages in identification. The first stage is fused or primary identification in which the infant fails to distinguish between himself and the significant social objects in his environment, particularly the mother. The second stage comes about when differentiation is made between self and significant others but when a strong emotional tie or dependency exists between the child and certain social objects. Freud saw two basic processes operating in the third stage, and he seems to have given varying degrees of importance to each in different writings. In the third stage one process is perhaps an exaggeration of the second stage, for there is a loss of the loved object in growing up and identification of the ego with the abandoned but *desired* object. Part of the individual's personality becomes like the lost object, perhaps to fill the felt void. The other process in this third stage is an identification with the stern and perhaps aggressive authority figure, the powerful but *feared* father. This whole latter stage is involved in the resolution of the Oedipal problem and the development of an adult and "socially mature" superego.

Another interesting theory and set of stages is proposed by Sears (1957a). The process begins with the infant's biological dependence on the mother and its psychological corollary of gratification or dissatisfaction. The condition of dissatisfaction is particularly important if it occurs when the mother is absent, as any mother occasionally will be. When this situation exists the infant attempts to reduce the tension and frustration by recreating stimuli similar to those produced by the mother. This attempt will sometimes produce actual satisfaction; probably the mere presence of familiar stimuli (or stimuli associated with gratification) will itself produce gratification on another level. This gratification will reinforce the imitating (modeling and identifying) behavior and the child will begin to become like the mother.

Sears points out that this reduces the problems of socializing the child because the process is intrapsychic to an important degree, even though the original stimuli were social in nature. He hypothesizes that socialization will take place most easily when (1) the mother (or socializing figure) provides great affection and nurturing, (2) the mother is occasionally absent, so that the child is required to create his own substitute satisfaction through imitation, (3) the socializing figure uses withdrawal of love as a means of disciplining the child (withdrawal of love being a psychological absence which requires imitating behavior just as the physical absence does).

Class and Patterns of Identification

Our data do not allow us to study these various kinds of identification (e.g., reciprocal versus similar), nor are we able to analyze the process of identification in terms of the special ideas of the theories just discussed. They require more detailed data on processes of an earlier period than our research provides.

Here we will look at the pattern and degree of positive identification as a consequence of variation in the emotional significance, power, and severity (hostility) of the two parents. The earlier discussion said that parents in lower status (reward) levels have less resources available for the process of socialization. We reasoned that this fact, plus special frustrations felt by the father which result in greater expression of hostility, make the process of identification with the paternal image less complete.

Two telling questions developed by Daniel J. Funkenstein and asked the subjects give evidence on this. The son was asked what relative he admired most (could take as a model) and which parent he was said to resemble more in personality. One might conjecture that the answer to the first question reveals the somewhat conscious attempt to identify with the parent and that the second question probes the consequences of this process. The responses at different class levels, given in Table 42, show a much stronger "identification" with the father than with the mother at the upper class levels. This decreases rather strikingly at the lower levels.

Table 42
Percentage of Sons Who Admire and Resemble Father More than Mother at Five Social Class Levels

Class Level (Hollingshead's)	Per Cent Who Admire Father More[a]		Per Cent Who Resemble Father More[b]	
I (Upper)	100	(10)[c]	72	(18)
II (Upper middle)	77	(30)	63	(46)
III (Lower middle)	69	(39)	67	(67)
IV (Working)	46	(28)	58	(52)
V (Lower)	44	(9)	45	(11)

a. The question asked, "Whom do you admire most in your family or among your relatives?"
b. The question asked, "Which parent are you said to resemble more in personality?"
c. Numbers in parentheses are total numbers of cases choosing father or mother, and exclude those choosing other relatives.

The difficulty of finding adequate masculine models among other relatives was also found in the lower levels. In the top class (Hollingshead's Class I) all boys who did not admire their father most chose another male relative as the most admired. In Classes IV and V only about 58 per cent of the sons admired their fathers or other male relatives most. The others chose female relatives. In order to simplify Table 42 this data is not presented.

Another way of looking at the data indicates that the two parents are less "admired" in the lower levels than in the upper levels. Instead, other relatives are chosen. Sixty-nine per cent of our upper class (Hollingshead's I and II) sons chose their fathers or mothers as most admired among their various relatives. This falls to 56 per cent in our middle class (III) and to 54 per cent in our lower class (IV and V). This perhaps creates problems of inculcating values and channeling the child according to parental ideals.

Table 42 provides evidence in support of the views we presented in Chaps. 4 and 6 that certain components of masculine identification, commitment to "mature" work and to the husband-father role, become problems through the lack of an "adequate" father figure and the presence of a powerful and adequate mother. One can imagine the conflicts and problems of a familial, sexual, and general social nature that this creates. It also creates problems which are sustained and exaggerated in the father-son relationship of the next generation.

The son's commitment to work (as an adult) may not be as impeded as one would think, for the mother (with whom he may be identifying) is more likely to be working in the lower classes. This leads us to expect that the working mother is more likely to be an identification figure for the son for two reasons: by working she becomes a more important figure in the family, and as a worker she may have a personality more consistent with the needs of a maturing son in an achievement-oriented society. Table 43 shows this to be true in the upper and middle classes but not true in the lower class. It is in this latter class where we had expected it to be most strikingly true. Evidently the controlling, expressive, and home-oriented mother who does not work is such an emotionally important figure at this level that the son "identifies" with her despite

Table 43
The Mother's Work Role and the Son's Identification
(Son's Report of What Others Say)

Class Level	Work Role	Number Resembling Mother	Number Resembling Father	Percentage Resembling Mother
Upper	Works	6	6	50.0
	Doesn't work	16	35	31.4
Middle	Works	10	17	37.0
	Doesn't work	12	28	30.0
Lower	Works	14	18	43.7
	Doesn't work	14	15	48.2

her probable inappropriateness for the son. This factor might increase rather than ameliorate the problem of identification with and commitment to the adult work role.

This general area of interest leads to a more specific concern: what influence do emotional relationships between mother and son or father and son have on the choice of (1) level and (2) type of occupation? We will discuss these problems later in this chapter.

IDENTIFICATION AND FAMILY STRUCTURE

The position has been that the lack of identification with the lower-class father is a consequence of his poverty in resources and power in society and the resulting emotional distance, lack of authority in the family, and severity in dealing with the son. Tables 44, 45, and 46 give evidence on these matters. These conditions and these consequences for the son are not limited to the lower class. Only because of social experiences and the distribution of social rewards is it more likely that certain father-son relationships impeding identification will occur in the lower classes than in the higher strata of society.

Severity of Socialization
and Identification

Table 44 shows that if the father's methods of socialization are severe the son is less likely to resemble the father (75 and 66 per cent versus 56 and 59 per cent). This suggests that identification with the "aggressor" is not operating, or at least not to the degree that identification with mild disciplinarians is occurring.

The figures of Table 44 bring to mind but hardly support other interesting ideas concerning the mothers' role and the son's identi-

Table 44
General Level of Severity of Socialization Techniques
and "Identification"

Father's Level	Mother's Level	Son Resembles Mother (Number)	Son Resembles Father (Number)	Son Resembles Father (Per Cent)
Mild	Mild	11	33	75.0
	Severe	10	19	65.5
Severe	Mild	18	23	56.1
	Severe	32	46	59.0

fication. If the mother is severe the son may be insufficiently confident to take the Oedipal step from identification with the mother to identification with the father. Or in the terms of George Mead, the mother's harshness produces anxiety in the son. This anxiety inhibits flexible symbolic behavior and impedes the kind of imaginative role-taking necessary if identification with the husband-father role is to occur. The son is anxiously frozen in a kind of femininity or "immaturity." It may be that nonhostile socialization by the mother is in this primary stage more important for the son in transferring identification from the mother to the father. In later years the tone of the father's socialization gains in importance and becomes more influential.

Emotional Support and Identification

Table 45 shows that though social class is an important condition in explaining whether identification with the father will or will not occur, the emotional relationship that exists between father and son is even more predictive of "identification." If the father operates

Table 45
Relationship Between Emotional Support from Father and Tendency for Son to Admire and Resemble Father More Than Mother

Class Level	Emotional Support from Father	Per Cent Admire Father		Per Cent Resemble Father[a]	
Upper	High	100	(11)	92.9	(14)[b]
	Low	74.7	(27)	53.4	(45)
Middle	High	100	(10)	78.9	(19)
	Low	61.5	(26)	62.5	(48)
Lower	High	66.7	(6)	70.0	(10)
	Low	41.9	(31)	54.9	(51)

a. Son's report of what others say.
b. Numbers in parentheses equal total cases.

effectively in the area of emotional support then the son has high identification with him ("admires" and resembles him) rather than with the mother at all three levels. In a general way this evidence is parallel to the findings of Sears, Maccoby, and Levin (1957) cited in Table 6, Chap. 4, which showed that the development of a conscience (a measure of identification for them) occurs more frequently for the child when the parent is warm and accepting.

Results similar to these for adolescent boys were obtained by

Pauline Sears (1953) in a study of 379 kindergarten children. She found that boys who chose to play the father in projective doll play (and were thus adjudged appropriately sex-typed and identified with their fathers) came from families where the fathers were reported to be warmer than the fathers of other subjects. Boys who chose the mother role in doll play tended to come from families where the mothers (but not the fathers) were high in warmth, where the mothers were quite permissive generally but tended to restrict the boys to the home area. This restriction increased the mothers' authority over their sons. These mothers also tended to be critical of the fathers in interviews.

Though the emotional relationship between father and son is more predictive of identification than social class, this does not mean that social status is an unimportant factor in identification. The whole framework of the research should be recalled. We have reasoned that the amount of positive affect the father has to direct toward the son is a consequence of the amount of positive sanctions (power, possessions, and prestige) that his status in society provides him. It is thus partially the amount of emotional support received from the father *as structured by the father's status* which brings about the son's resemblance to the father as a model. Again, we see that a warm and relatively intimate relationship between father and son brings about identification with the father rather than the mother. Warm support and rather mild discipline create the "emotional bridge" between father and son which facilitates an acceptance of the parental model.

The Structure of Authority
and Identification

It would seem that if the father plays the significant role in the area of authority, this would be another factor bringing about the son's identification with him. If the father is making decisions about behavior and the distribution of sanctions within the family, then identification might come about for two reasons. If the father is powerful he becomes admired as a respected and adequate person to be copied. Secondly, if he is controlling and sanctioning behavior then it would become advantageous for the son to accept the father's ideals and modes of behavior as his own. This would bring about harmonious and rewarded social interaction in his presence, and following Sears, security and gratification in his absence. Table 46 shows that this expectation is strongly confirmed in the middle and upper classes.

Table 46
Relationship Between Parental Authority Over Son and Tendency for Son to Admire and Resemble Father More Than Mother

Class Level	Authority Over Son	Per Cent Admire Father		Per Cent Resemble Father[a]	
Upper	Father	88.5	(26)	70.0	(30)[b]
	Mother	64.3	(13)	61.3	(31)
Middle	Father	78.6	(28)	78.6	(28)
	Mother	45.5	(11)	52.9	(34)
Lower	Father	41.7	(24)	51.7	(29)
	Mother	53.8	(13)	59.4	(32)

a. Son's report of what others say.
b. Numbers in parentheses equal total cases.

The opposite is found to be the case in the lower class. The reversal also holds when the authority structure is measured in a somewhat different manner (using additional questions) and when the source of authority is trichotomized into these categories: father, parents equal, and mother.

Though we should again avoid explaining away every exception, we do feel that we may get these results at the lower level because the father's authority and control are here particularly hostile and rigid in nature. Again, this may be indirect evidence in opposition to theories of identification with the aggressor.

STATUS, IDENTIFICATION, AND SEXUAL BEHAVIOR

Sexual behavior, like other physiological functions, is not met without social and psychological experiences and norms controlling its expression and molding its meaning. The child's training in areas of body function, the parental attitude expressed toward his body and toward pleasure at this level, his early feelings toward adult individuals of the same and opposite sex in society and in the family, and his relationships to sibs and peers of both sexes interact to channel sexual behavior and to create varying sexual interests and attitudes.

The child begins life in a situation of intimate body care, and with a focus on care in certain more sensitive areas. This intimate attention and its derivative emotional attitudes of encompassing approval and security must be given up, to a certain extent, in the process of maturing. Body care becomes less and less intimate, the child is expected to become *independent*, to express and be satisfied with verbal and symbolic expressions of love and interest in him, to accept criticisms, and to respond to increasing expectations for achievement. As the child matures, some of the intimacy lost in the family is regained in the latency peer group. Individuals are able to move from the natal family as their intimate reference group to the peer group with varying success. Similarly, individuals are with varying success able to move from the natal family or the peer group to the behavior system of adult sexuality (dating, courtship, heterosexual love and activity, and marriage).

For those who achieve adult behavior there remain certain rather overlaid needs to recapture the intimate emotional nature of the parent-child or family relationships and the peer-group relationships. This motivation, when combined with the operation of the incest taboo, interests in validating one's adult sex status, and development of genital sexuality on a physiological level, provide the impetus for sexual behavior, dating, marriage, and having children of one's own.

These needs for physical and emotional intimacy and regression must be met, it would seem, if the level of adult performance is to be maintained. The absence of an approved social situation in which the single individual can express these needs may account for part of the higher mental disorder rate of this group (see Table 26).

Achieved Status and the Emergence of Subcultural Sexual Norms

This sociopsychological interpretation of the development of erotic interests allows us to view sexual behavior as not merely a release of physical tension and needs but as the expression of attitudes and social desires learned in a particular subculture, and of needs resulting from a particular social situation. Patterns of sexual behavior, and here we use data from one of the Kinsey reports (Kinsey et al., 1948) as a test of our predictive interpretation, should be related to an achieved social status, education.

In the strictest sense this is not an interpretation but a group of hypotheses. Our theoretical perspective led us to look for something like the pattern which Tables 9, 47, 48, 61 and other tables from the report reveal. What do these tables indicate? Here are some basic findings relevant to our interest in this section and our approach:

1. The percentage of heterosexual acts expressed extramaritally is greater in the lower social-class levels than in the upper-class levels, but with age this pattern reverses. That is, by the age of 40

or 45 the lower-class male is relatively more faithful than the upper-class male (Table 47).

Table 47
Percentage of Total Sexual Outlet Obtained by Marital Intercourse Among Married Males by Age and Educational Level

Years of Education				Age			
	16-20	21-25	26-30	31-35	36-40	41-45	46-50
13+	85.4	83.9	82.8	78.3	74.4	76.4	—
	(3.47)[a]	(3.07)	(2.61)	(2.05)	(1.89)	(1.48)	
9-12	82.2	81.6	81.7	85.2	88.2	—	—
	(4.10)	(3.35)	(2.88)	(2.83)	(2.29)		
0-8	79.9	81.0	86.2	88.1	88.1	90.0	—
	(3.74)	(3.28)	(3.00)	(2.26)	(1.95)	(1.72)	

a. Numbers in parentheses equal mean frequency per week.
Source: Selected columns from Alfred Kinsey, Wardell Pomeroy, and Clyde Martin, *Sexual Behavior in the Human Male* (Philadelphia: W. B. Saunders Company, 1948), p. 356.

2. The percentage of total outlets homosexual in nature among married men is greater in the lower classes than in the upper classes at the early ages, but again this relationship has been reversed by 35 or 40 years of age (Table 48).

3. The percentage of homosexual outlets among single men is greatest among those with some high school education (and nearly as great among those with only elementary schooling) but least in the upper-status level (Table 48).

Why did we look for these kinds of trends and how do we interpret them from our general position? Let us look at sexual behavior as it interacts with social status and identification in the family.

Identification and Extrafamilial
Sexual Expression

Though findings (1), (2), and (3) deal with both homosexual and heterosexual behavior of married and single individuals, they are all related to the degree of erotic expression occurring *extrafamilially*. This common quality of the several kinds of sexual behavior, which are quite different in other ways, requires some common explanatory device.

During his younger years the lower-class man engages in more extrafamilial sexual activity, but this relationship becomes reversed after 20 or 25 years of married life. We were led to expect this for reasons already spelled out to some degree. The situation of the lower-class father makes it particularly difficult for him to direct the kind of warmth necessary for appropriate intimacy and the son's identification with the father-husband role. Thus, the high extra-marital heterosexual and homosexual behavior is a manifestation of absence of identification with the father-as-husband role, aliena-tion from the family group, and a relatively strong involvement in the same sex peer group. This latter group takes over much of the socialization function and it is here that many needs are satisfied and sexual interests first molded.

The peer group has its own incest taboo also, the homosexual taboo. If we generalize many of the proposed reasons for the func-tional relationship between the family as a socializing group and the incest taboo to the socializing processes and emotional needs in the peer group, we would be led to make certain predictions. We would predict that many of the erotic impulses do not find expres-sion in the intimate peer group as a personality-maintaining and socializing "family" where much of the motivation originates, but with females and occasionally males outside this group.

Within the peer group the individual in the lower levels of society learns certain conceptions of sexuality (of both heterosexual and homosexual nature) independent of the family situation. This force-ful, emotional, and extrafamilial socialization leads to an extrafa-milial expression of eros on the adult level.

By contrast, the problem for the upper-level male is freeing himself libidinally from a more secure and emotionally consistent family. He is sexually more restrained (both heterosexually and homosexually), but the sex that is expressed shows a greater inte-

Table 48
Percentage of Total Sexual Outlet Obtained Homosexually
by Age and Educational Level

Years of Education	Marital Status	Adol. -15	16-20	21-25	26-30	31-35	36-40	41-45	46-50
13+	Married	—	.16	.53	.96	.75	.89	1.64	3.0
	Single	3.14	2.43	3.72	8.82	17.90	—	—	—
9-12	Married	—	2.11	1.05	.96	1.38	.73	—	—
	Single	8.73	10.81	16.31	25.95	18.83	—	—	—
0-8	Married	—	3.08	1.33	.46	.14	.30	.08	—
	Single	8.03	6.85	8.06	14.04	27.43	18.60	—	—

Source: Selected columns from Alfred Kinsey, Wardell Pomeroy, and Clyde Martin, *Sexual Be-havior in the Human Male* (Philadelphia: W. B. Saunders Company, 1948), pp. 378, 382.

gration of his family role (married status) and his sexual role (lower rate of extramarital intercourse and homosexual behavior).

It is true that solitary sexual activity among the higher-status (college-educated) groups carries over into marriage at a higher rate for both males (Kinsey et al., 1948, p. 382) and females (Kinsey et al., 1953, p. 181). Perhaps they are at some psychosexual level still much more involved with their natal families, indicating the strong sense of satisfaction and obligation there. Perhaps they are also still involved psychosexually with themselves, a behavioral consequence of a cultural philosophy of individualism.

We would explain the reversing trends in fidelity at the different status levels in this way: with increasing age the lower-level married male, despite certain problems, is placed in a situation which socializes him increasingly for fusion of the family role and sex role activity. Thus the decrease in extramarital and homosexual activity. With increasing age the higher-level married male is increasingly freed from the emotional control and definition of behavior learned in his natal family. This freeing attitude is carried over into his attitude toward his marital family and he begins to express himself emotionally and sexually in other ways. Thus, the increased extramarital heterosexual and homosexual behavior with increasing age in the higher level male. This, we feel, indicates a learning to separate the father-husband sex role, which he learned by strong identification with his father, from an extrafamilial erotic role which had been relatively inhibited in development. The evidence is indirect and not beyond dispute.

It is difficult to make a similar interpretation of the association between status and the sexual behavior of women. This seems to result primarily from the fact that the sexual behavior of women seems to vary less by educational level and is associated less with such achieved statuses (Kinsey et al., 1953, p. 685). These conditions may be an additional example of a general condition—the female and mother roles vary less from class to class. Intimate natal family experiences are more likely to be influential for the woman.

Summary

The various tables presented thus far in this chapter support our general orientation in several ways. First, they show that the expected consequences at various class levels do occur. The mother becomes a more important figure of identification at the lower levels of society and the father a more important figure at the upper levels. Secondly, within each class we see that identification takes place for the reasons we have hypothesized to be operating to vary-ing degrees in the different classes. We see that variation in the amounts of hostility expressed in socialization, of emotional inti-macy, and of authority exercised influence identification.

And finally, we find that adult erotic behavior, which is closely linked to the process of psychosexual identification in the family, can be interpreted as a consequence of certain patterns of family roles at different status levels.

To continue our chain of reasoning and analysis, we should expect that certain patterns of emotional relationship between father and son or mother and son, and certain patterns of identification, should result in the choice of particular levels and types of occu-pations by the socialized son. The next section investigates certain theoretically derived expectations in this area.

FACTORS AFFECTING LEVEL OF OCCUPATION CHOSEN: A REVIEW

It is not the purpose of this section to systematically analyze the ideological and social-structural conditions which support or inhibit occupational mobility. Nor will it be possible here to con-sider in a theoretically systematizing manner the body of research material concerning the social and psychological characteristics of individuals who are prone to ascending or descending mobility. To some degree these tasks have been carried out in other works. (See particularly Lipset and Bendix, 1960.) Here we will attempt only a brief outline of the kinds of problems raised and investigated in these areas. There will be a special focus on family structure and occupational choice, for in this area we have original data to intro-duce in a meaningful way. Within the phrase "occupational choice" we include both type of occupation, which we discuss later, and level (relative to the father's occupational level) of occupation, which we deal with here.

The writer has developed what he considers a reasonably ex-haustive and meaningful list of factors which may influence the type and rates of mobility in a society or for an individual.

1. *Cultural factors.* What values exist in the society or in various subgroups of the society that may influence the rate of up-ward and downward mobility? These values may have to do directly with mobility (such as the success theme in America, as opposed to India's emphasis on tradition and caste) or, they may influence mobility indirectly. An example of the

latter would be the influence of Calvinistic doctrine on industrial development and mobility.

2. *Factors of broad social structure.* These factors may result from the above values or they may lead to values which then provide a rationalizing ideology for society's structure. These social factors include such specific conditions as:

   a. *The degree to which placement is based on achieved ability* rather than ascribed (inherited) position. In societies where mobility flourishes the moral slogan becomes "It is not who you *are* but what you can *do.*

   b. *Variation of opportunity to achieve* because of variation either in education or, once trained, in opportunity for advancement.

   c. *Demographic factors* such as differential birth and death rates or migration. Thus, much upward mobility in industrial societies has come about as a consequence of birth rates in the upper levels insufficient to replace the older generation.

   d. *Degree of change in occupational structure.* Thus, the parents' wish, "I want him to have a better life than we did," often becomes reality in work because our economy now demands more professional workers and fewer unskilled people.

3. *The influence of intimate social structure and the individual's position in it.* This refers to such matters as the importance of the peer group, the peer group's structure and the individual's position in it, the family structure, and its extent and tightness of organization (Faris, 1950). Thus, societies which place a focus on a large kinship grouping and on the individual's lifelong obligations to play his traditional role in it, make geographical and social mobility much more difficult. Our concern and data will be an analysis of factors in this section.

4. *Personality characteristics.* Individuals as individuals have different motivations and find different degrees of opportunities for mobility. Why this is so is to an important degree a consequence of the idiosyncratic way in which the individual has experienced the conditions of the first three sections here. He handles these in his own special way, however, and he inherits certain biological resources (level of vitality or intelligence) which influence the occupational level he can achieve.

We see from this review of causes that they frequently intertwine and influence one another or are discussions of the same causes from different conceptual levels. Let us now turn to an analysis of factors in the family, for this is our focus. After a review of various areas of literature and approaches (especially Lipset and Bendix, 1960; Kahl, 1957; and E. Cohen, 1958) the writer has attempted to develop a classification of basic factors in this area that influence mobility.

Useful for 3-d part of essay

1. *The family's relationship to society.*
   a. *Its integration into or lack of involvement in a particular community or social structure.* Here studies indicate that high integration of the family into its own community at a particular level impedes mobility. Geographical mobility and conscious interaction with families outside the family's own class level foster upward mobility (Allen, 1955).
   b. *The family's status.* Numerous studies show that initial status in life determines to a high degree adult status. These studies, however, are seldom sufficiently refined for one to see the influence of status itself on the *rate* of mobility from level to level. There is some evidence that the step from manual to nonmanual (white collar) work is particularly difficult and that a low rate exists there (Lipset and Bendix, 1960, pp. 165-171). The family's status influences mobility by providing the child with certain kinds and numbers of opportunities. Its status also has many influences on the family's internal processes (as we have seen), and these in turn produce dispositions to upward or downward mobility.
2. *The internal structure of the family.*
   a. *Its demographic character.* There is considerable evidence that being an oldest or only child, or a child with few siblings facilitates upward mobility.
   b. *The family's values.* The family is one of the strongest and most immediate representatives of the culture or subculture for the child. If there is an anxiety about worth (Calvinism), a focus on learning, or an emphasis on doing well in life, this seems to be reflected in the chlid's occupational choice (Kahl, 1953; Strodtbeck, 1958).
   c. *Ascriptive role dissatisfaction* (or pathology) and compensating achievement role activity (upward mobility). Several studies (Ellis, 1952; Warner and Abegglen, 1955; Mc-

Clelland et al., 1953, p. 279) show that individuals who are exceptionally achieving report distance or alienation from their families, hostility to their families, or dissatisfaction with the families' statuses. However, other studies indicate that this may be true only of the highly mobile and not of the moderately mobile. Perhaps those who are mobile to the degree the general culture and occupational shifts demand are "normal" but those who exceed this modal pattern of mobility or fall below (the downwardly mobile) have special motivations derived from primary group "maladjustment." The maladjustments result in independence from the various ascriptive solidarities of the original statuses. It will be seen that this is a corollary of a basic idea in Chap. 6, which was that certain primary group or ascribed roles develop in the urban lower classes in a characteristically exaggerated manner to compensate for frustration and lack of accomplishment in occupational roles.

d. *Role structure in the family.* These studies deal largely with the influence on mobility of the patterns of authority and the quality of emotional relationships in the family. Strodtbeck (1958), after a review of several studies of the upwardly mobile individual's position in the family, concluded:

> The general impression to be drawn from these studies, however, is that striving for achievement is more frequently noticeable among boys who perceive their parents as reserved and their relationship with their parents as unsatisfying (p. 145).

Strodtbeck presents data which show that the son's probability of upward mobility is increased if the father *shares* authority with the mother. His interpretation of this is discussed later when we present similar data.

These studies do not seem to have always gotten at the specific emotional content of the relationship or its structure (e.g., was the distance greater between mother and child or between father and child?). In the next sections we look at the family role conditions which produce different patterns of occupational choice. These conditions are regarded as consequences of (1) the mother's and father's role in the methods of socialization, (2) the patterns of authority and, (3) the locus of affect in the family's life.

FAMILY EXPERIENCES AND MOBILITY

After asking for his ideal choice, the high-school-age subjects were asked:

Of course, there can be a big difference between anybody's day dreams and what, seriously, he really expects to be and do. When you are an adult—let's say around 35 or 40—what kind of work do you really expect to be doing?

The sons' responses were then coded for occupational level and type according to Roe.

The fathers' occupational levels were also known, and the relationships between the sons' realistic choices and the fathers' present levels created three groups of sons: those who *expected* upward mobility, those who *anticipated* downward mobility, and those who *expected* no change. Cases with fathers in the highest occupational category and in the lowest occupational category were eliminated so the sons could move in any direction. This prevented the direction of mobility from being a function of the father's status. For example, if the sons of fathers at the very top had been included, then high-status cases and their characteristics would be overly represented in the stable group because they could not be upwardly mobile. Tables 49, 50, and 51 show the relationship between three important dimensions of family behavior and expected mobility.

Mobility and Severity of Socialization Techniques

Table 49 shows that both the mothers and fathers of occupationally stable sons are most likely to be severe socializers. This table also shows that the mothers and fathers of downwardly mobile sons are least likely to be severe in the socialization techniques used. Upwardly mobile sons have parents of intermediate severity.

Table 49
Severity of Parents' Discipline and Son's Social Mobility

Son's Estimate of Social Mobility	PER CENT RELATIVELY SEVERE	
	Father	Mother
Upward (104 = 100%)	37.5	42.3
Stable (43 = 100%)	55.8	56.1
Downward (20 = 100%)	30.0	20.0

Why should this be so? Much of what we have said and have found led us to expect that the downwardly mobile sons would be most severely socialized. Perhaps this pattern can be explained in this way. Parents who are very mild and nonpunishing do not foster achievement and autonomy but create a relaxed child with little occupational drive. Parents who are very harsh and severe create a kind of rigid anxiety and inflexibility which make occupational adventure (upward mobility) threatening but also create a kind of status anxiety that makes downward mobility almost unthinkable.

The idea that the parents' hostility and severe socialization could lead to the sons' occupational rigidity and fear of occupational adventure seemed so intriguing that further analysis was made regarding the similarity in qualitative *type* of occupation chosen and degree of hostility and severity of socialization. This showed that those sons choosing occupations like their fathers' were more severely socialized than those choosing occupations unlike their fathers' (44 versus 40 per cent). This analysis also showed that those sons choosing occupations like their fathers' were more likely to have hostile fathers (using a different measure) than were sons choosing occupations unlike their fathers'. In the former group 63 per cent, and in the latter group only 50 per cent, of the fathers were rated in the more hostile group. This gives further evidence for our interpretation and for lines of thought developed, surprisingly, in *The Authoritarian Personality* (Adorno et al., 1950).

The data also show, however, that high emotional support from the father (which we now know leads to high identification) *also* leads to a choice of occupation like the father's.

All of the differences discussed here are rather small. In no cases are the differences so great that all these factors could not be operating to some degree. That is, a mildly socializing but emotionally distant father would minimize similarity in type of occupation chosen by the son. A father who was hostile, socialized severely, but played an important role in the boy's emotional life would maximize rigid identification and the choice of an occupation of the same level and kind as the father's. In fact, it is perhaps just this type of emotional climate in the family which sustains a fairly traditional society with occupational inheritance as a moral expectation.

It may be that this ordering (with the least severely socialized downwardly mobile, and the most severely socialized occupationally stable) will account for some of the varying results and interpretations regarding family experience and mobility. Some studies find warmth and support producing upward mobility, but other studies find rejection and coolness producing upward mobility. The variability of the findings may result from the fact that the studies have sometimes spoken of only two groups: (1) the upwardly mobile and (2) the remainder of the cases. This would tend to lump together individuals with quite opposite experiences: the very mildly socialized declining cases and the severely socialized stable group. If this second group was composed of an unusually large number of downwardly mobile sons, then by comparison the upwardly mobile would be more severely dealt with. If this group was composed of largely occupationally stable individuals, then the opposite results would be obtained.

Another point discussed earlier has application here. Some studies of upward mobility have looked at extreme mobility, others have not distinguished the degree of mobility. It may be that those manifesting extreme mobility (Warner and Abegglen's businessmen and Ellis' career women) display distance from their families but that those with more moderate mobility do not show this pattern.

Mobility and Authority Structure

A second factor in family structure has been found important in the mobility of the individual. Let us begin with the work of Strodtbeck which was discussed earlier. This study showed that upwardly mobile sons came from families in which the fathers exercised less authority and the mothers somewhat more. Strodtbeck (1958, pp. 188-190) interprets this relationship in this way: if the father is powerful and has an authoritative control over the family the son develops a kind of resignation about life which reduces mobility and achievement. He has been *controlled* and feels that he will be in the future also. This situation is also more highly structured than that of the family in which the parents *share* authority. This structured quality may make mobility difficult because it creates in the child a feeling of strong involvement in the family's life and also a feeling of anxiety or inadequacy in the more fluid and flexible social environments of occupations of higher social status.

Table 50 gives detailed support (i.e., for three mobility groups and three authority patterns) of Strodtbeck's findings and interpretation. It presents a rather consistent picture: critical factors in high occupational aspiration seem to be the absence of the father's dominating authority and the presence of shared parental authority *in the family generally and over the son*.

Table 50
Source of Authority and Son's Social Mobility

Son's Estimate of Social Mobility	SOURCE OF AUTHORITY			Total Number of Cases
	Father (Per Cent)	Parents Equal (Per Cent)	Mother (Per Cent)	
Upward	39.2 (29)[a]	32.5 (24)	28.4 (21)	74
Stable	48.8 (19)	28.2 (11)	23.1 (9)	39
Downward	53.4 (8)	13.3 (2)	33.1 (5)	15

a. Numbers in parentheses are numbers of cases.

Emotional Support, Identification, and Mobility

A third factor, the source of emotional support, also influences the son's mobility pattern. Table 51 shows that the son who expects that he will move to an occupational level above his father's is more likely to have a father who participates more in the affective life of the son. This may be in conflict with the results of Dynes, Clarke, and Dinitz discussed earlier, and the idea that ascribed role maladjustment produces upward mobility. The table shows that the downwardly mobile boy is particularly likely to obtain emotional support from his mother.

Earlier data (Table 45) showed that the parental source of emotional support for the son also tends to be the source of identification for the son. This has significance here, for occupational activity is an important component of the male role, and if identification with the father is weak, achievement is likely to suffer.

Further analysis of data by Forrest Dill provides concrete evidence for this interpretation of the relationship between parental identification and occupational aspiration (and possibly eventual achieve-

Table 51
Source of Affection and Son's Social Mobility

Son's Estimate of Social Mobility	SOURCE OF AFFECTION			Total Number of Cases
	Father (Per Cent)	Parents Equal (Per Cent)	Mother (Per Cent)	
Upward	23.0 (17)[a]	32.5 (24)	44.6 (33)	74
Stable	25.7 (10)	28.2 (11)	46.2 (18)	39
Downward	20.0 (3)	20.0 (3)	60.0 (9)	15

a. Numbers in parentheses are numbers of cases.

ment). Dill found that sons who admired (identified with) the father more than the mother aspired to higher levels of occupation. This was true for both their fantasy and realistic occupational choices. It was also true, holding class constant, at all class levels. The mean level (using Roe's six levels) of realistic occupational choice was higher for those identifying with the father rather than the mother in our upper class (a mean of 2.08 versus 2.60 where 1 is the highest occupational level and 6 is the lowest), middle class (2.27 versus 2.67), and lower class (2.09 versus 3.53). In a six-point scale, the 1.44 difference revealed in the lower class is particularly striking, and again suggests some of the difficult problems of work commitment that are experienced by the son in the working class. It is here that the emotional significance of "mom" may dominate the son's psyche and may be in conflict with his performance of instrumental tasks.

A somewhat more psychoanalytic perspective on this matter can be introduced. In an achievement-oriented society the line of development for the male child is from the point of great involvement, identification, and dependence on the mother, toward greater and greater autonomy, independence of the mother, and mature rational behavior appropriate for occupational pursuits. If the mother provides "too much" love and pleasure, and if she is admired too much, the pressure for masculine adult development (as the dominant culture defines it) may be ineffective. The son will remain involved in the "regressive" behavior system of mother-son love. This will reduce the probability of his upward mobility and will greatly increase the likelihood of his downward mobility (social regression).

Here one is reminded of the evolutionary principle that ontogeny (the life history of the individual organism) recapitulates phylogeny (the history of the phylum or species). If the child does not go through a series of developmental stages which in an abstract way may reflect the historical stages of societal development, then he cannot become a participating adult member in the complete society as now evolved. Instead, he will fall back to a position at a less differentiated and lower level of society.

Talcott Parsons (1959a) discusses how the school system aids in the achievement of these developmental stages. Higher school systems become increasingly more differentiated in terms of status rewards and subjects taught. They also become more and more specialized in function, for the primary grades include a number of activities which are emotionally supportive and familial in nature, whereas at the university level the student and professor are expected to suspend their diffuse primary group needs and focus on the exchange of interpretation and fact. This seems to be something of the pattern of man's recent development from ascriptive and traditional societies to impersonal, and complexly differentiated societies.

Family Roles and the Social Origins of Harvard Undergraduates

Data made available to and reanalyzed by the author indicate that some of these same conditions operate in the reports of older individuals who are further along in their career development. The questions regarding their families asked the Harvard students of this study were quite similar to the questions asked the high school students. These data (gathered in their original form by Henry Wechsler) also indicate that the associations between parental roles and mobility appear not only in the range of social classes of the senior high school data but also among those of higher status and of more pronounced mobility. Tables 52 and 53 show the parental roles of a sample of Harvard undergraduates of different class origins (Classes I, II, and III according to Hollingshead).

Table 52 shows that those sons who are upwardly mobile (Class

Table 52
Social Origin of Harvard Undergraduates and Reversal of Parental Roles (Father's Affection Greater Than Mother's, and Mother's Authority Greater Than Father's)

Year in School	Class I[a]		Class II		Class III	
Senior	15.5%	(45)[b]	25%	(24)	33%	(31)
Freshman	11.0%	(43)	23%	(35)	36%	(33)

a. Class I, II, and III are the three top classes of Hollingshead's five class system.
b. Numbers in parentheses are total numbers of cases falling in each category.

III sons who are attending Harvard) are much more likely to derive from a family structure in which there is a reversal of the traditional parental roles in the family. In contrast, those sons who can be interpreted as occupationally stable (sons of Class I origin who are attending Harvard) derive from families in which the fathers hold authority and the mothers give emotional support to the sons.

Table 53 shows that paternal authority decreases as one moves down the scale of social origin (those lowest on that scale being the most educationally and occupationally mobile) and that the fathers' emotional role *increases*. These results show the same patterns as those of Tables 50 and 51, which were developed from the high school data. They also lend further support to the interpretation developed there.

We do not have the type of data which would allow further substantiated interpretations in this area of interest—other than those that were developed previously in this chapter and by Strodtbeck. However, some of the theoretical framework developed in Chaps. 4 and 6 can be employed here. A son's downward mobility is associated with a father whose relationship with his son is relatively devoid of emotional support and warmth and may be to some extent hostile or at least indifferent. Also, a downwardly mobile son is most likely to identify with his mother and to feel during latency and adolescence the impelling need to find adult and masculine identification somewhere. He does this by rebelling against his mother, fleeing the home situation, and becoming involved in the peer-group situation. Here is where masculine and "adult" roles are learned, so he tends to become isolated from the conforming society-wide adult standards which are interpreted as nonpeer group, non-"good guy," and perhaps, therefore, feminine. This sociopsychological process (which does not take place only in the lower classes) leads to the belief that achievement in school, the men in the higher occupational groups, and the cultivated behavior of higher status groups are effete and "foreign" (i.e., are of the outgroup as the peer group divides the world). Therefore, to engage in behavior leading to a higher social level (school work) or to have goals of achieving higher status threatens the adolescent's loyalties to the peer group and his status in the ascribed male role.

Table 53
Parental Roles and Social Origins of Harvard Undergraduates

Family Structure	Year in School	Class I		Class II		Class III	
Father dominant source of authority	Senior	75%	(45)[a]	71%	(24)	53%	(31)
	Freshman	73%	(43)	58%	(35)	58%	(35)
Father dominant source of affection	Senior	20%	(45)	27%	(24)	36%	(31)
	Freshman	23%	(43)	30%	(35)	48%	(33)

a. Numbers in parentheses are total numbers of cases falling in each category.

The Father's Mobility and
His Role as Socializer

Though this chapter deals with the influence of family experiences on the behavior of the *son,* let us now reverse the orientation and see what influence the *father's* own social mobility has on his parental role. We do this because it will tell us not only how mobility influences the fathers to treat our subjects, the sons, but it also may give us some idea of how the sons of our sample with different mobility patterns will act when they become fathers of a new generation. In this way we may see dimly that "effect" becomes "cause" in the chain of generational ties that forms human history. We discuss in Chap. 9 the work of Bettelheim and Janowitz (1950) which found that the upwardly mobile were least ethnocentric (hostile to Jews and Negroes) and the downwardly mobile were most ethnocentric. Bettelheim and Janowitz interpreted the hostility to Negroes and anti-Semitism to be consequences of frustration in the area of achievement. (Later similar studies have not always given unqualified support for these results.) This frustration then led to a compensating emphasis on ascriptive qualities (e.g., Christian as opposed to Jewish) and a displacement of hostility onto the outgroup.

The earlier discussion and data have also shown that fathers who experience a lower *absolute* status in society may also experience frustration and then displace their hostility into the family. Do downwardly mobile fathers (like the subjects of Bettelheim and Janowitz) feel greater frustration and direct their hostility toward their sons? Table 54 shows that they do this to a rather striking degree. Upwardly mobile fathers are relatively severe in only about 37 per cent of the cases, but downwardly mobile fathers are severe in 60 per cent of the cases. A second measure (general degree of hostility) also showed this: only 39 per cent of the upwardly mobile fathers were hostile, but 55 per cent of the downwardly mobile

Table 54
Father's Social Mobility and Severity of Socialization Techniques

Father's Mobility (Relative to His Own Father's Status)	Low Severity (Number)	High Severity (Number)	Per Cent Severe
Upward	53	31	36.9
Stable	36	17	32.1
Downward	14	21	60.0

fathers were. This gives additional support to the theoretical approach here and to the Bettelheim and Janowitz study.

Curiously, this ordering of percentages is just the opposite of the magnitude of percentages in Table 49 which related the severity of the father's socialization and the son's expected mobility.

This *reversal* of the pattern, the association of these patterns with particular paths of mobility already shown, and the introduction of other qualifying conditions might provide some explanation for certain social processes. Perhaps alternate generations play their parental roles in similar ways, subjecting their sons to socialization techniques which are rather different from those which their progeny will use and from those which their fathers used before them. These alternating methods (from severe to mild and back again to severe) might explain such processes as the circulation of elites in stable societies and the alleged phenomenon that success comes to alternate generations in a family line.

Summary Statement

The findings of this research indicate that the probability of upward mobility is enhanced if the father is an important source of confidence and emotional support, if authority in the family is shared between the parents, and if socialization techniques are moderate —neither severe nor very mild. The probability of class-level stability is maximized if the father operates to a moderate degree as the source of authority and affection, and socializes severely. The son's downward mobility is maximized if the father predominates in the authority role (policy making and general control) and if his participation in the emotional life of the son is limited. (It should be recalled that emotional support and authority are relative measures.) These two factors combined with very mild socialization by father and mother lead the son to choose occupations below the father's.

FAMILY EXPERIENCES AND TYPE OF OCCUPATION CHOSEN: A REVIEW

Perhaps one of the earliest works which relate to our interest in this section was done by Levy (1943). In a study of children with problems of adjustment, Levy found that the children of highly protective and demanding mothers tended to score high in verbal skills. Children who were rejected by their mothers tended to have greater facility with mathematical concepts and to have fewer arithmetic problems (pp. 94-95). The mathematical facility would probably predispose the individual toward technical and scientific occupations. The verbal facility would provide for skill and satisfaction in occupations requiring verbal abilities such as business organization and contracts, general cultural, and personal service. At any rate, we have here some evidence of the relationship between early family atmosphere and future vocational skills.[1]

Roe did intensive studies of the personalities and social histories of very eminent scientists in the fields of physical science, biology, psychology, and anthropology. Let us present her summarizing comments on the relationships between family and the men in each of these groups. She says of the physical scientists (physicists, chemists, astrophysicists, etc.):

Attitudes towards their parents now and in earlier years seem to have been an important factor. They are largely free of present parental ties of any strongly emotional sort, and without guilt over this. Although there is frequently present an open or covert attitude of derogation of their mothers they almost universally respect their fathers profoundly although they seem never to have been very close to them. This situation may well have been a factor in their adoption of a profession which has more "masculine" values in our culture than have many of the learned professions. (Roe, 1956, p. 215.)

Of research biologists she says:

In many of the parental homes, there is no evidence of great warmth, and the incidence of death, divorce, or serious illness among parents of these men (resulting in considerable family disruption and stress for the children) was high, amounting to 40 per cent. The psychosocial development pattern is similar to that found for the physicists. (p. 217.)

Perhaps the presence of illness and death made problems on the biological level of human existence particularly acute and thus led to the focus on the biological and *life* sciences.

She also found that the psychosocial development of both biolo-

---

1. Maccoby and Rau (reported in Maccoby, 1961, p. 361) found parallel results among normal children. They found that those children who are relatively stronger in verbal skills, are in interaction with their mothers more than are those children who are stronger in numerical ability, holding general intelligence more or less constant. At least this was true in the situations observed by the researchers. These are not surprising results, for words are symbols nearer the ascriptive and expressive base of human interaction—a base closer to the female role. By contrast, numbers deal with a more abstract and external world—and as such are nearer the instrumental male role. Facility with numbers would be enhanced by lower rates of mother-child interaction, and through the resulting liberation from the hold of mother-child intimacy, such liberation would probably lead to increased involvement in the world outside this expressive area.

gists and physical scientists seems rather "inadequate" by conventional standards and that their sexual motivation is rather inhibited and mild. These conditions indicate certain emotional problems or at least a disinterest in social interaction. These factors would lead to choice of occupations which were nonsocial in nature.

Of the psychologists she says:

Family patterns involving overprotection and firm, if not overt control were very common in the group; present resentment and difficulty with parents are more frequent than for other scientists except for anthropologists. The pattern of psychosexual development is in marked contrast to that in the physical and biological science groups. (p. 219.)

The above quotes suggest that there are two continua along which these scientists may be placed: (1) the continuum of present parental hold on the adult child, and (2) the continuum of involvement in pursuits which are human and cultural in content. Roe's results also suggest that there is among her scientists a positive association between placement on the two dimensions. Using Parsons' hierarchy of systems of symbolic action (which places the cultural system at the top and the organism at the bottom), we would interpret these results in this way: just as the individual's choice of occupational *level* may be a function of the degree of his involvement in adult culture, so his choice among scholarly pursuits which vary as to level of symbolic control may be a function of the extent of his involvement with his parents. Those sciences which deal with the symbolic norms that are most powerful (e.g., the study of culture) appeal most to those individuals who are and probably were most emotionally involved with their parents—the adult representatives of "higher" culture.

In speaking of the anthropologists she says:

They are very like the psychologists in most respects, tending to extremer degrees of differences from the other groups. The average economic level of the parental family was higher and concern with social status was evident in all but one of them. In general family control was likely to be markedly over- or underprotective, and open hostility to the parents is common. (p. 220.)

If for the time we disregard the physical scientists, we observe a pattern which also becomes meaningful with the introduction of Parsons' ordering of systems of action. Though all the scientists studied are probably on rather high social levels and would fall in the same occupational strata as these are traditionally defined in the sociological literature, those of higher social origins are predisposed to choose occupations which deal with higher systems of symbolic action. Thus, 75 per cent of the anthropologists, 50 per cent of the psychologists, and only 45 per cent of the biologists have fathers who were of professional status.

Though one method of analysis shows that the percentage (84 per cent) of individuals of professional origin is highest among the *theoretical* physical scientists (this is not true of the *experimental* physicists), another manner of analysis indicates that on the average, anthropologists' origins are actually higher. Whatever may be the case, there is something of a linear or possibly curvilinear association between level of social origin and level of involvement in culture of the phenomena studied. The possibility that it is curvilinear is probably a consequence of the high logical and symbolic development in theoretical physics and astrophysics. The fact that the experimentalists in these fields show a distribution nearer the biologists provides some evidence for the view that those of higher social origins will tend to be in those sciences studying higher systems of symbolic control. If science is appealing and if occupational status is desired, the individual chooses those areas for which his past provides some preparation. Individuals of lower statuses probably lived in families that knew less about "what was going on" in society, in their community, and in culture than did those future scientists or scholars of higher origins. This would lead to less ability in developing and working with ideas in the human and cultural areas.

The data do not provide incontrovertible evidence for this interpretation, though it is given further support by the work of Hagen (1959). He finds that those individuals choosing technical or research work (in the physical sciences) tend to be of lower social origins than those choosing administrative positions in those or other areas of work. Hagen's work was based on a thorough study of interviews with Harvard graduates after ten to twenty years of actual work in some occupation. His group is thus far from being typical in terms of origin, degree of mobility, and type and level of occupation. With these cautions in mind let us see what he found.

Hagen's work grew out of an attempt to test some of Roe's basic ideas about family atmosphere and occupational choice. Most of the theory advanced by Anne Roe was not supported. Interesting associations did, however, emerge between social class, parental dominance, and reaction patterns on the one hand and choice of occupation on the other.

He found two basic and predictive dimensions: class, and the personal response of the subject to the dominant parent, "defensive or nondefensive." Further, he stated:

> Therefore with few exceptions, which will be noted, the placing of a sub-group toward the working class end of the continuum implies that the mother is the dominant parent; the converse applies in the case of the upper classes. (p. 140.)

The central importance of (1) class, and (2) response to the dominant parent led Hagen to make an analysis in terms of a two by two table with four quadrants, each quadrant with characteristic occupations, occupational attitudes, and family experiences. Here are some of the findings, taken from that detailed picture, which seem most appropriate for the presentation of our own findings.

1. Technology is an avenue of mobility for working-class boys. The casual atmosphere thought by Roe to be characteristic of families producing this occupational choice was found only in the upper levels of society.
2. Research scientists, who deal with fewer people, are likely to be from the working class and to have defensive reactions to the dominant parent, the mother. This description is considerably less applicable to administrative scientists who are engaged in little research.
3. For business executives or organizational administrators the general picture is one of a boy who felt great respect for and admired a dynamic but sometimes rather distant father. This family situation is probably favorable for the acceptance of the rather complex hierarchies of authority in this type of work.

Hagen found that those working in higher-status jobs (within most situses or types) were from families in which the father held authority. Hagen's finding appears to be in some respects in disagreement with the findings we presented earlier and with Strodtbeck's work, but the disagreement may be merely apparent, because Hagen based his work on a much more select part of the population.

Some of our earlier reflections concerning choice of occupational *level* have meaning in a discussion of the qualitative *type* of occupation chosen. First, there is a problem of method. Though the system of categories developed by Roe seems very helpful, it was developed with a psychological perspective in mind and without a basis in some sociological theory about the nature of society's organization and the organization of the work situation. It is felt by this writer that there is a pressing need for an adequate system of categories of occupations. Without such a meaningful system, we cannot make very intelligent sociological hypotheses about the kinds of occupations chosen.

The set of categories must be developed not merely through a study of the kinds of occupations one observes every day, or those that are presented, with little systematic rationale, in the occupational literature. Instead, the categories must be derived from some general theory about the kinds of basic collectivities and roles which form the structure of a social system. That is, an occupation is a kind of social role in some kind of work enterprise, each role involving the carrying out of certain functions for the social system within which it is involved. Further, this set of categories must not be simply a list of qualitatively different and discrete kinds of occupations; there must be some principle of organization (*fundamentum divisionis*) which systematically relates the occupations to one another as well as to society. The development of such a system is a present but as yet unsuccessful endeavor of the writer's; in the presentation of the data here we rely on Roe's system.

Second, future analysis should recognize more explicitly that the choice of a particular kind or level of occupation does not have the same meaning for each individual. The meaning of an occupation varies according to the chooser's position in society. Let us explain what is meant here by giving a number of examples. An individual with certain kinds of motivations and of lower-class origin may choose a particular occupation not because of any special interest in its content but because upward mobility is considerably easier in that occupation.

The individual's position vis-à-vis the family can also influence his choice. Alienation or close emotional ties to the natal family can direct his choice. If there is extreme hostility, then certain antisocial or asocial exploitative occupations may be chosen. Even here the relations with the family cannot be looked at in isolation. If the child is hostile and alienated from a family already engaged in occupations of an exploitative nature then he may turn to succorant occupations like political reform or social work.

Other conditions also open and close the doors to various choices. A person's ethnic group, degree of involvement in the peer group, attitude toward individuals of the same and opposite sexes all have bearing on the kind of occupation chosen or possible for the individual. Such matters have not been explored very systematically and thoroughly by more than a few behavioral scientists.

Let us now turn to an analysis of the data at hand concerning the occupational aspirations of our high school male subjects.

FAMILY STRUCTURE AND TYPE
OF OCCUPATION CHOSEN

Something of a division of labor and interest exists in the field of occupational choice. Sociologists have sought to discover the family and social conditions producing or allowing choice of occupational *level*. Psychologists (especially those with an industrial and vocational bent) have focused on the interests and life experiences that produce choices of particular *types* of occupations. Sociologists have neglected this problem of choice of type of occupation; this is rather unexpected, for occupations are certainly social roles.

The division of labor is not thoroughgoing. Certain psychologists, such as David McClelland et al. (1953), have dealt meaningfully with conditions producing mobility. Certain sociologists, such as Everett C. Hughes (1958) and his associates, have analyzed with insightful detail the structures of different types of occupations, the satisfactions obtained in each, and the motivations for their selection.

We have already analyzed some of the family patterns that are associated with choice of job level and direction of job mobility. The data derived from the high-school-age sons also are relevant to our second interest, type of occupation chosen. There were sufficient numbers of choices in five types (technology, science, organization, general cultural, and arts and entertainment) to permit an analysis. These five were ordered from most instrumental, most adaptive, and most conventionally masculine to most human oriented, and least masculine.[2]

2. Our ordering with regard to masculinity generally agrees with the masculinity scores compiled for these different occupational groups by Anne Roe in *The Psychology of Occupations* (New York: John Wiley and Sons, Inc., 1956), pp. 160-161.

Theoretical orientations developed since the analysis of this data and discussed in Chap. 10 (see "The Expressive-Instrumental Dimension in Social Behavior and Historical Process"), if applied to the analysis of data presented in the next five tables, might modify that analysis in two ways. (1) The ordering might focus on an internal-external dimension moving from (a) occupations or social roles focusing on the *external* and superordinate symbolic systems (the "superego" roles of the society, e.g., "general cultural"), through those (b) occupations focusing on the needs *internal* to the social system and its members (the "ego" roles of the society, e.g., "organizational" and "service" occupations), to (c) those specializing in dealing with the problems presented by the *external* subordinate environments (the "id" roles of the society, e.g., "technological" or "outdoor" occupations). (2) This ordering and these definitions would then require a review of all cases, reclassification of a number of occupations (e.g., many lawyers might fall into (b) with businessmen), and a recalculation of the associations. The results might be somewhat different, but the writer feels that this theoretical orientation should be developed further before additional empirical reanalysis is made. The reader should keep in mind the

This dimension for measurement was created and used for two main reasons. First, it is basic to many of the theoretical positions of Parsons (and is also suggested by Roe's work). Its use thus provides an approach for the development of hypotheses and the interpretation of results. Second, it was felt that this dimension was related to early social experiences and to salient psychological motivations in occupational choice: what happens to the child in the immediacy of human association in the family predisposes him to make occupational choices with regard to human-orientedness.

With the types of occupations ordered in this manner, certain associations are revealed; these are shown in the remaining five tables of this chapter.

Occupational Choice and Loci of Emotional Support and Authority

No clear pattern emerges in the association of locus of affection with occupational choice (Table 55). There is a slight tendency for the sons of families where the parents share the affectional role to make human-oriented and expressive occupational choices. There is also some indication that it is more probable for the sons of families where the fathers rather than mothers act as source of emotional support to make human-oriented and expressive choices.

Table 55
Source of Affection in Family and Son's Choice of Occupation Type (Realistic Estimate of Occupation at 35)

Source of Affection	TYPE OF OCCUPATION CHOSEN BY SON (PER CENT)				
	Technology	Science[a]	Organization	General Cultural	Arts and Entertainment
Father	27	0	27	12	33
Parents equal	29	33	35	41	33
Mother	44	67	38	47	33
	52 = 100%	15 = 100%	34 = 100%	17 = 100%	12 = 100%

a. The science category is a group composed of a large number of choices such as "chemist," "doctor," and "dentist." These occupations as stated *seem* to be closer to technology than to research science, in which there is participation in the more abstract cultural realm. If there were more research scientists the category might be moved to the right. This problem perhaps reflects a weakness of the typology developed by Roe.

shift in the orientation from this section to the views expressed in the critique of the instrumental-expressive (or instrumental-consummatory) dimension in Chap. 10.

This ordering and definition of occupational roles parallels somewhat the categories developed by Malinowski and by Parsons, and parallels closely Warner's three adaptive systems: the beliefs of the sacred order, the moral organization, and technology (1959, p. 486).

Those whose mothers are their sources of emotional support are more likely to be choosers at the other end of the instrumental-expressive dimension.

A very definite pattern emerges in the relationship between authority structure and occupational choice (Table 56). Fathers'

Table 56
Source of Authority in Family and Son's Choice of Occupation
(Realistic Estimate)

| | TYPE OF OCCUPATION CHOSEN BY SON (PER CENT) | | | | |
Source of Authority	Technology	Science	Organization	General Cultural	Arts and Entertainment
Father	54	47	29	35	25
Parents equal	17	20	29	53	58
Mother	29	33	41	12	17
	52 = 100%	15 = 100%	34 = 100%	17 = 100%	12 = 100%

authority roles decrease sharply as one moves from instrumental occupations chosen by the sons to expressive occupations. An even sharper increase and more consistent progression is observed in the percentage of parents who share authority as one moves from the instrumental occupations to the expressive ones. This is a strong pattern, of which we saw a faint reflection in the affectional role structure.[3]

The writer would explain these trends in this way. Those occupations in modern society which participate in the human, social, and cultural realm are ones which require a nontraditional and non-ascriptive orientation. Such an orientation is learned more easily in families in which there is a sharing of roles and a parental flexibility in the acceptance of traditionally sexually ascribed tasks. The sharing of parental roles may make the child less conscious of ascriptive roles (especially sexual ones) and of the sharp differentiation of the realms of the masculine and the feminine in traditional subcultures. The male child may therefore feel less concern about choosing occupations that are more expressive and human in orientation and have feminine overtones in achievement-"fixated" so-

3. A study of the figures of Table 56 shows a rather definite pattern in the mother's role. It shows mothers exercising greater authority over those boys who make instrumental choices. The pattern is, however, a rather irregular curve, for the greatest maternal authority is exercised over boys making organizational choices. What this pattern means, if anything, is difficult to ascertain, and our discussion does not deal with it.

cieties. Male children from more traditional families, with fathers and mothers playing specific roles, may be very aware of the conventional interpretations of different occupations and may feel that they must choose instrumental occupations to validate their ascribed sexual role.

It could, of course, be the case that those families in which there is some deviance in the family roles (father less the authority and more the locus of affection) produce sons with sex-role and peer-group-role maladjustments. These maladjustments produce curiosity or interest in people and emotional tensions, all of which find outlet in the human and expressive occupations.

If we combine the results concerning the locus of authority and the locus of affection with our earlier findings on the son's identification, a rather interesting but speculative idea emerges. The above findings led us to further analysis regarding the relationship between parental *identification* and instrumental-expressive occupational choice, but only slight, if any, support for our expectations was found. Why should this be so? It will be recalled that compared with the structure of authority, the structure of *emotional support* in the family showed a more predictive relationship to the son's *identification* as we have defined it. It will also be recalled that the *authority pattern* seemed more predictive than the emotional support pattern of the *kind of occupation chosen*. Probably the more expressive and intimate parent-child relationships tapped by questions on emotional support probe forces molding the deeper psychosexual nature of the personality (Whom do you resemble? Whom do you admire?). On the other hand, the more highly structured and impersonal relationships tapped by questions on authority get at the interpersonal forces in the family shaping interests that will lead to choices in the secondary relationships of life, the occupational ones.

Severity of Socialization and Occupational Choice

The immediately foregoing sections have presented data within a theoretical framework that was not always adequate. The writer was not completely prepared on a theoretical level for the empirical results of this chapter. This is an exploratory study (to repeat a cliché all researchers are fond of), and perhaps the theoretical poverty in some sections is to be expected.

The findings, however, are not random gleanings from a host of analyses but are things which the writer went looking for.[4] Certain "hunches" led him to expect the final results even though the theoretical basis for this expectation could not at the time (nor necessarily now) be made thoroughly explicit.

Tables 57 and 58 show the relationship between severity of

Table 57
Severity of Mother's Socialization and Type of Occupation Chosen

Social Class of Parent	Quality of Socialization	OCCUPATION CHOSEN BY SON		Per Cent Choosing Technology
		Organization (Number)	Technology (Number)	
Upper	Mild	7	11	61.1
	Severe	2	9	81.8
Middle	Mild	11	10	47.6
	Severe	8	9	52.9
Lower	Mild	10	16	61.5
	Severe	7	16	69.6

Table 58
Severity of Father's Socialization and Type of Occupation Chosen

Social Class of Parent	Quality of Socialization	OCCUPATION CHOSEN BY SON		Per Cent Choosing Technology
		Organization (Number)	Technology (Number)	
Upper	Mild	6	13	68.4
	Severe	3	7	70.0
Middle	Mild	11	10	47.6
	Severe	9	9	50.0
Lower	Mild	13	17	56.7
	Severe	4	15	78.9

socialization (by father and mother) and type of occupational choice (as regards organization and technology). It was our expectation that sons who were severely socialized would be more likely to choose technological occupations. This is true for both parents at each of the three social class levels. This pattern reflects the association found earlier in Chap. 7 where it was shown that fathers in technological occupations are more severe socializers. It also re-

---

4. The reader should not assume that all the analysis is presented. Analyses were made which are not reported but which the author felt were inconclusive due to weakness of the questions, data, etc. Some interesting and predicted findings are also omitted because they seem to be more appropriate for another statement.

flects some of the things said earlier about the technological occupations' participating less in the human and cultural realm. That is, the father's and mother's severe socialization of the son leads him to fear or move away from people and toward *things* in his work choice.

An additional and interesting pattern exists, though some of the differences are small. The mother's socialization is more predictive of type of choice at the upper level and the father's socialization is more predictive at the lower level.

Choices in other types of occupations were so few that no analysis could be made holding class origin constant. Nevertheless, the relationship between the severity of father's socialization and the instrumental-expressive ordering developed from Roe was sustained when social class origin was ignored. The figures are small, but the decrease in severity is sufficiently consistent as one moves from left to right in Table 59 for the writer to feel that the phenomenon observed is not a function of this particular group of subjects and their responses. Further, the difference between the percentages of sons who are severely socialized at the two extremes in the ordering (71 versus 15 per cent) is very great. Quite the same picture emerges, though to a lesser degree, when the mother's socialization techniques are analyzed in the same manner as in Table 59.

Table 59
An Expressive-Instrumental Ordering of Occupational Choices and the Severity of Socialization

Quality of Socialization (by Father)	Outdoor (Number)	Science (Number)	Business Contacts (Number)	General[a] Cultural (Number)	Service[a] (Number)	Arts and Entertainment (Number)
Mild	2	11	4	10	4	11
Severe	5	11	5	10	1	2
Per cent severely socialized	71.4	50	55.6	50	20	15.4

a. There is some question in the writer's mind as to which of these is more expressive-human.

A Theoretical Elaboration
and a Caution

Perhaps it is unwise to place great causal emphasis on severity of socialization in occupational choice. The question on parental techniques and the one on the son's choice may both tap a severe, conventional, and rigid subculture (or group of personalities) which both socializes with severity by tradition and channels work choices into conventional and "sensible" occupations. There may be a tendency in these subcultures to view manual labor and applied science as important work and the other occupations as suspect and "just a lot of fancy folderol."

This rigidly severe emotional climate and this social and occupational philosophy bring to mind "authoritarian" philosophies of both the right and left at various social levels. The nouveau riche oilman or industrialist embraces McCarthyism and an extreme laissez-faire philosophy and in doing so manifests a fear of humans, society, and the cultural realm (with the associated occupations). The clergy, political leaders, writers, professors, etc., become suspect. Social Darwinism is a suitable philosophy, with its portrayal of society as largely competitive and composed of hostile individuals (who are nearly animals) seeking personal survival.

The individual on the social and political left, especially the more naïve Socialist or Marxist, tends to agree in certain respects with the extreme laissez-faire industrialist or farmer on the right. Marx and Marxism also devalue the social and cultural realm as mere exploitative superstructure. True value is economic and material; it is produced by the one who works with his hands and by the technological expert. Managers and owners are mere expropriators. The clergy and intellectuals are likely to be their assistants in the development of the deceiving superstructure. And again the hostile and competitive view of society is present in the emphasis on nearly constant class struggle.

These philosophies cannot be explained by attributing them to "bad blood" or even to the "authoritarian" personalities of their advocates. The philosophies are themselves derivatives of class and value conflicts, of broad sociohistorical processes, of their advocates' holding relatively deprived positions in those processes and their having dissatisfying personal lives for various reasons unique to individuals.

This deprived position then leads to severe socialization of the child, hostility (influencing occupational choice) to whatever is human and emotional in nature, and general alienation from prevailing social norms. Such factors may in turn lead to a desire for either an extreme shift to the past or to some extreme reorganization of society.

If this analysis is accurate, it would be interesting to know what experiences (familial and otherwise) lead the socially disaffected to choose such different (in some ways) and yet similar (in other ways) solutions. The author would speculate on the basis of findings by Daniel Funkenstein et al. (*Mastery of Stress,* 1957) that a powerful and hostile father leads to the son's having a reactionary political position, while a powerful and overly controlling (and perhaps hostile) mother coupled with isolation from peers leads to extreme liberalism or Marxism. This would also fit in with interpretations of the association between the power of the German father and the rise of reactionary ideology in Germany, with the findings of Strodtbeck (that Jewish mothers are more dominant) and Lenski (that Jewish voters, despite their high economic and occupational status, are quite liberal in their political beliefs), the findings of Hagen and the present writer that those individuals who are gaining status in their *achieved* roles (and therefore possibly experiencing status inconsistency because their ascribed statuses are lagging behind) originate in families where the father is less powerful and the mother more powerful. These various interpretations and findings also give support for the idea to be developed later (in Chap. 9) that occupationally successful and mobile individuals tend to support liberal ideology because it deemphasizes their old *ascribed* statuses and emphasizes their newly achieved statuses. There are, of course, broader personal experiences and social forces directing them.

Both in the Marxian goals (e.g., the withering away of the state) and the goals of the reactionary right (e.g., the best government is that which governs least) there is an antagonism to the integrative function of authority and values. Perhaps such basic philosophies of life are also reflected in occupational choices. These are choices which move away from the human realm among the severely socialized (as we interpret our data) and toward the social and cultural occupations among the mildly socialized and humanly inclined.

CHAPTER 9

Status and Emerging Subcultural Themes

AN ORIENTATION TO THE PROBLEM

In this chapter we will try in somewhat more detail and in a somewhat more systematic manner to discuss the development of subcultural variation. Any observer with a structural inclination observes certain surviving modes of behavior in different parts of human society. With this structural inclination he finds explanations on the level of personality inadequate and incomplete. If the variation in behavior displays its variation structurally, then causal factors of a structural and cultural nature should be found. The emergence of subcultural specializations in American society does not result from accidental gatherings of various class, ethnic, and cultural groups. Nor are the subcultures simply the societal manifestation of the "natural" psychological inclinations of individuals who gravitate to responsible or irresponsible positions in the society.

These subcultural specializations and their position in the reward structure are a product of Western society, American history, and the selection involved in certain persons' emigrating to America (see Chap. 3). These factors and processes can be better understood if we briefly review the ethos of American society. The dominant culture emphasizes an effective mastery of man's external environment (social and physical) and the production of diverse resources. This prevailing ethos is the Protestant ethic in secularized form, just as Protestantism is a somewhat secularized version of earlier Christianity. The focus is on this-worldly industry, individualism, and individual responsibility to God rather than on obedience to sacred tradition and ritual.

As it is viewed here, this ethic makes productive activity and occupational role particularly critical in determining a person's status in society and feelings of worth. It is hypothesized that certain status groups turn to other roles and behavior systems where status may be obtained, if feelings of adequacy and status are not achieved in this sphere and in the dominant and society-wide system of evaluation. These status-motivated and patterned responses result in a special hierarchy of subcultures.

We discussed certain psychological responses to failure, particularly in Chap. 4. Such responses as aggression, apathy, regression, and anxiety become themes of behavior in the lower classes. If individuals within a particular segment of society feel such feelings sufficiently frequently and commonly, then certain adjustive norms emerge, fuse with old traditions, and become themselves traditional. Through such processes are the themes of subcultures born.

If the dominant culture were otherwise (for example, the passion- and soul-dominated culture of Spain) there would be a different coupling of excellence in various areas of life with a special distribution of rewards and power. The joining of a certain degree of ability in various areas with variation in rewards would lead to diverse but predictable psychological and behavior responses. Thus, a society which highly rewards intellectual ability but tends to ignore physical excellence would find among its highest status groups a subculture composed of highly intelligent and socially esteemed (and therefore relatively secure and free of aggression) individuals with rather mediocrè physical qualities. At the bottom would emerge subcultural norms to handle the special syndrome of problems felt by the unintelligent, the disesteemed, the deprived, and possibly those excelling in physical qualities (the stereotype of the mesomorphic lower-class worker and the aggressive gang member and his erotically attractive "dolls").

In a society which reversed the order of importance of these two attributes (intellect and physical excellence) the syndromes of norms of adjustment would be somewhat different (e.g., the tendency to equate meanness and evil with physical ugliness in the literature of traditional societies might be taken as evidence of such patterns).

It is out of such diversity of the dominant evaluative criteria and the ranking of other secondary criteria of a culture that the special orderings of subcultures are created and eventually characterize the strata and emotional fabric of different societies.

This is, to be sure, something of a reductionistic explanation, for cultures develop with a certain autonomy that is relatively independent of underlying personal motivations and social structure. It is not the only right explanation, but is one arrived at as a consequence of the author's greater facility with psychological processes than with the processes of cultural development. This greater facility is not altogether idiosyncratic but reflects the relative development of human knowledge in these two fields at this time in history.

We would like now to add a new analytical concept: the characteristic behavior in various classes is a consequence of the psychological response to status combined with the special types of *alternate routes* to "success" *available*. This is an extension of Merton's concept of anomie (1949, pp. 125-150). In Merton's analysis, deviant behavior is a consequence of the inaccessibility of skills required for accepted success. This results from the individual's position in society and it leads to various responses (e.g., innovation or rebellion) as modes of adjustment and of gaining new status. The alternate routes to variant and compensating responses are not randomly distributed but structured by society. Means as well as goals are shaped by the distribution of reward, power, and particular existing values.

This orientation is used skillfully by Cloward and Ohlin (1960) to explain various kinds of juvenile gangs and delinquency. Thus, members of certain ethnic groups (Italians, Anglo-Saxons, Poles, etc.) tend to gravitate to gangs which participate in profitable theft and extortion. This is partially because they have, through ethnic ties, contact with adult criminals—(for the distribution of their goods) and with legitimate political officials (for legal protection in their activities). Other ethnic groups without such contacts, largely Negroes, are blocked in their attempt to achieve success in this more acceptable criminal pattern. They turn, instead, to "senseless" assaults and robberies as a mode of releasing frustration. These seemingly "pointless" crimes also provide social status, for they give evidence that their performers are "tough."

Being "tough" is not an accessible goal for all, however, and it appears that "triple failures" retreat and turn to narcotics. From a certain perspective they are triple failures because (1) their low ethnic status (e.g., Negro) makes occupational success a difficult goal to seek, (2) the position of their ethnic group makes organized crime inaccessible, and (3) certain familial experiences (predominantly, close ties to the mother) make toughness and aggression a difficult channel for success. Thus we see that the aggressive crimes against persons constitute 31 per cent of the known crimes committed by nonnarcotics users, compared with only 3 per cent of the crimes committed by narcotics users (*Chicago Police Department Annual Report,* cited in Clausen, 1961, p. 203). For this group, status is achieved by being "cool," "hip," or "in the know," and by using narcotics skillfully.

ACHIEVED STATUS AND THE EMERGENCE
OF SUBCULTURAL THEMES

The various patterns discussed in the previous section seem to have validity. Let us see if we can refer to some general principle or concept which will order the particular pattern of subcultures that we observe in the classes of American society. As we have said, those individuals who fail to obtain status in our *achievement*-oriented society turn in exaggerated manner to certain *ascribed* roles as alternate routes to status and satisfaction within a narrower segment of society. This we have called *role compensation*. It also works in the other direction, for those individuals who fail to gain status and satisfaction in certain ascribed roles turn to achieved roles for status.

Possibly the bourgeoisies of seventeenth-century Europe are historical examples of role compensation on the group level. They were denied the socially ascribd status of the nobility and the ascribed status of "worthiness" as accepted human beings. The Calvinistic concept of predestination may be interpreted as a special example of a powerful, and here possibly threatening, ascribed status of cosmic proportions (eternal damnation of the soul). Their modification of the concept of predestination made "worthiness" and acceptance as a human being a state that had to be *achieved*. Even the child had the potential for evil. These conditions when combined with Protestant puritanism made erotic regression and its emphasis on the roles of intimate groups a morally unacceptable compensating response. Instead, they turned to thrifty and industrious effort in occupations—achieved roles.

The bourgeoisie in the course of two or three centuries has mellowed; there is now less stressful emphasis on thrift and hard work. This process of moderation and "conservative" retreat is often seen in various radical social and religious movements. Sociological analysis explains this reacceptance of conservative principles and norms as a functional necessity if unrealistic (to some degree) radical movements are going to deal with the realities of operating society.

The bourgeois Protestants' mellowing may also be explained within the concept of role compensation. Their successful positions in the power and prestige system of society reduce their needs to compensate for failures in other areas of social life. This may give a psychosociological perspective and explanation to the moderating retreat we see in various movements that become successful and powerful to some degree.

This mellowing is a fact bemoaned by the still striving and newly arrived (e.g., the more vociferous supporters of traditional Republican views). For them, the old virtues of thrift, hard work, competitiveness, and aggressiveness are disappearing from the work community and society.

What are some processes and further examples in contemporary society that provide some explanation of subcultures?

Most individuals have other memberships and roles of an ascriptive nature besides the important familial and occupational roles. These are the peer-group role, the sexual role, the neighborhood membership, the ethnic, religious, or national group membership. It appears that these roles and memberships are all more significant at the lower levels of an achievement-oriented society. One might respond that this is only to be expected, for these individuals have not yet accepted the norms of society, which is dominated by and evaluates the individual by certain norms of achievement. We will attempt, however, to describe the responses (and where possible refer to evidence) in these roles and behavior systems in a way that indicates that they are not only a "cultural lag" on the part of the lower class but are compensatory responses. They are "exaggerated" and actually more extreme than past norms.

The Sexual Role[1]

Two basic findings given earlier in several tables on sexual behavior have importance here in analyzing certain patterns of erotic acts as compensatory:

(1) The percentage of total outlets expressed socially (with another rather than in solitude) is greater at the lower social levels than in the higher status levels—especially among single adolescents (Table 9).

(2) Sexual outlet is somewhat greater at the lower levels of

---

1. Though a person's sexual role is intimately involved with his peer role (premaritally) and his family roles (postmaritally), it seems reasonable to discuss compensatory achievement in the sexual roles of maleness and femaleness as analytically independent of these other roles. Status can be achieved as an attractive, appealing, and if necessary accessible woman whatever her same sex peers think of her and whether or not she is a good wife-mother. The focus in this section is on the libidinal and pleasure aspects of sexual roles. We have already discussed the effect of status on identification and sexual behavior, and the discussion of that relationship has strong application in this section. The reader is referred to its analysis in the sections entitled, "An Interpretative Review of the Influence of Status on Particular Functions of the Family" (Chap. 6), and "Status, Identification, and Sexual Behavior" (Chap. 8).

education or social status (the association between education and class is so great that we will ignore the distinction at this point) in urban populations but *not generally in rural* populations.

Let us attend to an interpretation of the first general finding.

The number of outlets *social* in nature is much greater among the lower-status single adolescents for a number of reasons. The picture of greater impulsiveness generally and less sexual inhibition specifically does not really "explain" this phenomenon sociologically but only gives it a psychological terminology. As we have said earlier, these patterns emerge because the lower-class male is attempting to gain satisfaction and status in those areas of behavior in which success and its resulting esteem are still available for him. In a society which is predisposed to judge him, and frequently with considerable accuracy, incompetent and socially deviant by middle-class standards, he turns to certain traditional definitions of ascribed roles, such as maleness (and if female, femaleness) as a strategems for success. Obviously one does not gain much social or sexual status through masturbation.

Another perspective helps us gain possible understanding of these patterns. The lower-class individual does not grow up with, nor grasp with a kind of compulsive concern, the ideal of individualism and privacy. His personality is more permeable, in Cooley's terms. There is a kind of coming and going, of entering without knocking, of hugging and slugging, of slapping on the back, of sleeping in various beds at various places, of giving without keeping account which communicates to the observer relatively permeable ego boundaries. The actor (i.e., any individual in a social role), in his own neighborhood at least, is less self-aware. This makes the interpersonal sexual act a rather spontaneous and predictable behavior growing out of this affectional permeability or diffuse eroticism. By contrast, the upper-middle-class American adolescent is well on his way to developing his own private individuality—he is to some degree alone with himself. This may be changing, but we are now trying to interpret a report gathered about behavior of one and two generations ago.

Given this emotional aloofness, it is not surprising that the college-educated individual, as an adolescent, has a markedly greater percentage of sexual outlets of a solitary nature. The interpersonal sexual act requires an act of escape from American middle-class individualism.

During single adolescence the interpersonal sexual act also requires, in a way which the solitary act does not, an escape from the emotional hold of, and obligations to, one's natal family, particularly the parents. Traditionally, and relative to the lower levels of society, this was not easy for the upper-middle-class individual. This is true for a number of hypothesized reasons. Given his secure and esteemed position in society, the upper-middle-class or upper-class parent can direct love and patience to his child without the economy of maintaining his own personality suffering greatly. This results in a much closer intimacy, perhaps a kind of emotional incest which the lower class parent and child do not display.

This intimacy also results in a demanding identification with the parent which "tells" the child that the parental-spouse role is intensely important and that sexual expression does not take place outside this role. That is, the erotic role (male and female sexuality) per se is fused with the familial role and exists with greatly reduced salience as an avenue of social action.

The second finding given above states that there are a greater number of sexual outlets in the lower levels of society. If mere "cultural lag" of the urban lower class explained the greater focus on the sexual role of the lower strata, then we might predict that males of a culturally backward rural background would engage in even more heterosexual activity than would their urban and achievement-acculturated brothers at the same educational level. Kinsey (1948) reports the opposite to be true. The urban lower-status male engages in more sexual activity, and as we would expect, this rural-urban difference nearly disappears at the upper educational level. This difference is most noticeable in heterosexual behavior that is independent of the familial role, that is, nonmarital intercourse.

Part of this difference might be explained by a theory that sex is more available in urban than in rural situations. This does not explain why the different norms of availability developed, nor does it explain why a similarly higher rate isn't found among the urban dwellers at the higher educational levels. The perspective taken here leads to a certain line of thought. Generally, the lower levels of the urban population are more dissatisfied and alienated from society (e.g., Beer's data, Table 8). This is the case because daily, in work and other activity, they must interact with those clearly judged by society their superiors. To a greater degree the urban community, with its extremes of high and low, is their reference group. By contrast, the rural dweller is moderately isolated from depriving evaluations and from the rich and powerful's clear superiority. As a consequence, he feels less deprived, enjoys relatively higher status within his reference group. Given this perspective, we would suggest that he would be less prone to high activity in the dating-fun-erotic area as an avenue of "achievement." He would also be less prone to other "extreme" responses of an ascriptive or socially "regressive" nature which become parts of the subcultures and modes of adjustment of the various classes in the diverse urban situation.

For the male, in most and perhaps all societies, masculinity (again on the level of its libidinal or erotic definition) has a controlling and possibly aggressive element (Fromm, 1959). Again it appears that the lower-level male in the industrial culture exaggerates this component in his sexual role as well as in his family role. We have discussed the aggressive element in the family, and if this aggression is also involved in the sexual behavior system, we would predict a distortion of or fusion of eros with hostility. Sexually tinged assaults by males against females and actual rape would be greater in the *lower* occupational levels among the urban dwellers than in *comparable* levels of rural areas and the upper-status urbanites. Unfortunately data is not available which would provide a specific test of this idea. Such data would consist of crime rates at different occupational levels holding marital status and place of residence (rural or urban) constant. Our view would lead us to predict lower rates of rape, sexually motivated homicide, and especially sadism in the less industrialized and success-oriented societies.

It also appears that our general perspective regarding status and ascribed roles helps explain the greater hostility felt by members of the lower class toward the practicing homosexual who plays the receptive feminine role. Hostility is expressed toward the latter because he is failing in his "ascribed" sexual role, a role which is terribly important at this level. The relatively more tolerant attitudes of upper-level males and females may reflect less concern over deviation in a role considered somewhat less critical in evaluating people. For them occupational nonproductivity is the more condemnable.

The greater tolerance felt by the upper-status male is also a consequence of better father identification and probably less erotic and homoerotic interest. For the lower-class male, the homosexual is a more threatening seducer into homosexual behavior. In such acts, not only is his status damaged as a male capable of obtaining women, but he may also find himself acting out certain "feminine" submitting needs. At this point his status as a controlling and aggressive male is destroyed. This loss motivates occasional assaultive responses.

In addition to this aggression manifested in sexual behavior, it appears that the lower-level urban male generally exhibits greater hostility than the low-status rural male. Spinley (1953), after two years as a participant observer in a London slum, characterized the low-status urban male youth in this way:

He has marked aggression which is permitted violent expression, and his attitude towards authority is one of hostility and rebellion. (p. 130.)

Though there is certainly aggression in rural areas, this does not seem a typical summary impression one would give for rural youth. As is the case for woman's kinship role, rural conditions and isolation may provide some protection from the differential evaluation in an achievement-oriented society and its consequence for the psyche.

The Male and Female
in the Urban Family

Our general position has been that low status in American society, which focuses on the achieved occupational role, leads to numerous compensating responses in ascriptive roles. This is a focus on what you *are* rather than on what you do, though there are important achieving elements in the most ascribed role. If it is true that there is a heavy emphasis in the lower classes on ascription, one would also expect a heavy emphasis there on the familial role, which is an ascribed role *par excellence*. This seems to be true for the mother, and we see the prominent figure of "mom" in the lower levels of society. The compensating focus on the father role by the working class man in modern society seems less noteworthy.

It is perhaps true that there is greater emphasis on family and kin at the lower levels than at the upper-middle-class levels, though even in family roles ascriptive blood ties fare better than the relatively more achieved marital ties.

We will outline several reasons for the variation in the roles of males and females in the family at the various status levels in urban society. One reason rests simply on biology and its socially structured ramifications. Women play a more important or immediate and enduring role in the bearing, caring for, and socializing of the child. This has certain consequences. In terms of *compelling* emotional needs she seems to be sought by the husband more than she seeks. Her membership in the category of female gives her an ascribed access to certain libidinal or emotional resources. This is because she is seen, by the process of generalization, as a symbolic member of the group which answered those demanding needs during the impressionable period of infancy and childhood. Also, certain methods of socializing may make her a more emotional figure and, relative to the male, one with perhaps more positive affect. Mothers seem to be warmer toward daughters (i.e., the next generation's mothers) than toward sons (Sears et al., 1957, p. 514), and daughters are less severely disciplined (Table 60).

Table 60
Type of Punishment Received by Fourteen-to-Sixteen-Year-Old Males and Females, White and Negro

	Per Cent Physical[a]	Per Cent Other	Per Cent Never Punished	Per Cent Unknown	Number
White					
Boys	8.9	85.8	3.5	1.4	649
Girls	6.2	90.0	3.2	0.5	769
Negro					
Boys	50.0	50.0	0.0	0.0	40
Girls	22.0	73.2	4.9	4.9	41

a. Significance of difference in percentage of physical punishment given boys and girls: white, > .10; Negro, > .01.

Source: E. Douvan and S. Withey, *A Study of Adolescent Boys* (Ann Arbor: Institute for Social Research, 1955); E. Douvan, C. Kaye, and S. Withey, *A Study of Adolescent Girls* (Ann Arbor: Institute for Social Research, 1956). Cited in Gold (1958).

These conditions give the mother a pivotal position in the emotional structure of the family. In undifferentiated society this position of power is counterbalanced, to an important extent, by the position of control and authority exercised by the husband in other family activities, especially economic and politico-military activities (Fortes, 1949). This is true because these "nonemotional" or instrumental activities are conducted more within the family and kinship system. In the differentiated society these activities, which seem more in accord with masculine motivations, are no longer within the family but segregated from it. And it is largely in these traditionally masculine activities, outside the family, that the lower-status husband-father is now failing. His functions have been moved out of the family and his adequacy in these areas is less, giving him little transferable power and status in the family situation. His functions have been drawn out of the family, he has little society-wide status to "bargain" with, and he may be forced to maintain his traditional husband-father position of power as best he can by the only resource he has available: threats and physical force.

The more successful male, by contrast, is able to present needed resources (prestige, economic security) as well as more desirable sentiments to his family, and in turn he receives status and emotional support from the family members. This tends to draw him into greater involvement in the family than is the case for the lower-level husband-father.

Compensatory Response and the
Peer Group Role (the "Good Guy")

We have discussed the peer role earlier, but let us deal with it in further detail. It seems that the peer group or gang has as its most devoted members lower-class urban males in their teens.[2] This is true for a number of reasons. Due to the parents' status and their economy of positive affect, they have less to offer the child. Hostility, neglect, and powerlessness in the family lead the child to escape the status he experiences there and to seek situations in which his chances for interpersonal approval are improved. This is particularly true for sons with less adequate fathers and with problems in identification, and because sons (especially in lower-status groups) seem to receive more overt hostility from their parents. Data presented by Sears et al. (1957, p. 401) and Table 60 can be interpreted in this manner. They show that the boys, particularly among Negroes, are socialized by somewhat more severe techniques. Added to these are problems of adequacy in school activity. The lower-class son responds to these conditions by compensating in the peer group and by gaining approval as an all-around "good guy" in this group. This phrase seems to connote an emotional warmth toward in-group peers with an overtone of assertive masculinity and some hostility toward individuals outside the group.

The Peer Group and Its
Competition with the Family

The importance of this group and the strata of motivations developed by it does not disappear at the end of adolescence but continues, with varying degrees of strength, into adulthood, and it structures the leisure and family roles typical of different classes in an industrial society.

The upper-middle-class wife is typically alone or ignored because of the husband's emotional and time commitments to his work or community activities. The lower-class and even lower-middle-class

---

2. It is also very strong in the latency period. It does not *seem* to have such a striking association with class level, however, at this age. For this assumed reason we will ignore the latency-period peer group.

wife does not seem to suffer from the husband's "being married to his job." Instead, she is more likely to find herself alone because the husband is "out with the boys." As we have seen, this is sometimes a disguise for the more frequent extramarital sexual activity of husbands at this level. In the lower-class neighborhood the tavern, poolroom, or nearby restaurant may provide the locus for the continuation of behavior and satisfaction of certain needs developed in the latency period and teens. In levels somewhat higher the veterans club or fraternal organization may provide a functional equivalent. Though there is, of course, much social interaction with one's own sex in levels above these (the private club), it seems to take place in American society more frequently in occupational groups or in social situations where both sexes are present. And even the private male club is more likely to occur in the *upper upper* class, which we have said again partakes of some of the ascriptive emphasis of the lower classes.

This continuation of peer-group interaction seems to be a "prolonged" interest in the activities of and approval gained in the "good guy" role. The intense satisfaction it offers in the teen-age period as a source of escape and of emotional security in the rather impersonal environment of the typical lower-level urban community, gives it a much greater meaning than is true for the upper-level male. Its function as a socializing group for masculine behavior perhaps continues to create in the married male some feeling of separation of marital and sexual roles.

In this area the upper-level male's various masculine roles are more integrated. He has had a rather powerful, conforming, and adequate father. This has allowed an identification and integration of the roles of maleness, fatherness, and husbandness. This seems to be a particularly important factor in explaining the differences in sexual behavior at different levels in society.

If the married male in the lower levels continues to feel this separation of sexual roles and family roles, then he may need, on frequent occasions, to surround himself with those early cues such as the gang which gave him a feeling of status and virility in his youth.

The "good guy" role with its theme of hostility to individuals outside the peer group and warm affect toward members of the ingroup is combined with problems of identification with the husband-father in his natal family. This would seem to leave a pattern of needs; there would continue to be feelings of uncertainty about one's adequacy in the marital role, though love, good marital adjustment,

children, and occupational adequacy would alleviate much of this
concern. There might still remain stronger promiscuous heterosexual
and homosexual interests.

Table 61 shows the tendency for the lower-status male to con-

Table 61
Sources of Extramarital Orgasm: Married Males
Per Cent of Total Outlet

Sources	Education Level (Years)	16-20	21-25	26-30	31-35	36-40	41-45	46-50
	13+	2.91	2.09	2.92	5.92	10.38	6.39	14.1
Heterosexual	9-12	10.91	10.84	9.10	5.61	3.45	3.85	3.3
	0-8	11.52	12.42	7.54	6.97	8.17	6.30	6.1
	13+	.16	.53	.96	.75	.89	1.64	3.0
Homosexual	9-12	2.11	1.05	.96	1.38	.73	—	—
	0-8	3.08	1.33	.46	.14	.30	.08	.00

Source: Alfred Kinsey, Wardell Pomeroy, and Clyde Martin, Sexual Behavior in the Human
Male (Philadelphia: W. B. Saunders Company, 1948), p. 382.

tinue to act and gain rewards in the heterosexual behavior system
—a system independent of and competing with love and sexual
activity in his husband role. The higher rates of homosexual behavior shown in the table among the married lower-class males
during their earlier years is interpreted to be an expression of ca-
thetic attachments to peer-group males which continue to operate
and again compete with their husband roles. This table also shows
a reversing trend for these patterns in the older age groups. We
have given our interpretation of this in Chap. 8. Briefly, we said
that it was a process of resocialization with time.

Both heteroerotic and homoerotic behavior find support and
are precipitated by the peer group situation, where hostility is directed to others (promiscuous and exploitative heterosexual behavior) and in-group loyalty to the same-sex peer group is required.

In an earlier period, latency, the "others" or out-group are often
girls of the same age. Teasing and hostile rejection of their company seem to be the typical behavior. This attitude does not sud-
denly change with puberty and the development of sexual interest.
Even in the teen-age period, girls continue to be something of an
out-group. It seems that considerable early heterosexual activity
(particularly in the lower-status groups) is motivated by exploitative
sexual needs and the needs to achieve status within the peer group.
Girls who are known to be available receive considerable attention

but are also the focus of considerable ridicule when the peer group talks together. The war of the sexes has greater validity here.

That sex is seen to a somewhat greater degree as aggressive in the lower classes may be found in the attitudes toward premarital intercourse in the different levels as reported by Kinsey. For the upper-level male, premarital intercourse is more likely to occur with someone he likes or with whom he is having an affair. A more common pattern for the lower-status individual is sexual activity with many different girls. He probably has no lasting interest in many of them. In contrast to the higher-status male, this male feels that "if I like her I wouldn't touch her until we got married."

There is no doubt that much love and satisfaction are obtained at the lower levels in the family group. The problem, and this is particularly true for the husband-father, seems to be that the low position in society results in an accumulation of negative affect and fewer rewards. This results in the father's loss of power in the family with the behavioral consequences outlined.

The gathering of adult married men, in addition to being conventional, conforming behavior in the lower levels, is one which reestablishes a situation that (1) provided, and still does provide, an assertion of independence from the relatively more dominant female figure in the family (in youth this was the mother and in adulthood it is the wife); (2) provided, and still does provide, certain affective and quasi-erotic satisfactions (often of a mock hostile nature, such as "razzing").

Compensation in the Communal Role ("the Patriot")

Patriotism here should be understood in a general sense. It refers to loyalty to any ascribed group whose membership is defined by common habitation or similar ethnic heritage (which historically would indicate common habitation and some tenuous biological ties). Our prediction is that those individuals and groups who have difficulty gaining status in their achieved roles will exhibit a high commitment to certain ascriptive qualities and norms of the in-group. Often it appears to the outside observer that the individual's commitment is less often expressed in positive commitment to the group's ideals and more often expressed through hostility to out-groups. This is not surprising if we consider the over-all feelings of deprivation and inadequacy in the general society.[3] The analysis

3. These sentiments of hostility, the attack upon "Communists" and real Com-

of the membership of patriotic and veterans' organizations, Mc-
Carthyism, and the Nazi movement show the members to be predominantly of the lower levels of the middle class and probably to
some extent of the lower class, as well as other disesteemed and
frustrated elements in the society (Lipset, 1960, pp. 97-176).

Very helpful and concrete data on this line of thinking is provided by Bettelheim and Janowitz in their study of anti-Semitism,
racial intolerance, and social mobility among World War II veterans
(Table 62).

Table 62
Anti-Semitism and Social Mobility

	Downward Mobility Percentage	No Mobility Percentage	Upward Mobility Percentage
Tolerant	11	37	50
Stereotyped	17	38	18
Outspoken and intense	72	25	32
Total	100	100	100

Source: B. Bettelheim and M. Janowitz, Dynamics of Prejudice: A Psychological and Sociological
Study of Veterans (New York: Harper & Row, Publishers, 1950), p. 59.

These data show that those individuals who were moving up
the occupational ladder expressed less hostility toward ethnic out-
groups than did those who were stable or moving down. The latter
seemed particularly frustrated and prone to displace aggression to
an out-group. Hating the out-groups did not endanger their positions in their own groups, and hating the out-groups did make them
more loyal and better group members.

Another observation seems to fall into place regarding the personality characteristics of anti-Semites, Nazis, and hostile paranoid
individuals as analyzed by Freud. They are not only more likely to
occur in the lower levels of society, but they are thought to be trou-
bled with an undue amount of homosexual interest, usually of an
anxiously semirepressed nature. This may mean that motivations
for aggression are particularly strong, for the individual is deprived
not only in (1) his achieved occupational role but also in (2) his
adequacy as a male. This would be particularly severe and frustrating for the individual of lower status who is not a committed
or practicing homosexual and places great emphasis on the importance of the ascribed sex role. This frustration is translated into

---

munists, and their motivations as revealed in the McCarthy movement, are analyzed
from a somewhat different perspective by Talcott Parsons in *Social Structure
and Process in Modern Societies* (New York: The Free Press of Glencoe, 1960),
pp. 226-247.

hostility toward the Jew (as a symbol of secular success) or into hostile paranoid concern, often of a homosexual nature.

It seems that the situation would be somewhat different for the practicing homosexual. He is no longer attempting to achieve status in the male role of the heterosexual behavior system. Instead, he has responded by moving into a deviant behavior system. Here alternate satisfactions and status are obtained, and perhaps less stressful frustration is felt.

Extreme liberalism and moderation as well as extreme reaction (ethnically intolerant Fascists) should be explained. Perhaps our axis of achievement-ascription provides a general explaining principle. Those individuals with lower ascribed status (e.g., physical unattractiveness, peer-group problems, sexual-role difficulties, alienation from the dominant culture, membership in an unaccepted ethnic group, etc.) but with high achieved status (e.g., highly intellectual, high occupation, success in school or community activities, etc.) will tend to be very liberal. That is, they will be against those things which would keep society "as it was" (traditional attitudes toward women working, toward Negroes and Jews, toward the importance of religion and religious attitudes, toward clubs and fraternities, toward traditional morality, etc.). These traditional values all minimize the areas in which they excel. Instead, they will wish to propose and legitimize those attitudes that are congenial to their particular set of capacities and incapacities.

The highly reactionary group in society, by contrast, is perhaps disproportionately composed of those individuals who have low or declining achieved status but high ascribed status which they have inherited from their biological and social past. That is, they are probably disproportionately individuals with "good" ethnic background and good physical appearance, peer-group adjustment, and conventional and stable family and sex role adjustment.

If individuals or groups happen to be blocked in all but a few or one of their statuses, then they may foster the importance of that one area with a fanatic zeal. It is probably of such status patterns and the anxious pursuit of alternate routes of status that "nuts" are born. These individuals become zealots in religion, in physical culture, in the family, in work, in chess, sexuality, or entertaining, for it is the only escape from complete frustration and disesteem.

A Note of Caution

A caution should be introduced regarding our interpretive approach. It is a caution which, regretfully, has some application to our theoretical outline in general. We cannot be certain that achievement frustration does lead to a compensatory focus on ascriptive status and to an expression of hostility. For example, it may be that the typical personality pattern of authoritarianism which is often ethnocentric, concerned about sex, highly concrete in thought is also insufficiently flexible to move in the fluid occupational sphere and is rigid and hostile in dealings with people. Such authoritarian persons are, therefore, not likely to exhibit upward occupational mobility. Generalizing this caution, we might say that the anxious and rigid hostility hold the individual in his lower status. This hostility is then directed toward other family members, society in general, and particular out-groups. The individuals relatively free of hostility in most situations find occupational mobility an easy matter. Their hostility-free personalities then manifest themselves in various roles and situations.

The only reasonable stand is a recognition that empirically both personality and the structure of rewards and power (the status system) can explain much of the phenomena discussed. How much each contributes could only be determined by more detailed information and possibly controlled experiments. It seems appropriate to continue an analysis and our theoretical development of the processes from the perspective of social structure in the absence of such definitive data.

Religious Behavior and Compensation

For most people, religion is not a matter of choice. One is usually born into his religion—an ascriptive collectivity which can provide great satisfactions and enhanced status. Neither atheism nor simple failure to join a religious group is quite respectable. But modal and model behavior seem to vary considerably from level to level in society. In the upper classes of society, membership is more frequent and perhaps even attendance is more common (Mercer, 1958, pp. 302-303). The accepted pattern in this class is, however, to take "religion in stride" and not to become fanatical about it. In the lower and lower-middle classes, there seems to be a somewhat different pattern. Certain individuals seem either to reject or accept religion with a certain fanaticism. For example, one must "take a stand for Jesus" or be counted against him.

These extreme attitudes are reflected in the degree of church attendance, perhaps a rather mild and indirect index of these feelings. The percentage of moderate attendants (from approximately once a month to three times a month) decreases as we move down the class scale, and the number who either completely reject the church (never attend) or who attend every Sabbath increases (Mercer, 1958, p. 302).

This fanaticism, which is interpreted here as compensatory, seems most apparent among women and peer-isolated males. This may be true because religion, especially in its Protestant lower-class and more extreme forms, combines great emotionality with strict demands for high morality, especially in the areas of sex, drink, fun, slothfulness, gambling, and dancing.

This combination is not likely to appeal to the peer-oriented male in the working class. In fact, religion here seems to focus its energies against just those things that are the particular interest of the male group. Religion at this level is the instrument of the dominant culture which "conspires" with the more "adequate" women of the lower-class community to bring their socially regressive males into line.

Religion has quite a different role in the upper levels of society. To an important degree it functions to legitimize the morality and privileged position held by both men and women of this strata.

It is at the lower level of society that new religious movements of a rather fanatic and "unrealistic" bent get developed. Probably alienation from and failure in the dominant culture (morality) and in the dominant church which supports it lead to deviant religious positions. The movements are frequently very expressive and otherworldly. The wealth, power, and success of this world are deemphasized (Pope, 1942). The legitimacy of the present ethos is questioned, and another is proposed in which their status would or will greatly improve.

The behavior characteristic of members of these movements may be in opposition to the active dominant culture. In these new sects the emphasis is often on passive belief and complete faith in a new world. Or there may be a pattern which partakes of our activistic dominant culture. Here one thinks of the actively evangelistic Protestant denominations.

Breadth of Loyalty at Different Status Levels

It appears that different behavior systems or roles recruit their most loyal supporters at different class levels. Individuals at the lower levels of society are more particularistic, more emotional in their orientation. At the lowest levels the focus of loyalty seems to be the family, the peer group, and the immediate neighborhood.

As one moves up the class levels, loyalties become increasingly universalistic. In the upper-lower or lower-middle class there emerges a somewhat more universalistic norm—national patriotism in a rather parochial form. This leads to the high rates of voluntary enlistment in the military in this strata of society, for enlistment meets a number of needs. It is motivated by nationalistic feeling in which a major component seems to be hostility directed toward some out-group (another society). At this level the male feels strongly the disesteem of society brought on by failure in the achieved occupational role. It is also at this level that male identification is something of a problem.

The military role offers a situation in which aggression generated by status deprivation may be expressed. It is a situation in which the occupational role may be improved somewhat. The military also provides a situation which, as it is said, will "make a man of you" and in this way solve problems of sex role identification. It is also something of a continuation of the same-sex peer group, and as such provides a condition in which male roles are internalized and problems of latent erotic or quasi-erotic interests may be acted out and resolved.

In some ways the military service plays a similar function to the traumatic and isolating puberty rites and the men's houses in simple societies. This is discussed in "The Function of Male Initiation Ceremonies at Puberty" by Whiting, F. Kluckhohn, and Anthony (1958, pp. 369-370).

The strength of this patriotic role at the lower levels may have been an important factor in impeding Marx's plans for revolution through international identification and solidarity of the proletariat. Such international solidarity as Marx hoped for exists much more at the other end of the scale—among the scientists, the liberal professions, the artists, and the social elite.

In the upper middle class such loyalties of a more universalistic and inclusive nature emerge. The English Speaking Union, World Federalism, the United Nations, and belief in democratic principles for all evoke loyalties at this status.

Though other factors are undoubtedly operating, it appears that those individuals whose behavior and skills do not allow rewards in society as a whole withdraw from these more inclusive behavior systems and reject their norms and standards. They then focus on situations of a more limited scope in which their relative status is improved. These particularistic and ascriptive commitments are typical of the loyalties of the lower strata.

We have chosen to talk more about the lower levels in the interests of ease in communication. Much of our picture for the *upper middle* class is the opposite. There is less concern about maleness or femaleness, a diminution of the salience of "sexuality," the gang, "our block," patriotism (be it to one's ethnic group, city, region, or country), and religious commitment. These areas of life are not ignored but are placed in their "proper" perspective in relationship to the serious goal of life, occupational achievement. It appears to this observer that these other areas are attended to, not as ends in themselves, but as necessary conditions for the development of a productive society.

In some measure, the upper or upper-upper class partakes of the values of the lower class again. This is perhaps true for two reasons. First, its position (especially in the older areas of America and in industrial Europe) was gained during *an era* when ascriptive qualities were more prominent in evaluating persons and groups. Family, inherited position, religious membership, and "eros" all seem to have been somewhat more prominent aspects of life at that time.

Thus McArthur's research (1955) on the characteristics of upper-class and middle-class undergraduates at Harvard University reveals that the upper-class men developed stories in Thematic Apperception Tests (projective tests of motivational responses to unstructured pictures) which indicated that they have closer and warmer ties to their families, are less concerned about occupation as a route of achievement and status, and have ties to their fathers closer than those of middle-class men. Further research by Funkenstein (1957) indicates that students from "elite" origins discuss more openly and have more frequent premarital sexual intercourse than do individuals from middle-class origins who seem on their way to prestigious positions in society.

Second, the position of the upper class is already achieved, and thus begins to take on some of the quality of ascription. An emphasis on ascription pays, for it assures one a respected place in society and it does not introduce the risk of continuing in the field of competitive achievement.

Despite these similarities to the ascriptive focus of the lower class, it is different because it is a turning to ascription from a position of security, esteem, and affluence. This position allows a mode of "graceful living" and kindness (*noblesse oblige*), for the people of this class have both the economic and emotional resources for such behavior.

A Theoretical Digression

In a sense our use of role compensation may be misleading. Let us state it in more general and behavioral terms so that it might be a general explanation of behavior. Individuals who are unable to achieve status in one behavior system will tend to withdraw and deevaluate its standards and values and move into alternative behavior systems (with different standards and power structure) in which higher status is gained. The deevaluation of the previous standards is accompanied by a rather intolerant rejection of the validity of these standards and an anxiously emotional (sacred) commitment to the new standards. This solves two problems. It serves to convince the individual that his inability to gain status in the previous group was of no importance because its standards are not valid. It is also an attempt (and sometimes successful) to persuade society generally and himself that the behavior system in which he is now involved and its standards *are* very important. It is his reference group.

There is an informal and direct person to person value "lobbying" as well as political lobbying to have certain things accepted as good and true in the public domain of values. If the individual or group is successful in bringing about some agreement from a part or all of society on this point it serves to increase his standing in some crucial part or in all of society.

The hostilely treated child's response to adult culture and authority may be partially explained by this process. He wants nothing to do with it, for it has given him few rewards and he must reject its standards if he is to consider his behavior and status valid. The intellectual's response to the standards of success in the business world or the businessman's response to the standards of behavior in the academic community could be placed in this framework.

Nor does it seem that the "tolerant" individual (as he is comfortably defined by "liberals" in a way that abides by their own sentiments) escapes this analysis. He rejects with considerable hostility the standards of the "intolerant" while expressing a good deal of hostility toward other groups to whom it seems safe to do so and toward whom it may be unfashionable in contemporary "intellectual" society to express tolerance.

Though recognizing an over-all validity of the standards of other behavior systems, the person has vested interests in supporting the validity of the standards he accepts and the validity of his own status. This general process is perhaps something of what is meant by ego involvement.

This perspective also helps us understand why the individual who seems to land at the bottom of the heap by almost any standard becomes alienated from most standards, finds no status anywhere, and "don't believe in nothin'." Here resides the resentful, revengeful, and often isolated individual capable of numerous deviant forms of behavior in a desperate attempt to gain reward and respect somewhere or to counteraggress against a depriving society.

EMERGING AND RECRUITED SUBCULTURES

A statement about origins of subcultures should recognize that they do not exactly create themselves but are consequences of interacting influences within their domain. The social system (especially its economic system and technology), the personalities of its members, and the various aspects of the dominant culture itself produce new themes (or, more frequently, variations on the basic theme) as they interact.

It might be hypothesized that certain subcultural value systems emerge, especially in a highly differentiated society, in order to fill certain roles which are required by the economy, by demands for exotic aesthetic satisfactions, or by the general society (F. Kluckhohn, 1950).

If such variant value orientations don't emerge they may then be recruited from outside the society. From this perspective it would not be an accident of history that Jewish groups dealing in finances were drawn to medieval Europe and were able to maintain themselves. They were able to survive in this otherworldly Christian ethos (which condemned the this-worldly financial activities) because certain realities in the economic sphere required incumbents to satisfy them. Nor is it an accident, from this view, that Puerto Ricans are, despite hostility felt toward them, "accepted" into the United States. It is possible that certain aspects of American society (universal education, urbanization, general unionization) produce insufficient numbers of individuals motivated to work at unskilled and nonprestigeful jobs.

Though not all the members of a particular subcultural group will behave in the modal pattern, a statement and analysis of the values that structure the group's behavior will assist in explaining its members' behavior. The analysis cannot end there. It must continue and answer two questions: How do these special normative systems fit into the norms and the dominant values of the general society? And how do these special normative systems get developed or accepted into the society? What is it about the society and the subgroups' special positions in the society that sustain these subcultural specializations?

Thus, if studies find that certain ethnic groups in America behave differently in hospitals, have different attitudes toward their kin, socialize their children differently, suffer from different kinds of mental disorders, we should understand not only what values they have but what human relationships and social position they now have which produce the observed variations. For example, that a group's class position is as important as are the inherited values and norms of its special culture is shown by the proclivity to crime among diverse cultural and ethnic groups, such as the Germans, Scandinavians, Irish, Jews, Italians, and Negroes, as they entered urban areas of the United States through the lower social levels at different times in history (Shaw and McKay, 1942). Similarly, when holding class constant, the observed differences between Catholics and Protestants in family behavior or rates of suicide cannot be explained entirely by the use of values. Even within a social class as usually measured, there are differences between Catholics and Protestants in prestige and location in society.

An analysis of a group's special values and history, the way in which these make possible or eliminate various routes to status, and the present status of the group also help explain the development of special combinations of behavior—a subculture.

Sociology and Ideology

Before we begin our analysis of several ethnic groups in America, let us take an excursion into the sociology of knowledge in the hope that it will prepare us for discussion of this emotionally charged subject. Our excursion has certain dangers, for it is an analysis of the professional in-group, of the subculture of the liberal social scientist; here immediacy creates emotional involvement and makes it difficult for both the analyst and the reader to perceive objectively what is occurring and what is being said.

Our statements about the conventions of sociological thought in the area of minority groups and our discussions of the ideologies of various ethnic groups will not be particularly complimentary. Sometimes a writer appears to pay compliments to certain ethnic groups to reassure the reader that the writer is not uninformed and illiberal. It is hoped that the approach to be taken here is not motivated by malice, but I do not feel inclined to engage in professional in-group flattery through imitation, nor to engage in patronizing adulation of various ethnic groups from the position of a middle-class academic.

Such good-intentioned analyses are often supported by another kind of "it isn't really there" attitude which anxiously attempts to minimize or mask the interesting variety of ethnic and class subcultures that do exist. The behavioral scientist often tries as much as possible to present the upper-middle-class Jew or the lower-class Negro as "just like everyone"—a stereotype of universal proportions—while using in his personal and professional lives a number of relaxing prejudices of his own (e.g., "the bigoted Irish Catholic biddy," the country bumpkin, the terrible Southerners, Babbitts, etc.).

It is often the assumption of sociologists and psychologists that the likes and dislikes of individuals in the out-group (nonscientists or members of ethnic groups of which they are not members) are based on error and are thus dangerous prejudgments. The Irish Catholic, however, in terms of his values and approach to life may have quite accurate reasons for not liking Jews and, of course, vice versa. The Protestant may also have a realistic basis for preferring German Catholics and fearing Italian Catholics, etc. The scientific community in its attempts to weaken certain myths (exaggerated stereotypes) may introduce others ("we are really all working toward the same goals").

The patronizing adulation and the efforts to minimize the variety of certain ethnic groups in professional statements while directing hostility toward others may result from an egocentric assumption of the superiority of certain liberal and rational values. To admit differences, in such a moral climate, is to automatically evaluate negatively those cultures which deviate from liberal rationalism and to appear intolerant.

The intolerance of such patronizing and, I believe, incorrect views originates in an unwillingness to accept the living validity of other moral orders. Violent love and intense hate, ethnocentrism, human warmth and involvement (rather than "freedom" and rationality) cannot be accepted by the holders of these views as valid alternatives. To do so would create certain threats to their own philosophies of life.

This rationalistic and terribly serious approach to life results in the misinterpretation of several aspects of ethnic and subcultural interactions. A kind of hovering anxiety sees every ethnic joke as an example of great hostility. Such jokes and forms of hostility are, however, often expressions of repressed admiration and approaches to closer emotional ties.[4]

Real intolerance, hostility, and preferences of a particular kind have a legitimate place in everyday existence. Likes and dislikes create the emotional fabric of human action, and without them social order, social control, achievements, and human gratification would not be possible. Moral preferences which happen to be in accord with the special preferences of the scientific community, however, should not then be presented in the guise of scientific objectivity and fact.

The "it isn't really there" attitude about subcultural differences is also motivated by a kind of scornful indifference toward the peculiar or disesteemed. Such surface indifference may be born of the scientist's marginal origins and resulting anxieties about his own status and commitment to the dominant values of a rational society. There is a preference for orientations to and choices of subjects of study which will align him with the more or less dominant segments (in a much broader sense than, say, the business interests) of society and which will not reveal variant subcultures as seeming to appeal to him. Forms of behavior which are alien to the dominant elements of society are treated as "social deviations" or "social problems" in a rather kindly missionary manner. This implicit moral deevaluation makes it difficult to attribute them to an ethnic group's culture.

There may also be a fear that an "undue" and unapologetic interest in behavior characteristic of the lower class (promiscuity, violence, the gang) and other disesteemed elements (homosexuals, vegetarians, etc.) will indicate an undue and motivated interest in these rather childlike, lustful, or "perverse" aspects of life. Promiscuity, homosexuality, and violence are only "social problems" from the perspective of a rationally coordinated society and its ally, the social scientist. They are neither new nor (from the naturalist's perspective) problems. They all have an ancient history and they are as much a part of the social body as is the eye a part of the human body. These forms of behavior, their support and punishment, are both functional and dysfunctional in various areas of life.

The orientation (and it is something of a straw man or ideal type, for no one behaves fully in this way, though we all probably manifest its qualities at times) regards the cultural patterns of the

4. Dornbusch's analysis (1955) of the interaction of Coast Guard Cadets may be viewed this way. The interclass hostility and exploitation may actually be a means of expressing and gaining a kind of emotional intimacy and friendship.

libidinal, dramatic, and playful lower class as either pathetic and unfortunate or a code which, though it must be understood, is still some way discomforting and depraved. The unctuous eros of Jayne Mansfield or a rock n' roll star or the brutal pageantry of a football game are regarded with anxious contempt, while bizarre customs of faraway, and thus nonthreatening, cultures or the simple-minded folk songs of faraway times are accepted with xenophilic and intellectual interest. Their distance not only lends enchantment but practically eliminates their power to seduce the uncertainly committed.

In this writer's opinion a truly sympathetic and frank analysis of subcultural variations reveals not only their rationale but also the good and appealing modes of life quite outside the experience of the average striving intellectual. In this form, the analysis does threaten the intellectual's commitment to his *modus vivendi* if it is of a specialized nature. It should not, if his attempt is to understand in the broadest sense the complex aspects of the human situation.

Our attempt will be to analyze with an intelligent sympathy, above all with frankness, and even with a bit of humor. For humor relaxes righteous indignation cloaked in scientific objectivity. It brings into question the view that we are the good, tolerant in-group analyzing and gaining necessary moral power over the bad intolerant out-group. We have all sinned—in manners typical of our subcultural ways.

We will look at four ethnic groups in America: the Jews, the Irish, the Italians, and the Negroes. We will spare the poor Germans, who received their share of deflating analysis in the 1940s. We will also neglect the mysterious Slavs (they seem far too amorphous and diluted in the American scene) and numerous ethnic groups of less importance numerically. And we have already drawn our caricature of Northern and especially urban white Anglo-Saxon Protestants (Wasps, as they are called) in our discussion of the secularized Protestant ethic. This set of norms is their stereotype (they cannot relax, they worry, they have no soul, no sense of beauty, they are materialistic, etc.) and it has some validity for them.

Let us introduce two cautions. (1) The things to be said about the various ethnic groups have validity for only some of the members; they do not apply to all the members. The things said concerning some traits (e.g., membership in the Syndicate by Italo-Americans) may be true for only a small minority. The size of the minority is sufficiently large, however, that the rate exceeds that of other subcultural groups and it may be considered characteristic of that group. (2) Much of the content of the subcultures of various ethnic groups comes in response to the actions of the dominant group. This point has been made repeatedly, however, and the writer does not wish to add another brief "amen" to that approach. Instead we will tend to neglect that fact and look much more at what the ethnic group is doing as actor and not as mere responder.

It is not assumed that this section will be a basic contribution to the literature on minority groups, for this is a large and difficult field which the writer has not mastered. Rather, these brief and, we hope, meaningful comments are intended to show the use of our general perspective. They will attempt to show how an ethnic group's history, values, and present status in various areas of society all contribute to the blocking of certain routes to status and the increased access or compensation in other roles. To make this more comprehensible and link it with our earlier discussion, roles will frequently be viewed along an ascribed-achieved continuum.

The Jews in an Industrial Society

The Jew in America seems an example par excellence of role compensation in the direction of achievement rather than in the direction of ascription. Jews excel greatly in intellectual and occupational pursuits, as data on class and religious affiliation reveal (Simpson and Yinger, 1953, p. 384 and Hollingshead and Redlich, 1958, p. 204). This is a consequence of a blocking of certain ascriptive routes to status in the larger society *and* within their own intimate sphere, and compensation in achieved roles.

The Jews' values and their early history in Europe also predisposed them to this pattern. That is, the ascriptively oriented society of Europe in the Middle Ages allowed a disesteemed ethnic group to engage in activity of secondary importance and of a lower moral order (trading and finance). This specialization in such nonascriptive values and roles placed them in an advantageous position with the industrialization of Europe. This was further heightened within the free and differentiated society of the United States.

In Christian-dominated Europe their achieved roles were often highly circumscribed and limited largely to financial and economic endeavors. As the close tie between religion and other institutions in society dissolved, new differentiated institutional areas were opened to the Jews. The increasing withdrawal of religion to a private sphere of life made public participation by Jews increasingly available. Prior to this state he had in many ways been outside the social and moral order.

With the differentiation of church and state elected and appointed offices became increasingly available to Jews. Though intellectual effort has long been admired in Jewish culture, its manifestation, prior to the period of religious differentiation and secularization of society, occurred largely within the Jewish community. The situation in Spain may have been something of an exception, where Middle Eastern influence allowed for a different accommodation of multiple-ethnic communities. With the differentiation of religious institutions and the secularization of Christian Western civilization, many universities, institutes, and literary communities were opened to Jewish intellectuals (the "good Baptists" no longer really control Brown University, nor does the Church of England control Cambridge University).

This emphasis on symbolic activity plus certain universalistic themes in Judaism set the stage for success in modern industrial society. Despite these changes, ascriptive in-group loyalty (such as represented somewhat more by the Irish) might have remained a dominant standard and route to status. The conflictful decision about this matter took place within the struggle between Orthodox, Conservative, and Reform groups for the allegiance of the Jew. This standard probably does operate ("Jews are clannish") to some degree, but the emphasis on ascriptive solidarity would have only sustained in Western society a cultural outlook which would have worked to the detriment of the Jew. That is, the demands for ethnic loyalty manifested by traditional sentiments in conflict with mobility would have been in essential conflict with liberal efforts to make achievement the basis of evaluation in the society. Ascriptive evaluation in the larger society had, in the past in Christian societies, proven a costly and sometimes mortal handicap. Just as it is in the interest of the occupationally declining white Anglo-Saxon Protestant to emphasize ascriptive statuses, and in the interest of the occupationally secure college-educated Wasp to take a moderate position concerning the ascriptive vs. achieved problem (e.g., the *New York Times*-reading East Coast business executive), so it is in the interest of the Jew to take a liberal position firmly supporting the American ideal of emphasis upon achievement and not ascription. This is perhaps a key to the rapid Americanization of Judaism in America and the blocking of ascriptive allegiances in the Jewish subculture.

The Judaic deemphasis—not denial—of the body, of eros, and of impulsive gratification, supports present pain for future gain. Such a philosophy also leads into achievement and American success. Joseph Elder (unpublished paper, 1956), analyzes various religions in the world and throughout history. Nearly all have what he considers instrumental figures and expressive or dependency figures. Judaism is unusual in that it has no important aesthetic-expressive and protective figure such as Mary. There is no Holy Mother, nor even the understanding Christ asking that they be as little children. The coming of the Messiah, possibly a consummatory figure, is placed in the future and constantly postponed, perhaps symbolic of the postponement of earthly pleasure.

There is also in Judaism the taboo against picturing the human form, as there was in certain puritanical Protestant groups, and this may be taken as a strong deemphasis of and desire to control the appeal of human eros.

These bits of evidence suggest other reasons for a deemphasis of ascriptive and emotionally binding ties within intimate spheres of life (the peer group, sexuality, and possibly the ascribed family, though not the achieved *marital* family) in the Jewish subculture.[5] The absence of these binding ties makes possible mobility and rational action in the interests of achieved-role accomplishments.

The Jews' very success in manifesting the ideals of an achievement-oriented society also creates the anti-Semitism they experience. After all, the carefully just and universalistic, the rather compulsively rational and intellectual, the slightly anerotic can be irritating in intimate personal situations and in attempts to develop political solidarity. It can be even more disturbing and aggression-producing when it is used with hostility to correct real and imagined social deprivation. "Inappropriate" reliance on broad principles, fact, and hard work can be as aggressive as deviant relaxation. The Jew is regarded as distant, exploitative, shrewd, and likely to be disloyal despite skill and creativity. Such allegiance to achievement and universalism does seem to conflict with the sentiments necessary for communal solidarity and charisma.[6]

5. The writer recognizes that the "closeness of the Jewish family" is an accepted theme. This "closeness" does not seem to express itself in mobility-inhibiting geographical and behavioral ties to the natal family and its values (as among Italian families) but rather in an expression of closeness symbolically and by the parents' support of the values of their achieving children.

6. See Reichley (1959) for a discussion of the difficulties Protestants and Jews have in operating in the field of politics given their moral philosophies. The emotionally permeated and particularistic philosophies ("cronies," the machine, "deals," ethnic, class, and kin nepotism) of the Irish, Italians, and other lower-statused ethnics seem more akin to the noninstitutionalized emotional, and slightly amoral jockeying for power which is at the heart of elective politics.

Other traits characteristic of the Jewish stereotype may have some basis in fact and should be analyzed if this were our major effort in this work. They are "loud." Though their cultural traditions and present family structure would be likely to produce strong superegos, they do feel dissatisfactions and find the need to express aggression. Perhaps they choose to do it in those situations (verbal), (1) which are

The progressive morality, "justice," and the dominant ethical principles of our society are also used by the liberal intellectual (and other high-statused individuals whatever their religious affiliation) as tools of advantage and power in the exchange of prestige and approval in the societal market place.

The Irish in America[7]

The Jewish immigrant to America was, in Europe, a town dweller, and frequently came from areas where commerce and industry were moderately and sometimes highly developed. The Irish immigrant, by contrast, was frequently of peasant origin and from a country that was predominantly agricultural. These differences in origin probably made the Irish person, particularly the male, less well prepared for the urban gateway to American society taken by so many immigrants.

Though the Irish were largely Roman Catholic, several factors favored their developing a moderately successful adjustment and becoming part of American society. Their Catholicism was somewhat more puritanical than the Catholicism of most Europeans.[8] We might say that the expressive-to-instrumental revolution occurred in Ireland within Catholicism rather than with the introduction of the Protestant sects of the Reformation. This condition made their values somewhat more akin to the dominant Protestant Ethic in nineteenth- and twentieth-century America.

Other factors favored their transition to a relatively advantaged position in American society. These include an important degree

---

borderline in their deviance (thus reducing the likelihood of countersanctions given their minority status), (2) in which they excel (again verbal) and in which they could therefore maintain control, and (3) which would, given a high superego and prohibition against violence, create fewer feelings of guilt than would physical or direct verbal assault. They are "shrewd." This seems to again connote the use of borderline situations which, though not against the law (and thus protects them from countersanctions), provide a situation for the expression of aggression against its spirit and against a sometimes exploiting and exploited group. This is also done in areas where the Jew excels (business or legal activity) and in areas which are less guilt-producing than direct person-to-person aggression. The analysis of these stereotypes is made with the recognition that they often get exaggerated and may fail to discuss the positive traits of a particular group. For the Jew certain positive attributes seem rather clear: low rates of criminality, high family stability, and artistic and creative intellectual efforts.

7. This section owes some of its stimulus to Winston White. Its weaknesses are the writer's own, however.

8. This puritanism may be seen operating in the much greater premarital sexual restraint among Irish-American servicemen than among Italo-Americans (unpublished data from interviews and questionnaires, Daniel Funkenstein).

of cultural communication with England, from which America borrowed so many legal and moral attitudes, their English-speaking ability, and their being physiognomically almost indistinguishable from "Americans." Such conditions, as well as their somewhat earlier arrival, make for greater "success" at the present time in America than is true for other Catholics—say, the Italians.

However, other factors, especially the interplay of their cultural history and their special position as recent arrivals in an urban society, created tensions, impeded upward mobility, and produced a distinct subculture analyzable within the theoretical frame used in this work.

In Europe, the Irish society was, like most, patriarchal in kinship organization but with special norms which had significance there and which took on special meaning in American society. Central to these norms was a particular land-inheritance pattern. The father retained control over the land and over his wife and offspring until his death or long into old age (Arensberg, 1959). This meant that young Irishmen were without means of economic independence through their twenties and even into their late thirties. Without economic independence and with the hold of the natal family still strong, the young Irishman's adolescence and social impotence was prolonged, and this made marriage a difficult matter. Indeed, such unmarried men were called "boys" even though they might be thirty or forty years of age. This economic and kinship authority position created lasting self-images in regard to power and adult adequacy. Patriarchy was nevertheless an ideal, and what might have resulted in a female dominance was handled in two ways, premaritally and postmaritally.

Prior to marriage the "boy," much like the matriarchally controlled adolescent in the lower classes of American society, turned to the gang. There was a kind of wandering with the boys in the emotional hinterland of the pub and the town. This pattern was perhaps carried over into married life to some degree, but many of these "problems" were solved with the inheritance or development of economic independence and with resulting marriage. Postmaritally, the husband's power was safeguarded by a rather strict separation of the wife's domain (the house) and the husband's (the barn and fields).

In the American city, these various conditions seem to have been psychologically aggravated. The husband and father lost some adequacy in his authority and economic role as a consequence of migration to an unfamiliar society (Murdock, 1949, pp. 200-206).

This loss coupled with the sustained adequacy of the mother and wife in her generally unchanged kinship role resulted in an aggravated puritanical matriarchy.

It appears that it is just such conditions, for reasons which are not exactly clear, which create drunkenness cross-culturally (Field, 1961) and in the Irish subculture in America. Those societies in which the population is mobile, the kinship organization is bilineal, matriarchy dominates, there are numerous informal peer groups, and the child-rearing practices are indulgent but demanding (in terms of self restraint and achievement) and are characterized by considerable inebriety. All of these latter social qualities are in varying degrees typical of the Irish in America.

Societies where there are patrilocal rules of residence, unilinear kinship organization, and high corporate kin obligations with few loose and informal peer associations are most sober. Perhaps societies which are geographically stable, where the male has high status, and where achievements are not too demanding and are largely channeled by the highly organized kin group—not by the informal peer group or individual—reduce to a minimum the tensions and problems of carrying out the male role. When the opposite conditions prevail, tensions and feelings of inadequacy are increased. Inebriety (and other subcultural norms of the Irish) is one method of release.

Does this particular cultural structure when combined with our perspectives (e.g., aggression and role compensation) provide a new view of the Irish subculture in America? Let us investigate. The initially low status of the Irish in America might have led them to an ascriptive emphasis on all or one of the roles discussed: peer activity, sexuality, in-group loyalty, etc. Certain conditions led to the choice of some and the neglect of others. The puritanism probably led to a blocking of sexual activity as an avenue to status within the society or subculture. If erotic activity was not an outlet, however, it seems that masculinity and femininity (of a specifically nongenital quality and thus not so undermined by puritanical inhibition) were outlets.[9] Activities subject to conscious control, such as drinking and belligerence, became symbols of masculinity. Traditions already existed in Irish culture that made the tavern and drinking

---

9. Femininity seems less important as a role for compensation. The writer has some difficulty, however, in making an insightful analysis of the female role. Though this may result from his particular location in society it seems more likely that it is a consequence of the reduced differentiation and variation of the female role by class or public statuses—the independent variable here.

available outlets, and these were buttressed by the special processes just discussed operating in Irish-American ethnic communities.

In addition to the matriarchal-in-genesis factors, the alcohol served as a releasing mechanism allowing for the expression of aggression (the "Donnybrook") and the expression of otherwise inhibited eroticism. Puritanism itself may have contributed to the high incidence of drunkenness among the Irish in America. Burchard's attribution of "rum, Romanism, and rebellion" to the Democrats (then strongly controlled by the Irish Catholics) during Cleveland's campaign may have been more than Blaine's political epitaph. It may also have been validly epithetic, for the terms represented the alcoholism, devout Catholicism, and aggression then characteristic of the Irish.

Alcohol also may have brought into even stronger form those beguiling qualities considered characteristic of the Irish. The riotously good-natured joking, the humorous belligerence, the whimsy just this side of insanity (e.g., that of Brendan Behan) are all probably qualities which provide high status in primary groups and in particularistic association.

The earlier problems of achievement and the blocking of direct genital sexuality brought other avenues of status (role compensation) besides these particular forms of good-natured peer-group action, of belligerent masculinity, and of femininity for women.

These attributes (e.g., good-natured whimsy) provide rewards in not only the peer group, they also provide means of gaining compensating status in other areas: personal power and status in political activity. In fact, one might look at the political organization characteristic of the Irish of a generation or so ago as the peer group grown up into the particularistically organized political machine. Such approaches and skills of the Irish and other ethnic groups made it difficult for the universalistic, rational, and justice-oriented white Protestant to compete effectively in urban politics (Reichley, 1959).

Political action was one made of gaining status in and expressing loyalty to the Irish ethnic community and to the broader community. It appears that such ethnic loyalty is especially characteristic of the lower-statused Irish. It seems to get transformed into goals of respectable Catholicism at a somewhat higher level and into a high interest in Americanism among those with even higher occupational status and greater involvement in the American social system.

The Italo-Americans

Some cultural historians in their more romantic and unqualifying moods have said that the ordinary individual in Italy is still, in spirit, a pagan. There may be some truth in this, for modern Italy seems to partake of some of the same attitudes toward life that characterized classical pre-Christian life around the Mediterranean. Christianity, in contrast, focused on the aspect of higher morality. The classical view, though it held higher morality to be an important part of life, regarded the various areas of human concern—the body, human passion, family loyalty, etc.—as moral and legitimate demands on human action. The problem was not how to attain constantly higher goals but how to achieve a balance. This contemporary allegiance to the demands of the body and its needs (eros), particularistic compassion, and impulse seems to be reflected in Italo-Americans much more than is the case for the Jews, the white Protestants, or even the Roman Catholic Irish. We cannot really explain why this is so but can only make a few brief suggestions.

The values of Catholicism (compared to those of Protestantism and Judaism) may help explain certain distinctive patterns among the Italo-Americans. But the differences that exist between the Italians and Irish cannot be explained in this way, for both are Roman Catholic. Perhaps part of the explanation comes in the point of origin of each culture. That is, if we look at the trend of development of Western society over the past two or three thousand years as a gradual movement from diffuse expressiveness to increasing instrumental and rational action, we observe that Italy, as a culture, probably originated and perhaps split off (much as in biological evolution) approximately a millenium earlier than did the culture of Ireland and the British Isles. I do not suggest that it is thus a lower form of social order or that it has remained unchanged. Its structure of action, however, may be rooted much more in aesthetics and expressive action.

The Italian immigrants, like the Irish, originated in the more disadvantaged peasant elements of their own society and moved into deprived positions in the American urban setting. Though there are these parallels, their adjustment to American industrial society has followed a different pattern.

Part of this was the very fact that they arrived as Catholics in much the same areas as the Irish but at a later date. The Irish and other Catholics had already filled the positions of control in the

Roman Catholic hierarchy and had cast American Catholicism in accord with their own interests. The Irish had also come to dominate urban American politics and had blocked this as a possibility for achievement. These conditions and historical facts probably helped create and sustain the reduced Catholic devoutness and reduced striving Americanism (apolitical attitudes) among the Italo-Americans as compared with the Irish. The norms of devotion and patriotism of the Irish Americans were not only reinforced by their earlier arrival, control, and success in the church and in the political organization but probably also by the inhibiting puritanism of Irish Catholicism which blocked expressive impulse as a means of gaining status.

Preemptive control by the Irish necessitated the Italians' looking elsewhere for avenues of satisfaction and accomplishment. Other factors would probably have made this necessary. The somewhat more impulsive and passion-dominated (in its more general sense) way of life brought the Italian immigrant under suspicion in such areas. He "couldn't be trusted." Also, his physiognomy created certain problems during the earlier part of this century, for he was "dark and swarthy," and by cultural definition these provided valid reasons for withdrawing trust.

These various factors led to an emphasis not just on the quasi-illegal political activity characteristic of the Irish, but on unqualified and sometimes brutal crime. The syndicate, the gang, extortion and its violent consequences became situations ideally suited to an ethnic group with frustrated needs to achieve, with aggression to express, and with impulsive motivations. Other native-born groups and recently migrated ethnic groups had had their turn at such crime, but they had taken it with less zestful commitment. Actually only a small minority of the Italo-Americans were actively involved in this criminality, but the rate was sufficiently high to create with some validity a stereotype.

The problems of finding opportunities for legitimate upward mobility may have reinforced the emphasis on the ascriptive expressive focus, but the preexisting expressive focus introduced problems of acculturation from the very beginning. Narrower loyalties, ascribed roles, and eros for a time became exaggerated concerns and it is probably in the areas of expressiveness (love, athletics, sexuality, the arts, the good life, etc.) that the Italo-Americans still excel.

Though Italians in American society still hold a moderately low position, this situation is undoubtedly changing. Public education, the process of Americanization, increased opportunities for upward mobility, the influx of Negroes, Puerto Ricans, and "hillbillies" into the lowest levels of urban America, raise, in turn, the status of Italians. And as their status changes in the dominant area of evaluation in America, work, their subculture changes from "impulse" to responsible rational control. This does not seem to be either a decline or an improvement in any absolute sense.

The Negroes in America

The Negro is not of recent immigration, nor is he non-Christian. In fact, he is an old American Protestant. Two factors, however, explain much about his present position and ethnic culture. One is historical—his introduction into American society as a slave, and with it the disintegration of his original integrating values, and the dehumanizing and defamilizing processes of the slave status. The second is biological and contemporary—his physical recognizability and the negative evaluations his appearance evokes. Part of these negative evaluations relate directly to aesthetic reactions, but many more come about as a consequence of the cultural and social factors his appearance symbolizes. Above all, his recognizability assigns him ascriptively to a certain ethnic group with a known reputation and given "place" in the scheme of things, much as family reputation ties the individual to his family's past successes and failures and reduces mobility in small communities. Irresponsibility, incompetence, meanness, and childishness are attributed to the Negro, and this attribution operates in self-fulfilling manner (to some degree) and produces other consequences.

These factors create incapacities and, even more, restrictions on what he can do to achieve in the broader and more universal levels of society as compensation for deprivation in the ascriptive realm. Thus, the Negro's compensatory emphasis on religion, emotionality, sexuality, and the peer group (at least in the urban environment) may derive from a blocking in not only the legitimate occupational route to status but also in the illegitimate achieved route (the political machine and the syndicate) and in the patriotic in-group route. The blocking of the latter is a result of the dominant white group's rejection of the Negro on an ascriptive level as a bona fide first class citizen of the country.

The blocking of the former (the machine and the syndicate) comes about in the ethnographic present as a consequence of the Negroes' order of succession in the ecology of the urban area. The ecological niche of the political machine was occupied by the Irish and other ethnics, and the quasi-legal and illegal syndicate was held first by the Jews and Irish and later by the Italians. These conditions are not frozen but are undoubtedly changing.

The barriers to accomplishment in the more universal roles in society (occupation and politics) and even to accomplishment in roles of only moderate universality (machine politics and parochial patriotism) lead to a development of and definition of Negroes as particularistic libidinal specialists. The dominant syndrome of activities and values of the Negro (sexuality, joking, expressiveness, violence, religious sects, kin, and the peer group) may be viewed in this manner.[10]

When unusual need or talent provides the means of escape from the Negro subculture and its lower status, the dominant society may still channel it into such expressive realms. That is, there are few Negro businessmen or noted scientists but many prominent and accomplished Negro dancers, singers, artists, musicians, and athletes.

Probably certain puritanical suspicions present in a work-oriented society leave open such "second rate" avenues for fame and status. Their variant or deviant position in the value scheme of a work-oriented society also probably results in the recruitment of offbeat and nonconforming individuals into the power structure of the entertainment world. Such individuals would be more prone to accept

10. A somewhat subjective analysis by the author of five ethnic subcultures (Irish, Italian, WASP, Jewish, and Negro) showed that sexuality and peer-group roles were strongest among and most highly associated with those ethnic groups showing lowest status and least upward mobility. This analysis looked at the relative emphasis on the natal family, marital family, peer group, sexuality, particularisitic patriotism (ethnic loyalty), universalistic patriotism (Americanism), and occupational status in each ethnic group.

An emphasis on the natal family, though a primary and particularistic group, seemed moderately associated with upward mobility and status. Its function as a representative of the larger society in the socialization process and as a stabilizer of the personality for "mature" social accomplishment may make it more universalistic in its function than its concrete social structure would indicate. Again, in the family area a majority of the Negroes suffer certain problems and inadequacies. This is true for many of the reasons we have outlined concerning the consequences for the family of low status in the general society. Its matriarchy suggests that it may become an area of status and satisfaction among Negro women but not Negro men. These conditions when brought together suggest a reason for the alleged greater stability, greater responsibility, greater cooperativeness, lessened sexuality (relative to Negro men), and greater maturity of Negro women compared to Negro men. Their position and involvement in the family protects them from some of the harsh conditions faced by the Negro in the general society.

It should be pointed out that the peer group *can* function in some social settings as a socializing group in the interests of the more universal and higher roles in society as Eisenstadt's study (1956) indicates.

ethnic minorities in terms of their abilities and less in terms of their ascriptive qualities.

These patterns are not unique to Negroes. Several ethnic groups (especially the Italians and Jews) have been defined as libidinal specialists and entertainers. Analysts have found (Weinberg and Arond, 1952) a rather clear succession of various ethnic groups in show business and boxing (from the Irish to the Jews, to the Italians, to the Negroes). The dominance of each succeeding group comes to be regarded as so natural and permanent that at present the appearance of occasional Irish boxers (e.g., Tom McNeeley) is viewed with surprise and with predictions of "most likely to fail." What is unique for the Negro is his long (over 250 years) and almost frozen position in the lowest levels of American society. This long history coupled with very limited alternate routes to status and an understandable rejection of the American "dream" of upward mobility probably creates some of the specialized patterns characteristic of the Negro subculture.

If evaluation in the public sphere in terms of ascriptive qualities continues to decline in America (and this seems to be the heart of many contemporary liberal trends) then the Negro may be the "Jew" of the future in America. That is, the opening up of public achieved routes to status will lead to upward mobility as compensation for deprivations still felt in various ascriptive areas.

By contrast, as religion declines in terms of its significance as a basis of ascriptive evaluation and as history provides evidence for the capabilities and contributions of the Jew to American society, the Jew may relax. He may relax, as have the genteel progeny of striving Protestant forebears of earlier days, in his achieved role pursuits.

The ascriptively deprived become the achievement compensating. With time (and some decline) those who have successfully achieved become the ascriptive elite of a new age.

These things are all said with a recognition of the lack of systematic facts. They attempt only to explain some commonly held views and observations of various ethnic groups. The views and observations seem to be stereotypes which are in certain cases true to this observer. Human scientists, caught in liberal ideology, often reject commonly held beliefs about various ethnic groups just because they are the beliefs of the masses and because they are— at least from the perspective of their own and most middle-class values, unflattering to certain groups. These commonly held beliefs are, after all, not completely determined by the emotions of the unsophisticated believer. Though they undoubtedly get slanted to assist the believer's adjustment to the social world, they are derived from countless everyday observations and everyday analysis.

Also, our position is in opposition to that taken by Merton (1949): "Superficial appearance notwithstanding, prejudice and discrimination aimed at the out-group are not a result of what the out-group does, but are rooted deep in the structure of our society and the social psychology of its members" (p. 186). But surely the members of the minority or out-group are themselves part of the society, and what they do as well as what the dominant groups do become the basis of just and unjust hostility. In our intellectual analysis we should not commit an error which is rooted in moral prejudices and a tradition of *apartheid*. Instead we should admit the minority group and individual into active membership in the society under analysis and into the category of "human." They are neither morally pure nor passive recipients of exploitation by the dominant community. They are capable of deceit, charity, exploitation, love, and sacrifice. They are immune to neither the vices nor the virtues of humanity.

THE SYMBIOTIC TIES OF NATIONAL CULTURES

The subcultures within a society do not arise by accident, but emerge as a consequence of society's need and symbiotic specializations. This analytic orientation can be carried over to an analysis of the ecology of cross-cultural variations. That is, just as certain roles, subcultures, or classes develop into specializations as a consequence of the society's functional needs, so certain geographical entities—nations—may develop certain characteristic national cultures as specializations within their civilization (in the Toynbean sense) or within the community of nations. According to this view, Great Britain's industrial and political emphases (the Commonwealth which spread the influence of the European Christian civilization over much of the non-Christian world) and Italy's artistic and religious emphases are not independent and accidental specializations but the consequence of *implicit* decisions on an international level ("civilizations") and the sometimes cooperative exchange of sanctions to maintain these specializations. Even the cultures characteristic of the Orient and the Occident might be viewed as expressive diffuse (feminine) and instrumental differentiated (masculine) specializations which were created and sustained by not only local values and conditions but through the intercivilization exchange of certain products and sanctions of approval, alliances, disapproval, and hostility. These exchanges are not only of an economic and political nature but also of an emotional and prestige nature.

This view, though perhaps beyond the level of present conceptual development and thus difficult to put into analytical practice, might give new insights into certain past and present international processes. Thus, just as parents sometimes implicitly encourage the development of delinquency in their children, who then become specialists in the expression of the parents' own hostility toward society, so various countries in Western society may have implicitly motivated or encouraged the twentieth-century acts of Germany (an exchange of implicit approval and aggressive acts). Vicarious but strongly denied satisfaction may have been obtained (even among the most liberal elements) in the observation of Germany's aggressive and regressive militarism and anti-Semitism. This might explain the long delay in taking action to control Germany. Only when they became fearful that they would also become victims of the "delinquency" did the stronger European and American nations apply the sanctions of war.

And if this orientation has some validity and if the community of nations is truly a community or society at some thin level, it raises questions about the realism (or sincerity) of the attempts to more or less equalize the level of development of all nations. "Underdeveloped" nations may be an inevitable part of the international community just as "the poor are always with us."

If nations were truly independent cultural and social entities then equalization might be possible and profitable. But if there is some social interdependence and if they do form an interdependent system, then certain features of a social structure are to be expected. One of these is specialization and its resulting differentiation in status (by various criteria). Some countries will be highly developed industrially and enjoy a high standard of living in at least a material sense. Other countries, like certain regions and classes within a nation, must provide the raw materials and the relatively less skilled labor. Though less developed in a material and in a differentiated cultural sense, these countries or regions may reap certain rewards in their emotional and communal lives. These are the rewards which come from an absence of bureaucratic organization and rationalization of a broad segment of life and from the presence of intimate and lasting human ties.

So long as these countries remain relatively isolated from the centers of the dominant civilization (France in A.D. 300, Peru in 1900) their material disadvantages are less apparent. The esteem disadvantage does not really exist in any important degree because they are not interacting in the same esteem exchange system as are the centers of civilization. These areas in the hinterland of the dominant civilization are a parallel of the relatively isolated and contented rural dwellers studied by Beers and shown in Table 8. As they are drawn within the economic systems and the systems of social approval and disapproval of the centers of civilization, their reference groups change. Different standards are introduced and they may begin to feel dissatisfaction. The attitudes and actions of such "have not" nations begin to take on the qualities of the alienated urban proletariat. Hostility is expressed in the form of political pressure, political subversion, and military probes. There is also, just as is true for the lower classes, a failure to live up to international "law." This is not surprising, for international law is partially a set of formal and informal rules about the relations between nations which may tend to serve the interests of the established and "respectable" nations (e.g., Great Britain in the twentieth century). The views of Thrasymachus and Marx give the observer new insights into the processes of international as well as national power.

In this situation, the established "have" nations view with critical eyes the almost barbaric actions of the newly arrived (the Soviet Union in 1960) and of the poorer and dissatisfied nations (China on the contemporary scene). The statesmen of the "have" countries must, if they are to protect their position, treat with a certain paternal forbearance the inferiority-motivated aggressions of the statesmen from the provinces of civilization (e.g., Adlai Stevenson's response to Khrushchev's shoe pounding and rattling verbal rockets).

The elite nations also take action to maintain the international status quo (e.g., the policy of containment) and condemn certain processes, which are the essence of power and politics, as immoral. It is not surprising, however, that they wish to maintain the international status quo, for it is a system of international relations which gives them considerable power and wealth. It also defines the morals of international life from an ethical base (Christian democracy) that is consistent with their own actions and sentiments. This consistency between action and the dominant moral code of international life provides these nations with prestige, and feelings of worth and moral superiority as well.

From this view America in the early 1960s is the powerful and almost respectable elite nation wedded to slightly faded aristocracy, France and Great Britain. The Soviet Union is the boorish *nouveau arriviste* who attempts to redefine the basis of international life in a way that will improve its moral position. These powerful and newly arrived nations find rocking the international status quo quite to their liking (e.g., Soviet diplomatic "barbarisms" and militarism). They right certain military wrongs and cultural slights they may have felt in the past within their international reference group (Western civilization).

Such military action may also improve the nations' power positions. And since power often begets respectability, the international moral positions of the nations may be improved as well.

China is the urban proletariat recently recruited from the provinces—"the provinces" in relation to the dominant centers of esteem and power. Given this position, it is engaged in numerous "senseless" aggressions and threats born of frustration and impotence (much like Cloward and Ohlin's "bopping" gangs). Meanwhile Micronesia slumbers in provincial (rural) isolation relatively content with its lot and not sufficiently informed or in contact with the rest of the world to suffer dissatisfying comparisons.

We do not intend to reduce the relationships between nations to just another case of the relations between classes. The analogy is only developed to suggest that certain processes operating within a society if abstractly conceptualized operate on the international scene.

Nor does this perspective ignore many seemingly nonmotivational factors of world politics such as population density, economic exchange, geographical boundaries, military treaties, and military strength. Though such factors can be looked at in terms of status (specifically prestige) needs, they probably provide much more explanatory power as they are usually employed by political scientists. The suggested approach only tries to look at them in terms of status motivation and status politicking.

Terms and concepts in such a view tend to be couched in psychological or motivational language. This does not necessarily mean that a reductionist attempt is being made to explain cultural and historical processes in terms of psychology. Rather the attempt is to show the society-wide motivational base of the processes of international exchange and affairs. International affairs are more than the rather "impersonal" matters of power, wealth, and money. There is the desire for international esteem and respectability, and the resulting national specialization of activity to gain such resources. This, in turn, leads to the interdependence which suffuses the affairs of the international society. When motivational factors arise and emotional sanctions are exchanged between social systems, their analysis becomes the legitimate concern of the various sciences of human action.

• CHAPTER 10

Summary and Postscript

Logical thinking does not go far enough. Surveying all the treasures of the mind and all the splendours of its achievements we shall still find, at the bottom of every serious judgement, something problematical left. In our heart of hearts we know that none of our pronouncements is absolutely conclusive. At that point, where judgement begins to waver, the feeling that the world is serious after all wavers with it. Instead of the old saw: "All is vanity", the more positive conclusion forces itself upon us that "All is play". A cheap metaphor, no doubt, mere impotence of the mind; yet it is the wisdom Plato arrived at when he called man the plaything of the gods.

—Johan Huizinga, 1960, p. 212.

SOCIOLOGICAL AND SCIENTIFIC NORMS

Some reflection brings to mind certain actions and approaches in this study somewhat outside the norms of scientific endeavor as presently and generally defined. At times we have introduced everyday observations and their interpretations. At other times we have speculated rather freely about what these observations (e.g., commonly held stereotypes) and our more empirical data "really" mean. And at times the writer has moralized with some self-awareness.

It has not been possible to prove or give convincing evidence for all of the ideas presented. They are not all stated as facts or firmly held conclusions but as reasonable interpretations arrived at after thought and criticism. At least the author is aware to some degree of their several weaknesses.

To develop theory, systematic ideas, and understanding requires neither a completely free flow of personal hunches and perspectives (though this helps at times) nor a battery of empirical data to in-

234

controvertibly support each statement in the system of ideas. When it has served the goal of understanding, the strict norms of science have been abandoned, for we feel that science should be a useful tool, not intellectual dogma.

These actions introduce some concern about what this writer feels is the proper role of the sociologist if he is to give meaning to human life. He is, it seems, first a *human being* who is a member of a particular moral order (his society) and of his professional community. Given these positions, he cannot help but moralize (express preferences and propose action to implement these preferences) in the face of incomplete rational understanding. In fact, he may have an obligation to moralize from his vista "before all the evidence is in." However, an even stronger obligation is that he be explicitly aware of his evaluations and make it evident to his audience.

Secondly, he is something of an *intellectual* attempting to understand human behavior as it presents itself in organized form. As such, he is primarily committed to the use of the mind (rationality, intuition, the adduction of evidence, abstraction, organization, etc.) and only secondarily to the use of the special techniques of science (e.g., controlled observations).

And finally and importantly, the sociologist is a scientist, committed in some degree to those norms of action which the scientific method implies. He must theorize, observe empirically, test, communicate, and revise. These obligations of the sociologist are placed in this order of priority: as a moral and responsible member of society, as an intellectual, and as a scientist—because science is the servant of the intellect and the intellect is the servant of the human being, not the reverse.

And contrary to some modern positons, scientific endeavor and intellectual endeavor (or the effort to understand) are not equivalent domains. For the scientific method even when most liberally defined depends on the evidence provided by the five or six senses as it can be interpreted and organized by the rules of inductive and deductive logic. As it gets defined by certain strenuous methodologists or operationalists, science (and therefore understanding) can be brought about only through well "controlled" empirical situations where "all" factors are understood and measured.

In one sense this is humility in the extreme, for it suggests that the human mind is an untrustworthy instrument and that numerous social controls and external checks must be operating before much can be known. The role of the autonomous intellectual is largely abdicated, for rather precise rules and social agents of control are introduced.

Both the strenuous and liberal scientific positions, however, seem to manifest themselves in the scientific and sociological community in a manner that is sometimes far from humble. There is a tendency to reject the validity of other forms of knowledge, understanding, or tests of truth. Traditional norms of thought and behavior, though they have resulted from numerous encounters with and tests by reality, are rejected—given a little evidence from the laboratory (or a dash of Spencian psychology and an afternoon of critical thought).

Carefully reasoned introspection, intuited insights, traditional morality, and metaphysical analysis tend to be rejected as nearly worthless. This approach seems not to realize or wishes to ignore (in order to enhance its own method and status) those realms of being and experience outside those presented directly to the senses.

At this point it does not seem appropriate to give a thorough treatment of the problems of epistemology and the philosophy of science (which is in many ways really an analysis of the morals of scientific behavior) that will be convincing or even understandable to the skeptic who holds rather rigidly to his narrow rationalistic and scientific allegiances. The writer, however, would like to elaborate his protest by speaking through the quotations of two writers. W. Lloyd Warner says of truth, reality, and science:

Furthermore, the non-logical expressive symbols which make up most of our symbols used in daily action—particularly those of religion—will be valid for those who use them, not because they can be proved to be true or false or logically congruent, but because they make emotional sense and are emotionally valid for those who *feel* them.

Moreover, if this is true, rational and scientific truth can be no more than one form of "knowing" reality and—this being assumed—reality as now defined can be no more than one form of what is real. The non-symbolic species behavior is the result of millions of years of accumulated adaptation. What the species inherits biologically and each individual member learns socially at the non-symbolic level, and is felt and experienced by the individual organism and by the organized responses of the group—being outside the realm of reason and its logical and scientific operations—contains orders of significance and truth far removed from even the suppositions of rational thought. The accumulated, condensed experience transferred and integrated into the species and its behavior and felt intensely by its members, individually and collectively, has meanings and validities and forms of truth for men beyond the capacity of rational thought to conceive and to order into sense-making symbols. Man's sense of what he is cannot ever depend solely on rational thought; too much is left out of what we know.

And Norman Brown gives us revealing insight into the hostile motivations of the compulsive scientist, motivations shared to some extent, I suspect, by all who "reveal" or analyze, myself included:

There is an attack on the great god Science in psychoanalysis; but the nature of the attack needs careful explanation. What is being probed, and found to be in some sense morbid, is not knowledge as such, but the unconscious schemata governing the pursuit of knowledge in modern civilization—specifically the aim of possession or mastery over objects (Freud), and the principle of economizing in the means (Ferenczi). And the morbidity imputed to these schemata, if interpreted in the context of the whole libido theory, amounts to this: possessive mastery over nature and rigorously economical thinking are partial impulses in the human being (the human body) which in modern civilization have become tyrant organizers of the whole of human life; abstractions from the reality of the whole body and substitution of the abstracted impulse for the whole reality are inherent in *Homo economicus*. In contrast, what would a non-morbid science look like? It would presumably be erotic rather than (anal) sadistic in aim. Its aim would not be mastery over but union with nature. And its means would not be economizing but erotic exuberance. And finally, it would be based on the whole body and not just a part; that is to say it would be based on the polymorphous perverse body.

I am objecting not just to an extreme commitment to the scientific methods of research and experimentation at the expense of the method of the humanistically oriented intellect. I am instead protesting against the modern "tyranny" of method and rationality in either form and the modern social scientist's unwillingness to be guided at times by his heart and soul, those unconscious urges and "rationalities" inherited from man's biological and cultural past. If one is to be a good human scientist these unconscious motivations, we all agree, must at certain times be placed under scrutiny by man's conscious rationality. But can the human scientist be a creative interpreter of human behavior unless he at times subjects his conscous rationalities to the evaluations and tests of the id, the unconscious, and broad sociocultural assumptions (basic traditional morality)? To do this requires him, as I see it, *as a sociologist* sometimes to abandon the narrow morality of rational thought and science and to take another view of human existence and social life.

Nonetheless, this has been, to an important degree, a scientific endeavor. And a question arises in any scientific effort regarding the validity of the different conclusions reached, of the assumptions made, and of the interpretations concerning the meaning of behavior and data. All of these thoughts and conditions require a discussion of some of the methodological problems and some of the research

and theoretical limitations of the work. This discussion will attempt
to answer some anticipated criticisms.

Following that section, the chapter will be concerned with an
interpretive summary and a discussion of some possible special
contributions.

METHODOLOGICAL DISCUSSION

Though the over-all picture presented gives rather consistent
support to our views, the evidence is sometimes rather slight. This
may mean the support is spurious *or* it may be only a hint of much
stronger relationships than those revealed. That is, the crudity of
our measure may mask strong relationships of which we see only
pale shadows.

It may appear that some support was almost universal. This
was nearly true for the dominant interests, though it should be
recalled that occasionally the opposite of what we expected has
been reported. When this occurred we attempted some reinterpretation of a specific hypothesis and finding within the basic theoretical
framework and general trend of the data.

The Selection of Questions Used

The success of certain measures and questions in various areas
rests in part on the series of pretests which were interspersed with
trial analyses of results obtained. Perhaps even more important was
the fact that considerable reliance was placed on questions already
developed by other researchers or their associates (Daniel Funkenstein, Samuel A. Stouffer, Florence Kluckhohn, Daniel R. Miller,
Guy E. Swanson, R. Sears, E. Maccoby, and H. Levin). This suggests that sociologists should be less "original" in the development
of questionnaires. Originality can be a costly starting anew.

Statistical Analysis and
Statistical Ritual

There has also been an allocation of effort which deemphasized
detailed statistical analysis. This choice was not a simple personal
preference but the result of a study of the characteristics of the data,
the assumptions of statistical procedures, and personal conferences
with capable statisticians. This has probably resulted in the unwarranted aceptance of *some* data as evidence and failure to see
additional associations. This allocation, however, has allowed an ex-

penditure of effort in the exploration of various areas of the data and development of additional theoretical interpretations. These on occasion created further predictions which the data then supported.

This seems to recall another rather pressing norm developing in sociology. This new convention seems to say that before general interpretive statements can be made one must "do a study." This means gathering one's own data of a type and number which can be statistically manipulated by the typical procedures. Once this is done the individual can proceed on his interpretive way with a certain indifference to other data from other areas which might have strong bearing on what is being said.

This impression has led to another choice and allocation of effort. Rather than autistically focus on the data we have gathered, we have sought to rely at times on broad comparative perspectives introduced by historical analysts or cultural anthropologists. And at other times it has seemed necessary to look at data from areas of research (e.g., Bettelheim and Janowitz, or Kinsey) which have as much bearing on our theoretical framework as would a detailed pursuit of numerous correlations within the researcher's own data.

The writer is not suggesting that the "compleat" sociologist must deal in both theory and empirical research. It appears that science, like society, is a system of specialized kinds of behavior. In the social sciences above all there should be an acceptance of the individual who generally develops theory only, of the individual who generally researches, and of the individual who wishes to work a little or a lot in both areas.

Nor is the writer saying that this is necessarily *the* right approach. It is felt, however, that there is a certain orthodoxy about the treatment of data which develops into statistically inappropriate and time-consuming ritual. The attempt to develop predictions and meanings from the data (expected and unexpected) did, however, result in additional ideas. As a stimulus for theoretical development the data were quite valuable.

LIMITATIONS IN THE RESEARCH AND WORK

Alternative Research Problems

The writer was interested in a substantive area (the interaction of class, family, and subcultures) and for this reason the research was carried out in an *ex post facto* manner. Despite the points made earlier the value of the experimental method is recognized. Without a controlled experimental design one can never be certain the observed association between two variables would be maintained in the absence of some additional variable(s). This concern was experienced frequently even though we were able to hold one and sometimes two variables constant while observing the relationship between others.

How could this problem be met? It does not seem impossible to test some of our ideas by a small group experiment. Let us suppose we want to know if the differential distribution of sanctions "really causes" some of the observed associations between status and hostility. A small group design could be developed in which few rewards would be directed toward certain individuals (by design) and more toward others. Further, there would be a rotation of the kinds of recipients (in terms of types of personalities and general level of status expectation) such that the influence of their subjective variability could be ruled out. Thus if the individual with X personality and Y status expectations expresses only 2 units of hostility when he receives many rewards but this same XY individual expresses 20 units of hostility when he receives few rewards then we *might* attribute the variation to the difference in rewards.

Additional Variables and Family Areas Requiring Study

The general approach has led the writer to focus on a detailed analysis of certain variables (status, autonomy, occupation, hostility, etc.). This has meant the neglect of other important variables such as the personality of the parent, family size, and religion. To deal with these variables adequately, however, would require more than a question (e.g., "What is your father's religious preference?") and presentation of data. We would want to know how frequently he goes to church, his status in the church group, and something about his attitude toward going (Lenski, 1961). We do have detailed information on certain variables (occupation and autonomy). These became our focus not because we consider them necessarily the most important in understanding human behavior and because we felt other variables to be of little importance. Our over-all theoretical approach determined to an important degree the variables of central interest.

This research and work have focused on the father and son roles. This was done because we felt that insufficient empirical data were previously available on them in comparison with the mother-child relationship. This specific father-son relationship was emphasized because most studies have investigated the relationship between social class and socialization as simply a parent-child relation without pursuing in detail empirically and theoretically the ramifications of same-sex versus cross-sex parent-child relationships.[1]

Only occasionally have we touched on the role of the daughter. Here again, one is struck by the greater emphasis in the literature placed on the mother and son roles. Perhaps this contemporary neglect and Freud's earlier problems in dealing with the female result from the fact that most researchers are males and as such have greater difficulty in understanding the female role. They may also result from the fact that the female role is somewhat less explicitly differentiated and variable than the male. It is the haven of diffuse traditional expressiveness, and it is therefore less explicitly and symbolically codified. This may make scientific study of the role (the attempt to find normative organization symbolically) more difficult.

The reader learned less about the husband-wife relationship and its integration into the structure of the family. He also learned less about the problems and gratifications of higher-statused individuals. This is regrettable but unavoidable within the limitations of this study.

SUMMARY OF BASIC POSITIONS, RESULTS, AND INTERPRETIVE COMMENTS

We would like now to present a skeleton outline of the assumptions, lines of thought, results, and interpretations. This will provide the reader with a summary of what has been presented.

In beginning to understand the structure of behavior in the family it becomes important to understand how it fits into society and how it is influenced by the cultural system and the psychological processes of its members. Our basic concern is an attempt to clarify the class variation of family behavior and subcultures.

How do the defining characteristics of class or status impinge on the family? Given this interest, it becomes necessary to discuss analytically the meaning of "social class" or "status" and the intervening conditions which result in its influence on the family.

1. Status is defined as the position one occupies in the reward system of a society or system of behavior. As the members of a stratum (a number of individuals and kinship groups with more or less the same status) interact frequently, they begin to

1. One of several rewarding exceptions is Jerome K. Myers and Bertram K. Roberts, *Family and Class Dynamics in Mental Illness* (New York: John Wiley and Sons, Inc., 1959), esp. pp. 57-128, 268-287.

develop adjustive norms and feelings of commitment to these norms. This is, perhaps, the meaning of class and its subculture.

2. There is a dominant basis of evaluation in a society. In American society and to an important degree in most industrial societies, this is an ethos which emphasizes achievement and mastery of the environment. The ethos need not be the individual's personal values, but it is the one which dominates and determines more than any other who will get *how much* of the desired things (wealth, power, esteem, self-esteem, and autonomy) in the society.

3. The importance of achievement and mastery over the environment makes the occupation central in determining one's position in the social world.

4. This central significance of the work role in determining one's contribution to and status in society, and its differentiation from family life in industrial society leads to a focus on the father role. The father's role becomes the focus because it is the most diversified and is the most direct link (through his occupation) between a rewarding or depriving society and the emotional organization within the family.

5. The geographical and social structural separation of the work situation from other areas in the father's life makes reasonable the use of the personality and several psychological responses (e.g., frustration produces aggression, frustration produces compensations) as intervening variables between the reward structure and the role organization of the family. Though these are psychological processes in their raw form, they become, through time, traditions and normative modes of adjustment. For example, aggression becomes the norm of being "tough" and compensation is socially structured into the forms of role compensation discussed.

6. Given several special interests (the attempt to explain the variation in socialization techniques, warmth, and the emergence of subcultures), we reasoned, and offered evidence to show that variation in class or status leads to variation in satisfaction. The variation in gratifications felt and frustrations experienced leads to two primary responses—aggression and compensating "achievement" in other areas of life, and to several secondary responses—regression, anxiety, and submission.

7. These emotional or behavioral responses have special effects on the ways in which the worker plays his familial roles. The variation in his action leads to adjustments in the various counterroles within the family. With time the role adjustments become moral expectations (e.g., Duvall, 1946).

8. These processes of thought and evidence help explain *varia-*

tions in family structure at difference class levels which the findings of other researchers and of this researcher reveal. Certain hypotheses about the structure of family behavior are supported, and in turn give support to the general "theory." Here are some of the basic findings in this area:

a. The socializing techniques used by parents of the lower class are more severe and aggressively tinged than at higher statuses, reflecting a family role response to the poverty of positive emotional sanctions and the frustrations and aggressions experienced by the parents themselves in the class system.

b. The father's role in various ways, especially in terms of the severity of socialization methods, is more highly associated with class than is the mother's. Thus, the mother is about as severe as the father at the upper levels but the father becomes increasingly more severe than the mother at the lower levels. This, it is reasoned, is the case because fathers are more exposed to the variability in resources received and aggression experienced.

c. Data from this study and other studies show that the father loses authority in the family at the lower levels as a consequence of his social and occupational inadequacy. In the upper levels of society the adequacy of the father in his extrafamilial occupation provides him with prestige and motivational resources that allow him to more frequently exercise benevolent authority.

d. The father's deprived social position in the lower levels of society also results in a greater general hostility toward and a reduced involvement in the emotional life of the adolescent son.

There is the assumption that variation in *type* of reward (e.g., power as opposed to esteem) brings, to some degree, variation in responses and different problems of adjustment. These different responses and needs lead to norms of a diverse nature. The special consequences of each type of reward are not spelled out, however.

e. There is also an assumption that many of the things said about status and the effects of status operate at different levels of social organization. That is, variation in the amounts of things desired will tend to bring about similar responses whether the status is one's position in the society-wide reward system (class), one's status among friends, or at work. (We even discussed some international processes as being akin to human action motivated by status). To provide a special test of this general perspective, details of the father's position in the structure of work were studied and predictions made about his probable family role response, holding general class constant. Generally, these findings show that fathers within the same occupational or prestige strata, who have in their work situations jobs providing more power, more satisfaction, more autonomy (as theoretically defined) tend to behave in predictable ways. Also, those fathers holding jobs which characteristically deal with areas higher in the hierarchy of symbolic systems of human action (cultural or business organization versus technological pursuits) tend to behave similarly. In all these types, fathers are less severe as socializers and are more likely to be emotionally supportive and involved in the boy's life.

We find then, holding general prestige or class constant, that lower status, of a very special sort, in the father's work acts as does lower society-wide status to produce similar family role responses.

9. These processes of thought and the evidence also help explain variations in the child's experiences in the family in different classes and their consequences.

    a. Class or status, its dependent conditions—the degree of frustration felt and the resources available—have certain familial consequences already shown: variation in severity of socialization, in the power of the parent over the child, and in the level of emotional support and warmth of the parent-child relationship. These, in turn, have important influences on patterns of identification with the two parents. As a father's severity increases, as his authority and emotional support for the son are reduced, the amount of identification with the father decreases and that with the mother increases. A decrease in the son's identifying with the father is particularly marked at the lower levels; perhaps for parallel reasons there is a problem for the upper-level daughter in her identification and relationship with the mother.

    b. These aspects of the family that correlate with status also have theoretically meaningful patterns of association with the level of adult occupation aspired to and the type of occupation expected. Upward mobility was maximized for the son when the socialization techniques were moderate, when parents shared authority, when the son identified with the father, and when the father was importantly involved in the boy's emotional life.

Occupations which are more human-oriented (expressive)

tend to be chosen more frequently than occupations which are traditionally defined as masculine (instrumental or technological) when the parental socialization is mild and when parents share the emotional and authority roles. It is suggested that mild socialization and a nontraditional role structure in the family maximizes the acceptance of "higher" areas of symbolic action (cultural versus technological) and their associated occupations. There also may be a lack of concern among these sons about ascriptively (or sexually) defined roles of behavior according to which women are concerned with the emotions of the family and men with the nonemotional and nonfamilial aspects of life.

10. These processes of thought and evidence also help explain the *interaction* between family status, family roles, the child's family experiences, and the emergence of subcultures in an industrial society.

    a. The variation in the amount of emotional resources available to families at different levels of socieity helps explain the power of the peer group and its cultural ways at the lower levels of society and the efficient induction of the child into adult culture at the upper levels.

    b. A detailed look at the absolute and relative positions of the male and female with regard to the distribution of sanctions in different classes provides a broad way of explaining some aspects of family life and sexual behavior. Variations in marriage rates, promiscuity, and homosexuality at different ages and at different levels of society are tentatively explained in terms of the resources available for socialization, the identification with each parental role that results, and the importance of the peer group as a means of socialization and an avenue of status. The peer group is especially important for the boy at the lower levels who seeks a masculine model, given the power of the mother and the inadequacy of the father. The psychological and social process of role compensation is also important here.

    c. Status, the psychological and role responses to it as it feeds through the family, the resulting socialized child, and the interaction between family structure, peer-group involvement, and general society are used to explain the *inception* of subcultures. It is recognized that these subcultures have been operating to some degree for generations but that the sustenance of traditions and the increasing differentiation of subcultures must also be explained.

11. This general orientation and certain special processes are

used to understand and analyze the location and development of subcultures in a society.

    a. Basic in understanding the emergence of subcultures is a recognition that each society has a dominant standard of evaluation and that this standard determines the placement at different levels of the society of individuals, possessing different amounts of the attributes specified by the standard. These two factors result in strata of modes of adjustment (or subcultures).

    b. One important process in the emergence of subcultures *in an achievement-oriented culture* is the emphasis on increasingly ascribed, parochial, and expressive roles as one moves down the class ladder. There is an increasing withdrawal from universalistic areas (disinterest in work, school, and perhaps political activity) where they are at a status disadvantage and an increasing involvement (role compensation) in these societally narrow areas of life where there is some possibility of gaining esteem in interaction with fellow men. They may look for eminence in their own religion, ethnic group, neighborhood, peer group, or sexual role. They may, of course, given their disesteemed position *in an achievement-dominated* society, develop heightened interest in more universalistic activity (e.g., politics) in order to bring about greater eminence of their ascriptively and expressively oriented philosophies. In political parlance such responses are usually called reactionary movements. This orientation also helps explain those social philosophies termed liberal or radical. Such individuals have exceptional status in achieved areas but low status in ascribed areas which they wish to deemphasize.

We have said earlier that failure in achieved roles leads to an emphasis on ascribed roles. There is a measure of unwarranted simplification in this bifurcation of the possible avenues of status. Though this simplification eases thinking about the matter and is in accord with traditional sociological usage, it might be better to realize that there are different kinds and degrees of ascriptiveness-to-achievedness. Thus, infantile and regressive-impulse-dominated eroticism may be the most given (ascriptive) and least achieved of all *social* roles. It is action which leads to gratification whatever the social object and regardless of the situation. For the average individual, roles and involvement in the *natal* family are probably next in the ascription-achievement scale, followed in order by roles and involvement in the peer group, heterosexual activity, the *marital* family, the occupation, and finally, the community. But one can readily see that in an individual case there might be significant changes in this ordering.

Earlier we talked of the functions of consumption in a highly productive and work-oriented society. Consumption or skillful styles of life may also become compensating responses for individuals who do not achieve.[2] The right amounts of the "right" goods and services may be the means to status and success. Thus "hip" (lower class), "sharp," "keen," or "nice" (lower middle or middle class), "elegant" (lower upper) and "tasteful" (upper upper) are suggestive of vocabularies (in American English) developed at different class levels to convey this interest and the relevant standards.

This does not, in this writer's view, vary so much from class to class (though a subjective impression indicates that it does develop special significance among the more expressively oriented ethnic groups of lower status—perhaps the Negroes, Italians, etc.). In fact, it may become a matter of greater concern at the upper levels of society where money and time allow the development and satisfaction of special tastes. Skillful consumption, as well as high production, requires work. One must keep informed and engage in purposeful and planned shopping.

12. It is finally suggested that some of the concepts developed concerning the motivations for status, for moral approval, and for esteem as they operate to influence the behavior and relations between classes and regional subcultures within a society, can be extended onto the intersocietal level. International relations then are seen as not simply the power struggles of morally isolated and autonomous units seeking non-social resources but are to some degree to the social interaction of members of a moral community, sensitive to the evaluations of other systems in the civilization. Many of their acts can be viewed as attempts to gain and maintain social approval and esteem. And even war has its proprieties.

ORIENTING MODES OF THOUGHT

Certain modes of thought have been particularly valuable intellectual tools in developing theoretical frameworks within which to interpret the data or for the development of meaningful hypotheses which could later be tested by the data. These may not always be evident to the reader and they are stated here, not as statements in the development of theory or of correct methodological procedure. They are not even on the level of codification of "intellectual

2. I am indebted to Kinje Ima for this criticism.

craftsmanship." They are more in the nature of helpful hints for the weary researcher.

I have found it helpful in attempting to explain my dependent variables, family behavior and subcultural development, to draw on not only sociology, psychology, and cultural concepts, but also to borrow, in a sufficiently abstract way, some of the orientations or analytical approaches of biology, economics, and history.

Biological Modes of Thought

From biology, I have tended to view society and various subcultures, much like life, as surviving *exploratory* organizations of behavior attempting to adjust to the social and nonsocial environment (Campbell, 1961). Given this view, society, and perhaps only in its Western form, develops in a particular cultural direction with its various levels (and individuals in those levels) more or less involved and socialized to the values indicated by that direction. Thus, ontogeny recapitulates philogeny but with varying degrees within a living system depending on the location of that particular unit in the system under study.

This rather Darwinian perspective also leads to a prediction of certain "degenerative" subcultures which will emerge to fill new ecological niches created in a changing and more highly differentiated (in terms of function and rank) society. This is much like the position held by some biologists that new "degenerative" forms of species arise in differentiating biotic communities. Perhaps I choose the term "degenerative" to communicate my explicit or implicit value judgments, but it is also the biological usage, and it suggests that society pays a price for its "higher" forms.

Psychosexuality and Social Structure

This biological cast is also reflected in a willingness to look at the interaction between biological variables (male versus female, or the demands for satisfaction on the somatic level, sexuality) as not mere givens in societal processes but as real causal variables and at the root of many variations, strains, and satisfactions within the social structure. The investigation of the relative status of *female* parents and *male* parents within supposedly the same prestige strata gives new clues to the development of male and female subcultures and the special ways in which they are brought together in the family in different classes (e.g., the relationship between spouses and between generations of the same and opposite sex).

A naturalist's perspective and a systematic view also regard the whole range of sexual behavior as within a general system of acts to satisfy somatic, psychological, and sociocultural needs. Many analysts of human behavior take a different approach. If the individual or group abides by the norms of family structure in Western society, then the behavior of that individual or group is analyzed within concepts of the family or personality development, or if the individual's or group's action is outside these norms (and there is a tendency to dichotomize and categorically place types of behavior and individuals) then the behavior is turned over to the behavior pathologist. However, these kinds of behavior and these individuals (the premaritally and postmaritally "promiscuous," the highly inhibited, the latently homosexual in varying degrees, and those individuals engaging in occasional or frequent homosexual acts) are too common to be cast out of our analysis of the normal processes of the family, the work group, dating habits, or society. We have tried instead to bring these norms and individuals into our analysis of the dynamics of the emotional structure of society. From this somatic perspective, the norms and expressions of psychosexuality are the emotional thread that holds society together on a very basic level. Man is a loving and a wanting-to-be-loved animal.

I do not believe this interest in the structural conditions channeling eros is peripheral to a study of social stratification or even society in its industrial form. This interest makes more understandable the essential condition which varies from the libidinally oriented lower class to the achievement-oriented and "responsible" upper middle class. It also reveals the dimension and problem which occupies the parent in his struggle with the willful child. Both the parent and the powerful instruments of the anerotic morality in a rationally coordinated society attempt to bring the spirit of play and love into line with the interests of work, long-range effort, and serious educational processes.

The agents of rationality do not necessarily try to crush play and eros, for that would probably have serious and disruptive consequences. Rather, they try to limit it to the private sphere of the family situation, where such motivations are *efficiently* satisfied for the adult and *efficiently* used in the socialization of a new and *productive* child.

This willingness to look at the structural aspects of eros also introduced some suggestive generalizations concerning Freudian and functional (e.g., K. Davis and B. Malinowski) concepts about the process and norms of psychosexuality in the family. For example, parallels in the family and the peer group as socializing groups suggested that there is probably a norm similar to the incest taboo of the family operating in the peer group for many of the same functional needs. In most societies the taboo against homosexuality serves the same function in the same sex peer group as the incest taboo serves in the family. It prevents the somewhat socially paralyzing erotic commitments to one group to the exclusion of the rest of society. This taboo also greatly restrains the expression of erotic needs which would be emotionally disruptive in the socialization process of the preadolescent and adolescent individual in the peer group. Such restraint, it is theorized, is also necessary in the family to prevent disruptive erotic ties.

Another taboo operates to the degree that the premarital peer group is heterosexual. This is the comparatively mild taboo against early love affairs and intimate sexual relations between individuals of opposite sex.

That these three taboos differ in strength may partially reflect the (1) importance attached to each group as a socializing instrument for society, and (2) the crucial necessity of freeing the individual from the more regressive and private (e.g., the family) and the reduced necessity of freeing him from the groups considered less regressive, more adult, and broader in scope (e.g., the heterosexual peer group).

This line of thought suggests that as a society becomes more achievement-oriented, more mobility-conscious (socially and geographically), the taboo against erotic expressions in the heterosexual peer group would increase. Society would act to reduce the competition of such emotional attachments with school, parental expectations and control, and free rational movement. Here the Kinsey report (1948, p. 411) provides very indirect evidence in conflict with either this line of thinking or with our position that America is becoming more work-oriented. That report shows that premarital heterosexual expression with companions (i.e., status and age peers rather than prostitutes) has increased in the last generation or two.

As a sociology-of-knowledge aside, the writer would suggest that the neglect of the level of biological structure and motivations, and the somewhat clinical and inhibited manner in which Freudian and psychosexual concepts have been introduced into an analysis of social structure, originate in the work-oriented antiascriptive (antibiological) and liberal cultural milieu surrounding the social scientist in American society.

It does appear to this writer that an understanding of the desires for love, for play, for some quasi-erotic communal attachments, and of the social structure of emotions and eros is a more basic concern for comprehension of the serious and playful aspects of life than is an understanding of the nature of bureaucracy, the nature of task-oriented groups, or the structure of the doctor-patient relationship. The former topics focus on the basic nature of social man and his emotional ties. The latter topics, however, typically deal with rather recent and perhaps temporary social conditions and structures. They are also the topics that increasingly occupy the efforts of human scientists, perhaps because they flourish on the money and prestige made available by the centers of power in American society. Or it may only be the fear of eros and the desire to be research-minded, to be empirical, to be "tough" (an adjustive norm among uncertain sociologists) and practical that lead to such pursuits (Shils, 1961, p. 1414).

This somewhat libidinal orientation to sociocultural problems generates a new perspective on the position of the family in the study of social structure in industrial societies. The antiascriptive bias, the "loss of function" orientation, the anerotic and intellectual climate, and the low state of theory in the area of the family—all present in contemporary sociology—lead to a relegation of the family to a rather unimportant and peripheral position in the development of theories of social organization. The position here would suggest that the family's position is fundamental and central. It is that diffuse biologically based social group where interaction between the diverse influences felt by the family's diversely placed members in a differentiated society takes place. It is also that intermediary which assists in communicating the influences among codified social structure, man's psyche, and man's diffuse biological past. It is perhaps this diffuseness and central position of the family that makes the development of a systematic theory difficult and the concepts of so many disciplines useful.

This central and intermediary position of the family has been used by this writer as a point of departure to make what he considers legitimate speculations and generalizations from this study's concepts and data to the field of sociocultural organization.

Orientations from Economics

What I have borrowed from economics and through Homans (1961) has been rather simple. I have on a number of occasions suggested that the individual personality can, by and large, only give out as it receives. Social life is an exchange of not only goods but emotional sanctions, and a position of high status means the receipt of large positive resources. The person of high status enjoys or has accumulated emotional "profit" which can be reinvested in the child to bring about socialization (or seduction) into the mode of life of the adult. The amount and kind of social and emotional resources available influence the product (i.e., the socialized child), just as in the economics of everyday business life. The family, as well as the personality, can only give out as it receives.

To understand much of what is going on in society, social analysts should look at the positions of members of various social categories (by age, sex, rural and urban, marital status, ethnic group, etc.) in the ecology or economy of the distribution and exchange of different kinds of emotional and social sanctions. This might tell us who can "buy" the support, allegiance, and love of other groups or individuals.

The Expressive-instrumental Dimension in Social Behavior and Historical Process

If the expressive-instrumental dimension is to have general utility in sociology and in the study of culture it must be stated in a way which is independent of exclusively psychological states or the individual's motivations. Analysts of human behavior should not define "expressive" or "instrumental" action by simple reference to the presence or absence (possibly postponement) of emotional gratification and consummatory states for the psyche. Instead, we should develop definitions that rest on systems and subsystems of various spheres of human action (e.g., the body, the culture, etc.) and the exchange of various sanctions between these systems.

The value of this dimension has been evident in this study on a number of occasions. It projects the meanings of Freud's pleasure and reality principles to the level of individuals or roles in social systems. There is some lack of clarity in its meaning, however, for it may remain too close to Freud; and though formally it is orthogonal to the internal-external dimension, actually it is defined and used (as I understand it) in a way which makes it not entirely independent of that dimension.

It seems to me that the term "expressive" (or "consummatory") has been variously used, or can be used, by General Action theorists to refer to (1) social action which is personally gratifying and emotionally satisfying (and sometimes impulsive) for the *psyche*, or (2) to action which is free from consciously precise and codified symbolic structure and increasingly regressive (in the sense of private) in nature. From the viewpoint of this second definition, expressive behavior at its "lower" levels moves out of the conscious psyche and into unconscious somatic processes. From this view death is perhaps the most expressive of all acts of life forms (Brown, 1959, p. 133) and is the least aware of "reality."[3] Or it may (especially when the term "consummatory" is used, rather than "expressive"—see Chap. 6 and Parsons, 1959) refer to (3) the consumption of resources (or sanctions) *within* a system rather than to an exchange of resources between the system under study and outside systems.

The third definition brings in several additional considerations: (*a*) the dimension is now related rather closely to the internal-external dimension or categories, but it refers to process (the exchange of sanctions) rather than to categorical structure (perhaps the internal and external categories). (*b*) If this statement of the meaning of instrumental and consummatory has some validity, then General Action theorists must define and communicate more explicitly that acts which are *socially* instrumental are exchanges with rather distant systems which may be either more "progressive" and symbolically developed (e.g., the science of politics) or more regressive, unconscious, and biophysical in nature (the act of sleep, or the psychosomatic orgasm). That is, any system being studied must instrumentally orient itself and communicate with two types of reality: an encompassing superordinate reality and an encapsulated subordinate reality. This dimension and recognition of different environments is seen occasionally among physiologists, for on the somatic level, the human body must relate itself not only to the laws of physiology (its own rules of action) but also to (1) the laws of the bisocial community (superordinate reality) and (2) the laws of biophysics (subordinate reality). (*c*) The fact that systems exist (persist and change) in time suggests that they communicate with another order of environments: they in some sense communicate with their encapsulated pasts (the id in Freud's theory of the personality) and their encompassing and future environments (the superego in Freud's theory). These "external" environments do not seem to be clearly introduced in the General Theory of Action.

---

3. Freud's definition of reality sometimes has a conscious rationalistic or individual personality bias. There are other levels of behavior (culture or the body) in which forms of behavior appear (e.g., political rituals or death) that are attuned to reality (e.g., the realistic demands of the state of the system *at that time*) even though they may seem irrational to the observer using rules of intellectual behavior (logic and science) passed through generations of Western scholars and the value prisms of their subculture (Warner, 1959, pp. 491-506).

It may be Parsons' failure to introduce with explicit strength the dimension of time into his theoretical statement of the structure and processes of human society that creates a concern among many analysts of human behavior. This failure creates a special uneasiness among certain future-oriented and historical and conflict-conscious social theorists (often with some Marxian orientation) who feel that Parsons is "static" and an apologist for the "status quo." This may produce special concern among them because Marxian theory says, to grossly simplify, that history consists in a tug-of-war between the traditional thesis (social needs of an *id* nature) and the "progressive" antithesis (new ideals parallel to the superego), producing some integrating and even newer synthesis (the rational and integrating ego).

With these considerations in mind, the writer would propose that "expressive" ("consummatory") and "instrumental" are matters of degree. Those situations which are increasingly consummatory or expressive are those in which sanctions are exchanged within increasingly narrow units (or systems) and within increasingly narrow spans of time. Those situations which are socially instrumental are those in which sanctions are exchanged within increasingly broad spans of social organization and within increasingly broad spans of time (postponement of gratification). Instrumental actions are apt to be more highly "symbolic" (in the specific sense in which this word is usually used) as a consequence of the broad range of time and social space encompassed within its endeavor (e.g., modern society). This requires highly symbolic and efficient means of exchanging information and sanctions between quite "distant" and differentiated subsystems.

Of course, all human action is on some level symbolic (neural impulses, a touch of the hand, an interpersonal push and its physiologically communicated consequences for the psyche and the soma), but acts often occur below the level of consciousness or have become so traditional as to operate implicitly. For this reason they are often expressive at the social level.

Despite this critical evaluation, it is this particular consummatory-instrumental dimension (of social acts) and the way it is related to the family and its sex roles (Parsons, 1955), to occupational levels (Parsons, 1959 and Roe, 1956), and to the specialized areas of life that are the concern of special systems of human action and social institutions (Parsons et al., 1961) that led the author into certain pursuits, hypotheses, and interpretations of data. For these I am highly indebted to the general approach of Parsons in ways that are not always explicit in the writing.

The lack of explicit organization of the problem in concepts and terms of the theory of action is true partially because Parsons' contributions are sometimes difficult to understand and they are not evident until one realizes that he has been using them. It is also true because Parsons' approach tends more to be suggestive of modes of attack or thought about a problem than to be specifically operationable. And finally, I have not seen this work as a test of Parsons but rather as the investigation of a particular area of social behavior.

This salience of the consummatory-instrumental dimension led to a particular analysis of the pattern of exchange of sanctions between the husband and wife. It also suggested that certain variables were central in our investigation. Thus, we studied the degree of emotional support as a manifestation of the consummatory realm and the nature of authority in the family as a part of instrumental action.

The interest in the consummatory-instrumental dimension also led to: (1) an investigation of the relationship between family experiences and the type of occupational choice ordered along something of a consummatory-instrumental dimension, and to (2) a brief discussion of kinds of status, peer-group involvement, and family experiences that might be related to particular political philosophies. We were even willing to look at national cultures as specialized in certain endeavors ranging along this same dimension and therefore interdependent subunits within a civilization.

As we stated earlier, it appears that Western society within the last 1000 or 2000 years has been moving in a particular direction. Many analysts have found this particular trend—and I do not suggest that any crucial evidence is presented in this study to support that view. Society is moving from a decreasing focus on the ascriptive-expressive realm and an increasing emphasis on achieved roles and instrumental action (symbolic action focused on the external physical and cultural environment which postpones the gratifications of the internal system, man's biosocial core). These trends seem particularly true of the emphasized norms of behavior in at least the public realm of social life.

This particular view of social change (from expressive and ascribed to instrumental and liberal) has the "smell" of evolution and ethnocentric optimism to some and is thoroughly rejected, sometimes for rather emotional reasons. This evolutionary view seems to connote for them not only change but an assumption of progress. But *whose* progress? To see this direction of change is not to assume that the theorist finds it good. In fact, this research has attempted to show some of the difficult social conditions it creates.

There is also the assumption that this evolutionary approach implies an irreversible and unilinear line of development. Not even biological theories of evolution say that. Here we probably should also be more historically aware and consider the long story of man and his variability. To say that specialization and rational integration has been the general trend in the last 2000 years is not to say that there have not been variations and movements back into the more consummatory or perhaps regressive modes (Romanticism, the Middle Ages, and modern Fascism). And to say that it has been true for the last several thousand years of that small phase of man's life fanning out from the Near East, Greece, Rome, and Western Europe is not to say that it has been, is, or will be man's be-all and end-all.

From this perspective, those individuals who object to such statements about such general trends are often individuals who are overly focused on the recent past and modern trends as the inevitable cast of man's fate. To accept as reasonably evident certain directions of development (which may be in conflict with their values) predetermines man's future in a manner which they dislike. Historical detachment indicates, however, that very fundamental conditions from a contemporary view (e.g., the modern position of the Southern Negro, the social position of the Victorian woman as seen in that age or even the long ascendance of rationality) may be but temporary conditions and small entries in the development of man.

Historical Process, Cultural Change, and the Interaction of Generations

This historical perspective might well be given added emphasis in sociological analysis (Shils, 1961) and especially in the analysis of class and family behavior. Schumpeter (1955), for example, indicates how mobility, power, and prestige in a society are not simply the consequences of a particular cultural theme (e.g., equal opportunity) and the works of the individual but can result from the organized (and disorganized) efforts and goals of family lines and class groups through several centuries. Our cultural climate of individualism and achievement and the scientist's frequent separation from his family's past do not predispose modern sociology to such outlooks and investigations.

Social change or the history of a society, however much easier they are to investigate and however much more they may be structured by broad societal and world events, are in a very deep and covert way the interaction of the strands of generations within families and within the society. A particularly fruitful beginning for such an approach might be an analysis of the dominant culture, the arrangement of subcultures, and the influence of these conditions on the emotional patterns within and between generations whose members are of the same and opposite sex. From a knowledge of these facts some idea of the new generation's values and cultural inclinations in different parts of the society might be anticipated. Basic variations of this sort in a society would then result in particular kinds of children of the new generation, variations in the motivations for power among the offspring in different segments of society, the recruitment or lack of circulation of elites, and the possible emergence of a new subculture as the dominant ethos of the society. As there develop new elites with new issue, the process of the maintenance of power and esteem *or* the loss to new elites begins all over again in the still newer generation. In this way cultural stability or change takes place.

The recruitment of not only new elites but also new criminals, new groups of "ordinary folks," new psychotics, new maritally well adjusted, new familially uninvolved, and new revolutionaries takes place not in the interaction of just two generations (parent and child). It is a consequence of emotional climates, resources, and values which are passed through several generations in exaggerated or modified form. Society recreates itself and modifies itself through the emotional prism of the interlinking of chains of family life. In this way social stability or change takes place.

From this view, the family acts somewhat as genetic structures (and their special combinations through generations of conception) act to recreate and modify the biological form of the species. If certain spouses with certain social pasts and motivational structures (parallels of the biological pasts and genetic structures) marry and live in a particular social environment, then certain traits may result in increasingly exaggerated form. Such traits may get ruled out as "submissive" if others marry as spouses and create other genetic combinations in the emotional structure of the new marital family. For example, the familial and intergenerational processes operating by the time one is the youngest daughter of the youngest daughter of the youngest daughter may be so strong that one can predict with high probability that such an individual will be a rather self-centered, self-loving, and oft-married woman unwilling to enter the role of mother. In this way society insures the not too frequent recreation of certain motivational extremes.

This view would allow us to look at the emotional "cadets," "princes," and "kings" of the family line and study their dominant patterns of behavior in the family and outside. A genetics of the psychosocial life of family lines as well as its biological life seems possible.

The Components of Class and Their Influence

Probably no variable or measure developed in sociology is as predictive of so many phenomena as is social class. Yet within each social class are included many kinds of life chances and social experiences. The data and theoretical development here indicate a strong need for an analysis of these basic types of experiences (and their interrelationship) and their specific effect on human behavior. Not only will this allow more accurate indices but it will also give greater understanding of the structure and functioning of society. The writer has tended to focus on the amount of rewards received and their consequences. This distribution may be the basic element in class or stratification. We have, however, tried to look specifically at several kinds of rewards and study their particular influence. Our discussion of autonomy gives a somewhat different and more detailed knowledge than do most analyses of the influence of status. The discussion of esteem gave a different perspective on the relationship between that kind of reward and behavior at different status levels.

Rewards, however, are not the only differential experiences at different levels of society. People have different *kinds* of roles at different levels (e.g., Parsons' technical or primary-type roles versus managerial roles). One individual may have a role whose range of social responsibility, focus of interest, and breadth of social information is rather narrow (e.g., a welder or a surgeon). Another may have a role which has broad social significance and must draw on information from diverse areas of society (a mayor). These individuals may have very different or approximately the same social status (as generally measured) but still occupy different life situations. This variation in breadth and the way in which people are interacted with in the role will influence attitudes, behavior, and values. We saw that this was true in the discussion of the type of occupation and its relationship to the parental role. That discussion also attempted a theoretical explanation for this relationship which was in some respects independent of our explanation of the effect of social status as usually defined.

This discussion and the analysis of types of occupations at different class levels also showed that there is an interdependence between type of role and class level. For example, technological occupations are disproportionately of lower status. The analysis also showed that the type of role may be as predictive of behavior as the amount of rewards received in a particular class. Not only may type of occupation be as predictive as class, but its association with class level may contribute much to the latter's apparent predictive power.

The point being made is this. Class or social stratification is not a single vertical continuum of rewards. Contributing to its predictive power and intertwined with it is a structure of organized levels of control, different kinds of social roles involved in society in different ways and to different degrees.

The Interplay of Statuses

In discussions of social class and human behavior there is this tendency to view status as a kind of unitary dimension. However, the individual is motivated not just to gain high status as it is defined in socioeconomic indices. These focus on certain specific achieved statuses such as occupation and education. Individuals (and classes) to varying degrees want approval in such roles as "a servant of the people," a "cultivated person," a "devout person," a "good wife," a "real man," or a wit. Some of these desires are present in all and compete with the achieved statuses for the individual's attention. What the individual or group will focus on depends on physical attributes, emotional experiences, the demands and norms of society, and personal or group decisions. Subcultures arise out of such interacting conditions.[4]

It seems that the status one holds in these neglected behavior systems (e.g., how *physically* appealing is this girl or this group?) might be as predictive in various areas as are such matters as the level of intelligence or the class level (Jones and Bayley, 1950). The neglect of such statuses (though race is an exception) in so-

---

4. For a discussion of the political response of individuals with inconsistent statuses (both achieved and ascribed) see Gerhard E. Lenski, "Status Crystallization: A Non-Vertical Dimension of Social Status," *American Sociological Review*, August, 1954, pp. 405-413.

ciology and to some degree in academic psychology, may result from an achievement bias.

The Interplay of Social Status and Personality

The writer has frequently drawn on psychological concepts. In discussing certain behavior at different status levels we often found parallels between our statements and the dimensions of the authoritarian personality. It is recognized that certain types of personalities sift and move into various classes, but we do not consider the norms of behavior at different levels as simply variations in the personalities of class members writ large. From a social structural perspective it seems more likely that the structure of power, distribution of autonomy, and demands for routinized behavior create the authoritatian subculture in various segments of the society. The definition given of autonomy contains societal dimensions which, when introjected into the personality, define the degree of the individual's "authoritarianism." Chart 3 indicates the parallel conditions that define lack of autonomy and authoritarianism.

Chart 3

Social Structure (Low Autonomy)	Personality Structure (Authoritarianism)
1. High specification of behavior and sanctions [focus on traditionalized modes of behavior and traditional (ascriptive) roles]	1. Rigidity in Behavior—rigid and severe sanctioning of "slight" deviations from conventions
2. Strong external control over individual from higher status positions	2. Hierarchical authority structure expected and acted out
3. External control, high specification, leads to greater frustration and externally expressed aggression (perhaps combined with status-compensating focus on ascriptive in-group)	3. Focus on in-group and hostility to those in ascriptively defined out-groups

In contrast to the picture presented in the chart, the individual in highly autonomous roles is expected to move in fluid social situations, using resources flexibly and exercising individual responsibility. There is a deemphasis of traditional specifications of behavior (the ascriptive sexual dichotomy). Similarly, the nonauthoritarian personality responds flexibly in social situations, is accepting of deviations from conventions and of *ascriptively* defined out-groups, tends to avoid strongly organized authority situations, and seeks self-responsibility.

It should be emphasized again that though the authoritarian personality may seek low-autonomy situations, it is felt that low-autonomy situations generate authoritarian personalities and high-autonomy situations generate the opposite. It may be a requirement of a differentiated and coordinated social system that certain policy-making and powerful roles be flexibly and autonomously defined. If this coordination is to operate successfully there may be a social-system demand that lower-status roles (e.g., enlisted men do not think, they obey) be relatively inflexibly defined and strongly controlled by others. Even though these conditions are necessities of the system and not necessarily motivated by desires of the powerful for emotional exploitation, they may have certain inevitable consequences for human behavior, such as the hostility produced in low-autonomy environments. On frequent occasions throughout this work we have tried to outline these consequences.

The Arena of Emotions
in an Anerotic Culture

Frequently it has appeared to this writer that the contemporary human scientist, when he has tried to analyze the more intimate and "regressive" spheres of life, has been caught and guided by his own rational and universalistic orientation. What is functional for the family, what is mature family behavior and sexual behavior, what is the mature personality seems very close to what serves and is efficient for a work-dominated society. The social scientist's orientation does not seem to be dominated by the values of the status quo (usually defined as the values of the business community); the social scientist is too sophisticated and alienated from those values for that to occur. Rather, it is the values which he shares with the conservative as a member of a rationally organized and achieving society that seem to obfuscate his analysis of the meaning of play, love, sexuality, strong loyalties, popular art (pornography and popular fads), and even instrumental acts.

How is such action, especially in its more "deviant," aggressive, and emotional forms in the lower classes, to be understood? The social scientist is apt to solve this problem by placing such actions in the category of crime or social problems and turning again to an analysis of the organization of the conforming norms and behavior. They are, however, in any absolute sense no more nor less social problems than are urban renewal, the demands for increasing attention to education, and the demands of work and of sexual morality—problems for the less achieving segments of a society's population.

This fusion of emotionality and deviance is not, as we are apt to feel in our rationally and psychoanalytically dominated society, inevitable. It appears rather to come about as a consequence of the distribution of social resources and of the dominant values of our society. It is a society which tends to deemphasize emotionality, intense ascriptive loyalties, sexuality, communal solidarity, and dramatic and artistic expression of traditional ideals. Individuals who manifest these may get some esteem in our society, but it is recognized that first-rate approval and reward go to those who act efficiently, justly, and briskly to bring about solutions to presented problems.

It is these briskly rational individuals and their activities which become the focus of the entire society. Social resources (e.g., esteem, money, etc.) are invested to bring about greater conformity to norms for increasingly efficient behavior. If our reasoning has been correct, it is also the conforming individuals who therefore have the emotional resources to socialize their children in their own image. The child becomes as an adult an individual who will also accept the importance of rationality, efficiency, and mastery over the world about him. He also has had a reasonably pleasant family life and this should provide for the development of motivations to carry out adequately his own family responsibility. It is very likely, however, that the parent in creating in his child the ideal of rationality and adaptive mastery over the external world, undermines or inhibits the development of the strong flow of normatively organized and spontaneous inner emotions which lie behind that range of behavior we call psychologically expressive. This includes religious faith, art, the art of play, love, passion, and awe at the baffling mystery of the cosmos and man's inner being. These can be brought into social enhancement and cultural fruition by normative organization and social concern just as industrialization, science, and other instrumental-universalistic activities have prospered given our ethic of productivity. The enhancement of expressive action is done with moving and gratifying results in some cultures (perhaps classical Greece or contemporary Italy).

This expressive area also includes many aspects of the family. At the rationalistic levels of society the family is much better organized and stable from all external appearances (e.g., divorce rate, number of husbands poisoned or wives beaten) but it appears to proceed through life with a relatively pleasant and untroubling lack of commitment by both spouses and children when other duties arise. It can hardly be otherwise, given our procedures of socialization (thoughtfully professional) and the commitment of family members to PTA, occupation, conventions in other towns, scout work, school, summer camp, etc.

Meanwhile, down in the lower levels of society where the id rears its head in social forms, its expressiveness is combined with an undue amount of discord and absence of normative organization. This forms what is thought to be an inevitable and unlovely syndrome of ascriptive loyalties-expressiveness-aggression. It is perhaps not surprising that interpersonal expressiveness (parades, strong interpersonal bonds outside marriage, art in its more seductive forms) carries a bad reputation and suffers disesteem.

It is possible that the analyst "finds" anomie in social groups which live by well-organized norms but norms which the analyst happens not to like. Empirical rates indicate, however, that anomie does vary in the family as a consequence of its status in the society and perhaps for reasons discussed throughout this work. Those occupationally inadequate social groups who turn to the ascriptive-expressive-aggressive modes of life as compensating adjustments to their status in a work-focused society and to the subtle aggression they receive, are also the parents who find themselves with few material or emotional resources with which to train the child. The result is a heightened difficulty in socializing the child into the traditional norms of the parent generation in both the expressive and instrumental realm. This greatly weakened hold of the parent generation and of its traditions over the child *and* the child's compensation in expressive behavior help explain the intense fads that fleetly move through working-class adolescent subcultures. Such "nonsense" probably did not occur down on the farm where the family's high functionality and relatively undeprived position fostered the parent's traditions and their ability to hold the child normatively. The greatly weakened ability of the urban proletariat's parent generation to give expressive order may also explain the intense and fleeting emotional and sexual involvements and the lack of emotional order (high rates of psychological problems and mental illness) among their adolescents. In adulthood, this normative and emotional disorder of the psychosexual realm is reflected in adult sexual deviation from the dominating ideal and in family discord.

It is not surprising that American society is worried about "What should be done with our families?" Even at the upper level, divorce rates are high and a cool pleasantness prevails (compared with the intense involvements of a family-oriented society like Lebanon) born of our dominant ideal of rational achievement and mobility. In the urban lower classes, discord, instability, and aggression seem much more common than in rural areas of traditionally organized social orders. These are perhaps predictable consequences of an anerotic society. It is a culture which is in conflict with the needs of the individual as he leaves the completely biological realm and is guided through the psychosocial realm. It is a culture that is also in important conflict with the functioning requisites of the intimate social group that provides support during these transitions, the family.

A FINAL PERSPECTIVE

Anthropologists have institutionalized a method of decreasing cultural bias. Field work and the life experienced there on an emotional and immediate level weaken certain "natural" modes of thought derived from Western society and the anthropologist's own scientific subculture. Though some comparative work has been done, the typical American sociologist has not created a similarly institutionalized corrective. Perhaps because he feels it unnecessary. He is, after all, analyzing American or Western society which he knows as a member. But the sociologist's (and also the psychologist's) origins (preponderantly Protestant and Jewish of the lower middle class and upper middle class) and also his present position mean that he is a participating member of only a small part of the society. This creates a moral and intellectual interpretation of social phenomena that is probably not really corrected by reading, for example, Whyte's *Street Corner Society*. In the writer's opinion some equivalent to the anthropologist's field work should be a rather general expectation. The sociologist should not merely interview but should engage in immediate and prolonged participant observation, or simply live in some alien segment of his own society or some other society.

A Functional Equivalent
of Ethnocentrism

Without the kinds of experience discussed in the previous section, it appears likely that the analyst of human behavior may fall victim to a kind of class or intellectual parochialism. This parochial view often manifests itself in the academic community by a condemnation and rejection (as ignorant, primitive, and *unjust*) of values and behavior which are not in accord with a kind of utilitarian liberalism where rationality, free choice, individual planning, and tolerance (of a particular kind) play dominating roles. This parochialism also influences his choice and the manner of analysis of some fields (e.g., the topic of religion or minority groups).

Not only are the modes of life of nonprofessionals and other classes rejected with some lack of sympathy, but the values and modes of analysis of other disciplines are rejected with some hostility. This is not usually thought to have a parallel to the narrow bigotry characteristic of the intolerant out-group. Instead, such action and hostility are justified and expressed in the interest of "correct" scientific or intellectual procedure. These personal attitudes and professional ideologies, however, seem to be the functional equivalents of ethnocentrism on both an individual and professional group level.

In sociology, this parochialism or ethnocentrism, if you like, shows itself in a rather hostile rejection of certain biological concepts (society as an organic system in even a very general way or in evolutionary principles of change), of the use of psychological principles (the fear of reductionism), and critical stereotypes of cultural anthropologists. They are considered romantic escapists who may escape modern culture but who do not escape their own private intuitions. Special criticism is directed toward those who attempt to find very general patterns. The humanities are almost beneath contempt in the view of certain positivists.

I do not mean to say that sociology is alone guilty of this narrow "nationalism" (or that I am entirely free of guilt and not susceptible to a similar analysis). Some of the more critical views of *cultural* anthropologists come from their fellow anthropologists. Similarly, some psychologists of the more experimental and behavioristic bent almost read out of scientific respectability the intellectual efforts of the personality theorists and researchers. The clinical psychologist in turn has certain protective conceptions of experimental and physiological psychologists (e.g., "Are they really *psych*ologists?").

Perhaps as sociologists we should recognize the development of these intimate loyalties and the rejection of others as an inevitable consequence of the development of a professional community. That is, each nation, ethnic group, social class and professional group develops certain explanations of the world which enhance their own status and protect their own vanity. Most groups, not being primarily committed to "truth," can accept this old principle of social life without their own reputation and self-esteem suffering too greatly. The intellectual community is, however, committed to some concept of the truth which makes such protective theories narrow definitions of virtue and truth, inappropriate in terms of its own norms.

Perhaps as intellectuals and as scientists we should engage in some intellectual irredentism and regain the breadth of thought of earlier analysts of the social scene.

The Liberal Ethic and Modern Society

"The slums always seek their revenge."
CARL SANDBURG

The moral of this story is rather simple. It says that perhaps Marx was, in part, right. Exploitation does lead to alienation and rebellious counteraggression. His focus on exploitation was, however, too narrowly economic, and his predicted aggressive counter-response, too narrowly political. Perhaps more importantly, the exploitation in a highly industrialized and differentiated society is of an emotional and moral nature and the alienated and aggressive response is of a like kind—family disorganization, crime, and political apathy.

This is not an especially common view, even in the field of social stratification. Studies and statistics are often cited to show how universal education, a narrowing range of income, and an increasing living wage are ushering in the abundant and equalitarian life. That these should be taken as rather convincing evidence of such a grand new era may only reflect our achievement and money orientation. Such data do not look behind the life experiences of an emotional and communal nature that make such decreased class variation and increased achievement in some areas possible. If economic and educational rewards are becoming less variable, and there is even some question here (Mills, 1959, pp. 147-170), social approval and moral evaluation for individuals in different occupational strata of our society are becoming more variable.

Why should this be so? It seems likely that as society becomes more highly differentiated and complex, it requires, in turn, a greater range of power and prestige in various positions to bring about the reintegration of these specialized activities. There must be increasingly powerful and prestigeful positions to bring about control over an increasingly broad scale of social organization. And within these broad organizations are roles of decreasing autonomy and probably decreasing prestige.

That these increases in the range of status in life are not reflected in objective indexes means only that not all of life's rewards or significance can be tied to the amount of money one has at his command or the years of cultural enlightenment in his past (mean years of education).

If the new rationally organized society and its attendant liberal morality ushers in the "abundant" life economically for nearly all (and it is generally agreed that this is an economic necessity and not compassionate humanitarianism) and emotionally for the fortunate few, it must be understood what price our society pays as a whole.

Marx, fervent revolutionary that he was, saw part of the price in these revealing and perhaps exaggerated characterizations of modern industrial society:

> The bourgeoisie, wherever it has got the upper hand, has put an end to all feudal, patriarchal, idyllic relations. It has pitilessly torn asunder the motley feudal ties that bound man to his "natural superiors," and has left remaining no other nexus between man and man than naked self-interest, than callous "cash payment." It has drowned the most heavenly ecstasies of religious fervour, of chivalrous enthusiasm, of Philistine sentimentalism in the icy water of egotistical calculation. It has resolved personal worth into exchange value, and in place of the numberless indefeasible chartered freedoms, has set up that single, unconscionable freedom—Free Trade. In one word, for exploitation, veiled by religious and political illusions, it has substituted naked, shameless, direct, brutal exploitation. (1959, pp. 9-10.)

It is the price of a loss of social drama, of emotionally meaningful ties and traditions, of even the illusion of social love, and of a sense of moral solidarity. There results a drabness in social ties, an anxiety about self-identity, and emotional privatism. This price is emotional privacy or isolation among the fortunate at best (for this has some creative and gratifying consequences) and murderous and revengeful crime among the most exploited (the urban Negro in industrial America).

Crime consists of a double tragedy. Perhaps the greater horror is experienced not by the victim but by the criminal himself. Behind each brutally aggressive crime must lie gross deprivation of feelings of worth and a grave lack of love and the ability to value other individuals.

Though we can, as a pragmatic method of social control, hold the individual morally responsible, we can no longer "blame" him from a scientific position, this is now recognized. Psychiatric and even popular literature now find the family or the class-defined neighborhood to be the *bête noire*. We have shown, however, that the family roles and family's members are to an important degree the products of the operation of the entire society, especially the family position in the reward structure of a society concerned with achievement. It is this system of moral evaluation which produces the creative excellence and the brutal deviance within a work-dominated society.

Though the liberal may be quite concerned that certain *rational* and ameliorative actions be taken to cushion failure, such as minimum wages, social work, and rehabilitative therapy for the criminal and ill, to the degree that liberal and conservative elements support this achieving ideology they participate in the resentful deprivation of the disesteemed and murderous elements of a society. "We are all murderers?"

America is a functioning and emotionally rewarding society for many. There can be little doubt of that. There are nonetheless deep problems and strong alienations, far beyond common concern, which will not necessarily be solved by strengthening the virtues of equal opportunity for all (liberal justice) and its ideological partner, individual initiative. Lack of opportunity to succeed occupationally and individual sloth are not the only evils in society. The lack of purpose and the lack of social love and approval are perhaps even more strongly felt deprivations in our very secular and impersonal society.

Much of the stress and emptiness of American life perhaps results from the prevailing preoccupation with the privacy of family life. Even more important may be the preoccupation with work and its institutional companion and aid, education.

Man is not, however, just a "family man" and an "economic man." He is a social or political man and many of his most gratifying experiences can be found outside the institutions emphasized in American society. They are found in organized and spontaneous communal life with its heterogeneous and binding emotional experiences and roles. This is still possible in the small towns of rural America, among enclaves of ethnics within American cities, and to some degree among the esteemed and civic-minded in the urban community. But our urban and industrial social organization dooms many to the office or factory, to the home, and to a strange and rather fluid society outside.

Specialized and segmental investments are possible here and

there (e.g., the Knights of Columbus or the steady date) but they are clutched with a kind of compulsiveness sustained by a fragmentation of the social soul—the community. And it is sustained by the fragmentation of the community internalized in the personality, great status anxiety.

If we are to avoid some of the distressing conditions in modern society we must institutionalize and place in cultural preeminence the compassionate concern for others. For aggression and rational exploitation beget aggression and irrational assault. The slums do seek their revenge.

Values and Rational Analysis

Each family, group, profession, and nation then has its own values which provide, from a naturalist's view, a legitimate mode of adjustment to the cruelties and gratifications of life and society. If this is true, sociologists as progressive intellectuals should be engaged less in finding out what is "wrong" with juvenile delinquents, the McCarthyites, Fascists, and the capitalists, and engaged more in understanding what it is about our supposedly just (universalistic), free, and rational society that is seen as so depriving. These very conditions which are virtues and assets for the intellectual community are probably just those that deny the often reasonable needs of certain traditionally minded groups.

This is a position in considerable conflict with the social role that the liberal usually defines for himself. He usually regards his values and actions as those which will save the proletariat from the exploiting business interests in society or will even save the proletariat from himself. The values and interests of the liberal may be near realization as the dominant values in our society and as such the ruling values of the new era. In this new era the organizational specialist, the academic, and the "liberal" *may be* the new exploiting elite and should be subject to the same analysis Marx applied to the capitalist of another day.

America and industrial societies tend to be dominated to a greater degree by the "reality principle." This has certain advantages, for it allows for detailed knowledge of the environment and foresightful control over it and over oneself (in some areas). Not only does the reality principle do this but it allows sufficient accumulation of resources so that *at certain times* the individual can relax and obtain some aesthetic gratification. The degree to which the individual can differentiate these roles is a problem, and the degree to which he can achieve some over-all satisfying personal integration of these two roles is another problem. Some difficulties may arise in such a society in creating a general cultural climate that will allow for the cultivation of the world of emotions. There may develop an aesthetic poverty that manifests itself on the individual level and on the community or social level.

It appears that each era, society, social class, and individual solves this instrumental-gratificatory dilemma by a choice at different points on the continuum. Each choice has consequences which create particular tensions and certain gratifying rewards in life.

The Questionnaire[1]

This is part of a survey of students and their families in the Boston area. Some of the questions ask for facts about yourself and your family. Some questions ask about your father's work. *All of the information will be held strictly confidential*, so please answer the questions as accurately as you can. Absolutely no one will see the answers except one or two people at Harvard who are doing the study.

This questionnaire is not as long as it appears and all the questions we ask we believe are important. For this reason we would like you to answer each question as carefully and accurately as you are able. It is very important for our study that you do this seriously.

For some questions we have listed several possible answers and you can just put a check (✔) in front of the one that comes closest to your feelings or answer. Be sure to read all the alternatives and choose the best one. Please use pencil and erase if you have to.

We hope you will be able to finish, so work carefully but do not spend too much time on any one question. Please do not discuss the questions or your answers with anyone while you are working. If the meaning of a question really puzzles you, just raise your hand and I will help you.

In order that the study be successful, your serious cooperation is very important. Thank you.

If you like, you may give your name. If you prefer, feel free *not* to give your name.

---

1. The questionnaire here is not in the exact form in which it was presented to the subject: alternatives occasionally are omitted and space provided the respondent for answers has been omitted. A few questions (75, 76, and 77) were not used in the final analysis and presentation of data.

NAME ——————————————————————— (Please print)

1. Your age at your last birthday?
2. What program are you enrolled in?
 1. ——— Commercial
 2. ——— Scientific (College)
 3. ——— General
 4. ——— Classical (College)

NOTE: If you are not now living with both your parents, please answer the questions in this survey in terms of the people you do live with.

3. Is either of your parents a step-parent?
 1. ——— Yes, mother
 2. ——— Yes, father
 3. ——— Yes, both
 4. ——— No, neither
4. What is your mother's age?
5. What is your father's age?
6. Does anyone besides your parents and brothers and sisters live with you?
 1. YES. Who? ———————————————, ——————————————
 · 2. No.
7. How many sisters do you have? ———
8. Are your sister(s): (1) Older than you ——— ? (2) Younger than you ——— ? (3) Some older and some younger ——— ? (4) No sisters ——— .
9. How many brothers do you have? ———
10. Are your brother(s): (as in question 8)
11. Circle the number that shows the last year of school your *father* completed.
 Grade school: 1 2 3 4 5 6 7 8
 High school: 9 10 11 12
 Beyond high school: 1 2 3 4 5 6 or more
 Nature of school(s) attended beyond high school?
12. Circle the number that shows the last year of school your *mother* completed. (alternatives as question 11)
13. a. Where did your *father* live most of the time when he was growing up?
 b. Where did your *mother* live most of the time when she was growing up?

Now we want to talk about one of the jobs your father has held in the past 10 or 12 years but we want to pick the one that your father has held the longest or the one that is most typical of your father's work. In picking the one, follow these rules:

1. If your father has held his present job for *3 years or* more you can go directly to question 14 and answer the following questions in terms of his present job.
2. If your father has held his present job at least one or two years and it is *very* similar and typical of the work he has usually done during his life then go directly to question 14 and answer the following questions in terms of his present job.
3. If he has held his present job less than one year or if the job he now holds is not typical of the work he has usually done then raise your hand and we will discuss which job you should choose in order to answer the rest of the questions.

NOTE: In describing your father's job remember that we want to understand what kind of job he has and we will be completely in the dark unless you describe it well. *Please* don't use general terms if you can help it. Be as specific and detailed as you can be.

14. How long has your father held this job? .
    From ——, ——to——, ——.
         Mo. Year Mo. Year
15. In what kind of firm or organization does your father work (if it is a store tell us what kind of store, if it is a factory tell what they make, etc.)?
    Its location? (city or town) ————————————
16. Does your father:
    1. —— work for a company owned by others?
    2. —— work for city, state, or federal government?
    3. —— own his own business (or have a partnership)?
    4. —— do professional work (like doctor or lawyer) by himself or in partnership?
    5. —— OTHER. (What? ——————————)
    6. —— Father does not work.
17. About how many people work in the place (company, store, organization) where your father works?
    1. —— less than 10
    2. —— 10– 29
    3. —— 30– 99
    4. —— 100–499
    5. —— Over 500
    6. —— I don't know at all
18. What is the name or title of his job? ————————————
19. Just what is his work? Please explain very carefully. For example, don't just say he runs a machine if he does, but tell what kind of machine. Or if he is a salesman, don't just say salesman, but tell us what kind of goods he sells. If he is a foreman or manager, be sure and tell us that. In other words be as exact as you can be in four or so sentences. (Space provided for answer.)

Now we want to know how your father's work fits into the total picture at work. To do this tell us what other workers your father deals with, tell us what tasks these people perform, tell us how your father's work is related to their work. (Space provided for answer.)

If he deals with outside people (like customers, clients, the public, people in other businesses) tell us about these—who does he deal with, for what reasons, in what way, how much of his working time, etc. (Space provided for answer.)

20. What do you think are your father's general, overall feelings about his job?
    I would say that he *usually* (check one)
    1. _____ Likes it extremely well
    2. _____ Likes it very much
    3. _____ Likes it quite a bit
    4. _____ Likes it fairly well
    5. _____ Likes it just a little
    6. _____ Neither likes it nor dislikes it
    7. _____ Dislikes it
    8. _____ Hates it
21. Does your father have people working under him in his job?
    1. _____ Yes.   How many? _____
    2. _____ No.
22. If your answer is "YES" to the above (21), please tell us what kind of work these people do. (Be specific)
23. Is your father supervised by others? 1. _____ Yes 2. _____ No

If your father *isn't supervised* by anyone, then you are to skip the next six questions (24 to 29) and go directly to question 30. If your father *is supervised* then answer all the following questions (from 24 on).

24. Who is your father's immediate supervisor? That is, what is this man's occupation or the name of his job?
25. Tell us how he supervises your father. Tell us by what means (conferences, by letter, by talking to him while working, by phone, etc.) and how often.
26. How often does your father communicate or talk with his supervisor about the work?

1. _____ They are in almost constant communication about the work
2. _____ Frequently during each day
3. _____ Four or five times during each day
4. _____ Once or twice a day
5. _____ Once or twice a week
6. _____ Once or twice a month or less
7. _____ I don't know at all

27. How much of your father's working time is he in the presence (say within talking distance) of his supervisor?
    1. _____ Nearly all the time or all the time
    2. _____ Much of the time
    3. _____ About half the time
    4. _____ Only a part of the time
    5. _____ Seldom in his presence
    6. _____ Almost never or never
    7. _____ I don't know at all

28. Please read these two descriptions (descriptions A and B) and decide which describes your father's supervisor better.
    A. This supervisor tends to be a little bossy. He tells those who work under him just how to do things and he expects them to do it just that way. He usually doesn't explain why he wants something done—he just wants them to do it. He may be a little critical too. He watches everyone a little too closely and he checks on them quite a bit. He doesn't seem to want people to think for themselves much.
    B. This supervisor tells those who work for him what he wants done but he usually explains why he wants it done. He also gives those who work under him a chance to ask questions and make suggestions about how things should be done. He also gives people quite a bit of freedom in the way they handle parts of their job.
    My father's supervisor(s) is:
    1. _____ much more like A   5. _____ somewhat more like B
    2. _____ somewhat more like A   6. _____ much more like B
    3. _____ a little more like A   7. _____ I don't know at all
    4. _____ a little more like B

29. How often does your father complain about his supervision?
    1. _____ Frequently
    2. _____ Fairly often
    3. _____ Once in awhile
    4. _____ Seldom
    5. _____ Never
    6. _____ I don't know at all

30. How many hours does your father work *per week*? _____ hours.

31. Is there a specific time when he arrives at work?
    1. _____ Yes
    2. _____ No
    3. _____ Don't know

32. Does he punch in when he arrives?
    1. _____ Yes
    2. _____ No
    3. _____ Don't know

33. Does your father have a lot of tight schedules or tight deadlines to meet? Does he experience a lot of pressure to get things done in a hurry or at a particular time?
    1. _____ Yes, frequently
    2. _____ Yes, fairly often
    3. _____ Yes, once in awhile
    4. _____ Seldom
    5. _____ Almost never
    6. _____ I don't know at all

34. Please read these two descriptions of jobs (descriptions A and B) and decide which describes your father's work better.

    A. This father's job has things arranged and planned in advance. He carries out what has been decided by someone else OR he follows a pretty definite schedule or routine which the nature of the work requires. This means he isn't always able to do things in a way that would be most efficient for himself but his work fits in with other work. He doesn't often have to or it isn't often possible for him to decide on matters that come up in his work. The work flows in and he does his part of the work.

    B. In his job this father may sometimes do what others have decided or planned for him but usually he schedules or decides when or how he will do a sizable part of his work. Also, his job requires him to act and think on his own a great deal. Though there may be some routine and scheduling he has quite a bit of opportunity to shift things or do things in a way that is most efficient for himself. He frequently has the chance to decide on matters and solve things that come up at work.

    My father's work is:
        1. _____ much more like A
        2. _____ somewhat more like A
        3. _____ a little more like A
        4. _____ a little more like B
        5. _____ somewhat more like B
        6. _____ much more like B
        0. _____ I don't know at all

If your father has had a job different from the one described above in the last 10 or 12 years, we would like you to tell us briefly about it. Other than the one above, pick the job or work he did for the longest time in the last ten or twelve years.

35. How long did he have that job? From _____, _____ to _____, _____
Mo.   Year   Mo.   Year
36. Title or name of job: _____
37. Tell us briefly what this work consisted of—what were his duties?

Now we would like to turn to some questions about you and your family.
38. Below is a list of things a *father** might do when a boy about 10 or 12
    years old had done something the father regarded as definitely bad
    or wrong. Read the list, and thinking about your punishment during
    that period, decide which three things in the list describe best what your
    father was likely to do when you had done something he regarded as
    definitely bad or wrong.
    Answer by circling the letter in front of the 3 things your father
    was most likely to do.
    _____ a. Not punish you directly, but act hurt or disappointed in you.
    _____ b. Not punish you directly, but ignore you and act angry.
    _____ c. Reason with you calmly.
    _____ d. Ask you to apologize or show that you are sorry.
    _____ e. Not really raise his voice, but talk to you in a way that made
             you feel terrible.
    _____ f. Spank or hit or shake you.
    _____ g. Spank or hit or shake you, but only as a last resort.
    _____ h. Warn you not to ever do it again and tell you what would
             happen if you did.
    _____ i. Yell at you or scold you or really bawl you out.
    _____ j. Punish you in some definite way like not letting you go to
             the movies, making you stay in the house, or not giving you
             any spending money.
39. Now go back to the list above and look only at the three things you
    circled. Put a "1" on the line next to the thing you circled that your
    father was most likely to do, put a "2" by the thing he was next most
    likely to do, and put a "3" by the third most likely.
40. In your family when both your parents are around who do you
    usually talk over your worries with?
    1. _____ Nearly always with my mother
    2. _____ Generally with my mother
    3. _____ A little more often with my mother
    4. _____ A little more often with my father
    5. _____ Generally with my father
    6. _____ Nearly always with my father
41. Who is the main source of authority regarding most matters in the
    family?
    1. _____ Nearly always my father
    2. _____ Generally my father

* After question 49, exactly the same question (with the same alternatives) was
asked regarding the mother.

3. _____ My father, a little more often
4. _____ My mother, a little more often
5. _____ Generally my mother
6. _____ Nearly always my mother

Some parents show their warmth and affection openly while other parents
are quite reserved in showing that they like someone.

42. Would you say your *mother* is:
    1. _____ quite reserved in showing affection
    2. _____ a little reserved in showing affection
    3. _____ rather open in showing affection
    4. _____ very open in showing affection

43. Would you say your *father* is:
    1. _____ quite reserved in showing affection
    2._____ a little reserved in showing affection
    3. _____ rather open in showing affection
    4. _____ very open in showing affection

44. If something nice happened to you (you get a good grade, you get
    into a club or sport you wanted, etc.) and both your parents are
    around, who do you usually talk it over with the most?
    1. _____ My mother, much more
    2. _____ My mother, somewhat more
    3. _____ My mother, a little more
    4. _____ My father, a little more
    5. _____ My father, somewhat more
    6. _____ My father, much more

45. Who do you enjoy spending the most time with?
    1. _____ My mother, mostly
    2. _____ My mother, a little bit more
    3. _____ My father, a little bit more
    4. _____ My father, mostly

46. In your family when both your parents are around who usually exer-
    cises discipline over you?
    (alternatives as in question 41)

There are many things that have to be decided in every family. Some of
them are decided by one person, some by another. The following questions are about how things are decided in your family. Check the answer
that tells what happens in your family.

47. A mother and father are discussing whether they should buy a radio
    or television set now, or whether they should save the money for
    something really necessary. They can't decide. If this were your fam-
    ily, who would have the most say in deciding?
    1. _____ Father, mostly
    2. _____ Father, a little bit more
    3. _____ Mother and father would have *exactly* equal say
    4. _____ Mother, a little bit more
    5. _____ Mother, mostly

48. A family is thinking about plans for their vacation. They are wondering what to do, where to go, and things like that. Who would have the most say in deciding about this in your family?
    (alternatives as in question 47)
49. In the last 3 or 4 years, who in your family has generally had the final say in what you should do (how often you should go out, and where, how much homework you should do, etc.)?
    1. _____ My father generally
    2. _____ My father, a little more often
    3. _____ My mother, a little more often
    4. _____ My mother generally

PLEASE READ THESE TWO DESCRIPTIONS AND DECIDE WHICH IS MORE LIKE YOUR FATHER.

50. A. This father keeps close tabs on his son. He is pretty concerned about where his son is, who his son is going around with, and what he is doing. He feels his son is one of his important responsibilities. In general this father feels that in order to prepare his son for life he has to watch him carefully and closely. He has pretty definite goals and definite things he wants his son to do. When the son fails to do these he lets the son know how he feels by the way he reacts.

   B. This father doesn't keep tabs on his son much at all. He doesn't seem so concerned about where his son is, or who he is with, or what he is doing. The father feels others are as important or more important than himself in guiding the son through life. He usually lets other people tell the son what is expected of him. In general he goes his way and he lets his son go his way so long as he doesn't get into special difficulties.

   My father is:
    1. _____ much more like A
    2. _____ somewhat more like A
    3. _____ a little bit more like A
    4. _____ a little bit more like B
    5. _____ somewhat more like B
    6. _____ much more like B

PLEASE READ THESE TWO DESCRIPTIONS AND DECIDE WHICH IS MORE LIKE YOUR FATHER.

51. A. This father tells his son what to do and how to do it. He expects his son to do it just that way or else. He usually doesn't explain why he wants his son to behave in a certain way and he usually doesn't listen to what his son might want to say.

   B. This father tells his son what he wants him to do but feels the son should have quite a bit of choice about how he does it—and whether he always does it or not. This father explains why he wants his son to do something and he always listens to ideas his son has about the matter.

My father is: (alternatives as in question 50)

PLEASE READ THESE TWO DESCRIPTIONS AND ANSWER.

52. A. This father has interests and does things which take him outside the family quite a bit. Sometimes he talks with his children about school or he talks with the mother about how money should be spent or what needs to be done, but not so often. Also he doesn't do things with the family so often. Because of this he feels the mother knows most situations in the family best and he lets her make many decisions by herself.

B. This father is pretty involved in what goes on in the family. He talks with the children about what they are doing in school and outside. He often talks with the mother about how best to spend their money, what things they might do for recreation and also does these things with the family quite a lot. Not only is he involved in the family, but he is inclined to make decisions about things in the family—usually with the mother's help or by himself.

My father is: (alternatives as in question 50)

53. What is your *mother's* religious preference?
   1. _____ Catholic (Roman)
   2. _____ Jewish
   3. _____ Protestant. What denomination? _____
   4. _____ Eastern Orthodox (Greek, Armenian, Russian Orthodox)
   5. _____ Other (please specify): _____
   6. _____ No religious preference

54. What is your *father's* religious preference?
   1. _____ Catholic (Roman)
   2. _____ Jewish
   3. _____ Protestant. What denomination? _____
   4. _____ Eastern Orthodox (Greek, Armenian, Russian Orthodox)
   5. _____ Other (please specify): _____
   6. _____ No religious preference

55. Does your mother have a paying job (other than keeping house and taking care of the family)?
   1. _____ Yes, she has such a job now. What is its title?
   _____
   2. _____ No, not now, but she has had such a job within the past five years.
   3. _____ No, she has not had such a job within the past five years.
   4. _____ She has not worked since her marriage.

56. Would you check the amount which comes closest to your family's total income in 1957. Consider all sources:—rents, wages of all immediate family, etc.

1. ——— Less than $2000   6. ——— $6000 to $7999
2. ——— $2000 to $2999   7. ——— $8000 to $9,999
3. ——— $3000 to $3999   8. ——— $10,000 to $14,999
4. ——— $4000 to $4999   9. ——— $15,000 to $25,000
5. ——— $5000 to $5999   10. ——— Over $25,000
                        0. ——— I don't know at all

If you are not sure of the answers to these questions, make the best guess you can. If you do not know the complete answer, give as much information as you can.

57. What kind of work did your father's father do most of his life? (Give title of the job and describe briefly) ———————————

———————————————————————————————

58. Where was your father's father born?

——————————————————, ———————————
     (City or town)   *(State or country)*

59. What kind of work did your mother's father do most of his life? (Give title of the job and describe briefly.) ———————————

60. Where was your mother's father born?

——————————————————, ———————————
     (City or town)   *(State or country)*

61. Where was your mother's mother born?

——————————————————, ———————————
     (City or town)   *(State or country)*

62. Where was your father's mother born?

——————————————————, ———————————
     (City or town)   *(State or country)*

63. Most people have some daydreams about what they would like to be and do when they are adults. What would you like most to be and do if you could be whatever you chose?

64. Of course, there can be a big difference between anybody's daydreams and what, seriously, he really expects to be and do. When you are an adult—let's say around 35 or 40—what kind of work do you really expect to be doing?

65. Which parent are you said to resemble more in personality?
    1. ——— mother
    2. ——— father

66. This father often makes his son feel bad by ignoring him or refusing to talk to him and by acting cold and distant.
My father is:
    1. ——— very much like this

2. _____ quite a bit like this
3. _____ somewhat like this
4. _____ very slightly like this
5. _____ not at all like this

67. Whom do you admire most in your family or among your relatives?
1. _____ sister   6. _____ aunt
2. _____ brother   7. _____ grandmother
3. _____ mother   8. _____ grandfather
4. _____ father   9. _____ other. Who? _____
5. _____ uncle

68. This father often makes the son feel bad by the way he talks to him.
For example he may sometimes make fun or tease the son. Maybe
he tells the son what a disappointment he is or how he is failing his
mother and father. Just by talking in some way like this he makes
the son feel pretty bad.
My father is: (Alternatives as in question 66)

69. When requiring me to do something, my mother:
1. _____ always explains the reason
2. _____ usually explains the reason
3. _____ explains about as often as not
4. _____ seldom explains
5. _____ thinks explanations are unnecessary

70. When requiring me to do something, my father:
1. _____ always explains the reason
2. _____ usually explains the reason
3. _____ explains about as often as not
4. _____ seldom explains
5. _____ thinks explanations are unnecessary

71. When this son was a child, this father would often slap or shake or
spank his son—sometimes it seemed for sort of unimportant things.
My father was: (Alternatives as in question 66)

72. With regard to family problems, my mother discusses them with me:
1. _____ always
2. _____ usually
3. _____ about half the time
4. _____ seldom
5. _____ never

73. With regard to family problems, my father discusses them with me:
1. _____ always
2. _____ usually
3. _____ about half the time
4. _____ seldom
5. _____ never

74. This father yells at his son and often bawls him out for what he's done.
My father is: (Alternatives as in question 66)

We would like you to read these stories and then answer each question
in 3 or 4 sentences. If something like this has never happened, try
to imagine what would happen if it did occur. Tell us what your
father would probably do or say. Be as specific about what he would say

and do as you can be. Write not only what he does or says, but how he does it—in what mood or with what attitude towards you.

75. Suppose you had been going around with a group of three or four fellows your parents disapproved of. Several times your father talked with you—trying to get you to stop seeing them. Finally, they get into some serious trouble. The police come to ask you some questions and the neighbors begin to talk. Several days later your father comes home saying some of the people he works with heard you were taken to the police station and held. Even though this is not true, your father was angry and embarrassed.

In this situation, what would your father do and say to you?

What would be your father's feelings towards you?

How would you feel?

76. AGAIN READ THESE TWO DESCRIPTIONS AND DECIDE WHICH IS MORE LIKE YOUR FATHER.
    A. This father seems to worry about things quite a bit—about whether he is doing his work right, whether he is a good father and husband, etc. Maybe he worries and blames himself too much. Just the same he does the best he can.
    B. This father worries once in awhile about his work, or about whether he is a good father and husband, but not so often. Generally, if problems come up, he doesn't blame himself so often—others are "what's the matter." Just the same he does the best he can.
    My father is: (Alternatives as in question 50)˙

77. Imagine that your grades this year were about like they had always been. However, the past month or so you had been working hard and you brought home the best report card you ever had gotten. You are really pleased about it and you showed it to your parents.

What would your father do and say to you in such a situation?

What would be your father's feeling towards you?

How would you feel?

78. Now we all realize that parents have the responsibility of helping you to do the right things and keeping you from doing wrong. Here are a number of things parents often do. Some may not bother you at all and some hurt you more than others. Some hurt you physically and some hurt you in other ways—your feelings. Tell us how you feel.

Answer by putting a 1, 2, or 3 on the line in front of *each* way listed below.

Put a 1 if this way doesn't really hurt or bother you and you don't mind when they use it.

Put a 2 if this way hurts you or bothers you some. You dislike it and wish they wouldn't use it.

Put a 3 if this way hurts you or bothers you an awful lot. You hate it and wish they wouldn't use it.

_____ Not punish you directly, but act hurt or disappointed in you. (alternatives continue as in question 38)

Bibliography

Adorno, T. W., et al. *The Authoritarian Personality.* New York: Harper & Row, Publishers, 1950.

Allen, Phillip J. "Childhood Backgrounds of Success in a Profession." *American Sociological Review,* vol. XX, no. 2, April, 1955, pp. 186-190.

Anshen, Ruth Nanda. "The Family in Transition," in Ruth N. Anshen (Ed.), *The Family: Its Function and Destiny.* New York: Harper & Row, Publishers, 1959, pp. 3-19.

Arensberg, Conrad M. *The Irish Countryman.* Gloucester, Mass.: Peter Smith, 1959.

Argyris, Chris. *Personality and Organization.* New York: Harper & Row, Publishers, 1957.

Bakke, E. W. *The Unemployed Worker.* New Haven: Yale University Press, 1940.

Barber, Elinor G. *The Bourgeoisie in Eighteenth Century France.* Princeton: Princeton University Press, 1955.

Barker, R. G., T. Dembo, and K. Lewin. "Frustration and Regression: An Experiment with Young Children." *University of Iowa Studies in Child Welfare,* vol. XVIII, no. 386, 1941.

Barnard, Chester L. *The Functions of the Executive.* Cambridge: Harvard University Press, 1938.

Beers, Howard W. "Rural Urban Differences: Some Evidence from Public Opinion Polls." *Rural Sociology,* vol. XVIII, no. 1, 1953, pp. 1-11.

Bellah, Robert N. "The Religion of India: The Sociology of Hinduism and Buddhism, By Max Weber" (a book review). *American Sociological Review,* vol. 24, no. 5, 1959, pp. 731-732.

Bettelheim, B., and M. Janowitz. *Dynamics of Prejudice: A Psychological and Sociological Study of Veterans.* New York: Harper & Row, Publishers, 1950.

Blau, Peter. *Bureaucracy in Modern Society.* New York: Random House, Inc., 1946.

285

Blood, Robert O., Jr., and Donald M. Wolfe. *Husbands and Wives: The Dynamics of Married Living.* New York: The Free Press of Glencoe, 1960.

Bott, Elizabeth. "The Concept of Class as a Reference Group." *Human Relations,* August, 1954, pp. 259-286.

————. *Family and Social Networks: Roles, Norms, and External Relationships in Ordinary Urban Families.* London: Tavistock Publications, 1957.

Bronfenbrenner, Urie. "Socialization and Social Class through Time and Space," in E. Maccoby, T. Newcomb, and E. Hartley (Eds.), *Readings in Social Psychology.* New York: Holt, Rinehart and Winston, Inc., 1958, pp. 400-425.

Brown, Norman O. *Life Against Death: The Psychoanalytic Meaning of History.* New York: Vintage Books, 1959.

Campbell, Donald T. "Evolutionary Theory in Social Science: A Reappraisal." Unpublished paper read before the conference, *Social Science and the Underdeveloped Areas.* Northwestern University, June, 1961.

Centers, Richard. "Children of the New Deal: Social Stratification and Adolescent Attitudes," in Reinhard Bendix and S. M. Lipset (Eds.), *Class, Status, and Power.* New York: The Free Press of Glencoe, 1953, pp. 359-370.

Clausen, John A. "Drug Addiction," in Robert K. Merton and Robert A. Nisbet (Eds.), *Contemporary Social Problems.* New York: Harcourt, Brace & World, Inc., 1961, pp. 181-221.

Cloward, Richard A., and Lloyd E. Ohlin. *Delinquency and Opportunity.* New York: The Free Press of Glencoe, 1960.

Cohen, Albert. *Delinquent Boys: The Culture of the Gang.* New York: The Free Press of Glencoe, 1955.

Cohen, Elizabeth. "Parental Factors in Educational Mobility." Unpublished Ph.D. dissertation, Radcliffe College, 1958.

Cooley, Charles H. *Human Nature and the Social Order.* New York: Charles Scribner's Sons, 1922.

Davis, Allison, B. B. Gardner, and M. R. Gardner. *Deep South.* Chicago: University of Chicago Press, 1941.

Davis, Allison, and R. J. Havighurst. "A Comparison of the Chicago and the Harvard Studies of Social Class Differences in Child Rearing." *American Sociological Review,* August, 1955, pp. 438-442.

de Tocqueville, Alexis, *Democracy in America* (Richard D. Heffner, Ed.). New York: Oxford University Press, 1947.

Dollard, John, et al. *Frustration and Aggression.* New Haven: Yale University Press, 1939.

Dornbusch, S. M. "The Military Academy as an Assimilating Institution," *Social Forces,* vol. 33, 1955, pp. 316-321.

Durkheim, Emile. *The Division of Labor in Society.* Translated by George Simpson. New York: The Macmillan Company, 1933.

Duvall, E. M. "Conceptions of Parenthood," *American Journal of Sociology*, vol. LII, 1946-1947, pp. 193-203.

Dynes, Russell R., Alfred C. Clarke, and Simon Dinitz. "Levels of Occupational Aspiration. Some Aspects of Family Experience as a Variable." *American Sociological Review*, April, 1956, pp. 212-215.

Edin, Karl Arvid, and Edward P. Hutchinson. *Studies of Differential Fertility in Sweden*. London: P. S. King and Son, Ltd., 1935.

Eisenstadt, S. N. *From Generation to Generation*. New York: The Free Press of Glencoe, 1956.

Elder, Joseph. "Anthropomorphic Symbolism in World Religions." Unpublished paper, May, 1956.

Ellis, Evelyn. "Social Psychological Correlates of Upward Social Mobility among Unmarried Career Women." *American Sociological Review*, October, 1952, pp. 558-63.

Faris, Robert E. L. "Sociological Causes of Genius." *American Sociological Review*, vol. 15, 1950, pp. 689-99.

Field, Peter B. "Social and Psychological Correlates of Drunkenness in Primitive Tribes." Unpublished Ph.D. dissertation, Harvard University, 1961.

Firth, Raymond. *Primitive Polynesian Economy*. London: Routledge and Kegan Paul, Ltd., 1939.

———. *We, the Tikopia*. London: George Allen & Unwin Ltd., 1936.

Fortes, Meyer. *The Web of Kinship among the Tallensi*. New York: Oxford University Press, 1949.

Frazier, E. *The Negro Family in the United States*. Chicago: University of Chicago Press, 1939.

Frenkel-Brunswik, Else. "Explorations by a Contributor to the 'Authoritarian Personality,' " in R. Christie and M. Jahoda (Eds.), *Studies in the Scope and Method of "The Authoritarian Personality."* New York: The Free Press of Glencoe, 1954.

Fromm, Erich. *Escape from Freedom*. New York: Holt, Rinehart & Winston, Inc., 1941.

———. "Sex and Character," in Ruth N. Anshen (Ed.), *The Family: Its Function and Destiny*. New York: Harper & Row, Publishers, 1959, pp. 381-398.

Funkenstein, Daniel, Stanley H. King and Margaret E. Drolette. *The Mastery of Stress*. Cambridge: Harvard University Press, 1957.

Galbraith, John Kenneth. *The Affluent Society*. Boston: Houghton Mifflin Company, 1958.

Geiger, Kent. "Changing Political Attitudes in Totalitarian Society: A Case Study of the Role of the Family," in Norman W. Bell and Ezra F. Vogel (Eds.), *The Family*. New York: The Free Press of Glencoe, 1960, pp. 173-188.

Gillin, John L. *The Wisconsin Prisoner*. Madison, Wis.: University of Wisconsin Press, 1946.

Gold, Martin. "Suicide, Homicide, and the Socialization of Aggression." *American Journal of Sociology*, May, 1958, pp. 651-661. (Citing E. Douvan and S. Withey, *A Study of Adolescent Boys*, Ann Arbor: Institute for Social Research, 1955, and *ibid.*, *A Study of Adolescent Girls*, Ann Arbor: Institute for Social Research, 1956.)

Gough, E. Kathleen. "Is The Family Universal—The Nayar Case," in Norman Bell and Ezra Vogel (Eds.), *The Family*, New York: The Free Press of Glencoe, 1960, pp. 76-92.

Gouldner, Alvin W. "Reciprocity and Autonomy in Functional Theory," in L. Gross (Ed.), *Symposium on Sociological Theory*. New York: Harper & Row, Publishers, 1959, pp. 241-290.

————. "Organizational Analysis," in Robert K. Merton, Leonard Broom, and Leonard S. Cottrell, Jr. (Eds.), *Sociology Today*. New York: Basic Books, Inc., 1959, pp. 400-428.

Hagen, Douglas. "Family Atmosphere and other Childhood Patterns as Precursors of Career Interests." Unpublished Ph.D. dissertation, Harvard University, 1959.

Hammond, S. B. "Class and Family," in O. A. Oeser and S. B. Hammond (Eds.), *Social Structure and Personality in a City*. London: Routledge and Kegan Paul, Ltd., 1954, pp. 238-248.

Handlin, Oscar. *This Was America*. Cambridge: Harvard University Press, 1949.

Henry, Andrew F., and James F. Short, Jr. *Suicide and Homicide*. New York: The Free Press of Glencoe, 1954.

Hilgard, Ernest R. *Introduction to Psychology, 2d ed.* New York: Harcourt, Brace & World, Inc., 1957.

Hollingshead, A., and Redlich, F. *Social Class and Mental Illness*. New York: John Wiley and Sons, Inc., 1958.

Homans, George C. *The Human Group*. New York: Harcourt, Brace & World, Inc., 1950.

————. *Social Behavior: Its Elementary Forms*. New York: Harcourt, Brace & World, Inc., 1961.

Hughes, Everett C. *Men and Their Work*. New York: The Free Press of Glencoe, 1958.

Huizinga, Johan. *Homo Ludens*. Boston: Beacon Press, 1960.

Inkeles, Alex. "Personality and Social Structure," in Robert K. Merton, Leonard Broom, and Leonard S. Cottrell, Jr. (Eds.), *Sociology Today*. New York: Basic Books, Inc., 1959, pp. 249-276.

————. "Industrial Man: The Relation of Status to Experience, Perception and Value." *American Journal of Sociology*, vol. 66, no. 1, July, 1960, pp. 1-31.

————, and Peter H. Rossi. "National Comparisons of Occupational Prestige." *American Journal of Sociology*, January, 1956, pp. 329-339.

Johnson, Harry M. *Sociology: A Systematic Introduction*. New York: Harcourt, Brace & World, Inc., 1960.

Jones, Mary C., and Nancy Bayley. "Physical Maturing Among Boys As Related to Behavior." *Journal of Educational Psychology*, vol. 41, 1950, pp. 129-148.

Kahl, Joseph A. "Adolescent Ambition." Unpublished Ph.D. dissertation, Harvard University, 1952.

————. "Educational and Occupational Aspirations of 'Common Man' Boys." *Harvard Educational Review*, vol. 23, 1953, pp. 186-203.

————. *The American Class Structure*. New York: Holt, Rinehart & Winston, Inc., 1957.

————, and James A. Davis. "A Comparison of Indexes of Socio-Economic Status." *American Sociological Review*, June, 1955, pp. 317-325.

Kinsey, Alfred, Wardell Pomeroy, and Clyde Martin. *Sexual Behavior in the Human Male*. Philadelphia: W. B. Saunders Company, 1948.

Kinsey, Alfred, et al. *Sexual Behavior in the Human Female*. Philadelphia: W. B. Saunders Company, 1953.

Kluckhohn, Clyde and Florence Kluckhohn. "American Culture: Generalized Orientations and Class Patterns." The Conference on Science, Philosophy, and Religion. New York: Harper & Row, Publishers, 1947, pp. 106-128.

Kluckhohn, Florence R. "Dominant and Substitute Profiles of Cultural Orientation: Their Significance for Social Stratification." *Social Forces*, May, 1950, pp. 376-393.

Knupfer, Genevieve. "Portrait of the Underdog." *Public Opinion Quarterly*, vol. 11, 1947, pp. 103-114.

Kohn, Melvin L. "Social Class and the Exercise of Parental Authority." *American Sociological Review*, vol. 24, no. 3, 1959, pp. 352-366.

König, René. "Family and Authority: The German Father in 1955." *The Sociological Review*, July, 1957, pp. 107-127.

Kornhauser, Arthur. "Attitudes of Economic Groups." *Public Opinion Quarterly*, April, 1938, pp. 260-268.

Lang, Richard O. "The Rating of Happiness in Marriage." Unpublished Master's thesis, University of Chicago, 1932. Cited in Meyer Nimkoff, *Marriage and the Family*. Boston: Houghton Mifflin Company, 1947.

Lenski, Gerhard E. "Status Crystallization: A Non-Vertical Dimension of Social Status." *American Sociological Review*, August, 1954, pp. 405-413.

————. *The Religious Factor*. Garden City, N.Y.: Doubleday & Company, Inc., 1961.

Levinson, Daniel J., and Phyllis E. Huffman. "Traditional Family Ideology and Its Relation to Personality." *Journal of Personality*, March, 1955, pp. 251-273.

Levy, David. *Maternal Overprotection*. New York: Columbia University Press, 1943.

Linton, R., and A. Kardiner. "The Change from Dry to Wet Rice Culture in Tanala-Betsileo," in Theodore M. Newcomb and Eugene L. Hartley (Eds.), *Readings in Social Psychology*. New York: Holt, Rinehart & Winston, Inc., 1947, pp. 46-54.

Lipset, Seymour M. *Political Man*. Garden City, N.Y.: Doubleday & Company, Inc., 1960.

————, and Reinhard Bendix. *Social Mobility in Industrial Society*. Berkeley: University of California Press, 1960.

Locke, John. *Two Treatises on Civil Government*. London: George Routledge & Son, 1887.

Lynd, Robert S., and Helen M. Lynd. *Middletown*. New York: Harcourt, Brace and Company, 1929.

Maccoby, Eleanor E. "The Choice of Variables in the Study of Socialization," *Sociometry*, vol. 24, no. 4, December, 1961, pp. 357-371.

Malinowski, Bronislaw. *Sex and Repression in a Savage Society*. London: Routledge and Kegan Paul, 1927.

————. "The Group and Individual in Functional Analysis." *American Journal of Sociology*, May, 1939, pp. 938-963.

Marx, Karl, and Friedrich Engels. In Lewis S. Feuer (Ed.), *Basic Writings on Politics and Philosophy*. Garden City, N.Y.: Doubleday & Company, Inc., 1959.

McArthur, Charles. "Personality Differences Between Middle and Upper Classes." *Journal of Abnormal and Social Psychology*, vol. 50, 1955, pp. 247-258.

McClelland, David, et al. *The Achievement Motive*. New York: Appleton-Century-Crofts, Inc., 1953.

McKinley, Donald G. "Social Status and Parental Roles." Unpublished Ph.D. dissertation, Harvard University, 1960.

Mead, George H. *Mind, Self and Society*, Charles Morris (Ed.). Chicago: University of Chicago Press, 1934.

Mead, Margaret. *And Keep Your Powder Dry*. New York: William Morrow and Company, 1942.

Meier, Dorothy L., and Wendell Bell. "Anomia and Differential Access to the Achievement of Life Goals." *American Sociological Review*, April, 1959, pp. 189-202.

Mercer, Blaine E. *The Study of Society*. New York: Harcourt, Brace & World, Inc., 1958.

Merton, Robert K. "Bureaucratic Structure and Personality," in *Social Theory and Social Structure*. New York: The Free Press of Glencoe, 1949, pp. 151-160.

————. "Puritanism, Pietism, and Science," in *Social Theory and Social Structure*. New York: The Free Press of Glencoe, 1949, pp. 329-346.

————. "Social Structure and Anomie," in *Social Theory and Social Structure*. New York: The Free Press of Glencoe, 1949, pp. 125-149.

Miller, Daniel R., and Guy E. Swanson. *The Changing American Parent.* New York: John Wiley and Sons, Inc., 1958.

————. *Inner Conflict and Defense.* New York: Holt, Rinehart & Winston, Inc., 1960.

Miller, Neal F. "The Frustration Aggression Hypothesis," in Melvin Marx (Ed.), *Psychological Theory: Contemporary Readings.* New York: The Macmillan Company, 1951, pp. 482-486.

Mills, C. Wright. *White Collar: The American Middle Classes.* New York: Oxford University Press, 1951.

————. *The Power Elite.* New York: Oxford University Press, 1959.

Mosely, Philip E. "The Russian Family: Old Style and New," in Ruth N. Anshen (Ed.), *The Family: Its Function and Destiny.* New York: Harper & Row, Publishers, 1959, pp. 104-122.

Murdock, George P. *Social Structure.* New York: The Macmillan Company, 1949.

Myers, Jerome K., and Bertram H. Roberts. *Family and Class Dynamics in Mental Illness.* New York: John Wiley and Sons, Inc., 1959.

Nimkoff, Meyer F. *Marriage and the Family.* New York: Houghton Mifflin Company, 1947.

North, Cecil C., and Paul K. Hatt. "Jobs and Occupations: A Popular Evaluation." *Opinion News,* September, 1947, pp. 3-13.

Northrop, F. S. C. *The Meeting of East and West.* New York: The Macmillan Company, 1947.

Oeser, O. A., and S. B. Hammond. *Social Structure and Personality in a City: Volume I.* London: Routledge and Kegan Paul Ltd., 1957.

————, and F. E. Emery. *Social Structure and Personality in a Rural Community: Volume II.* London: Routledge and Kegan Paul Ltd., 1957.

Parsons, Talcott. *The Structure of Social Action.* New York: The Free Press of Glencoe, 1949.

————. *The Social System.* New York: The Free Press of Glencoe, 1951.

————. "Age and Sex in the Social Structure of the United States," *Essays in Sociological Theory.* New York: The Free Press of Glencoe, 1954, pp. 89-103.

————. "Certain Primary Sources and Patterns of Aggression in the Social Structure of the Western World," *Essays in Sociological Theory.* New York: The Free Press of Glencoe, 1954, pp. 298-322.

————. "The Kinship System of the Contemporary United States," *Essays in Sociological Theory.* New York: The Free Press of Glencoe, 1954, pp. 177-196.

————. "A Revised Analytical Approach to the Theory of Social Stratification," *Essays in Sociological Theory.* New York: The Free Press of Glencoe, 1954, pp. 386-439.

————. "General Theory in Sociology," in Robert K. Merton, Leonard Broom, and Leonard Cottrell, Jr. (Eds.), *Sociology Today.* New York: Basic Books, Inc., 1959, pp. 3-38.

Parsons, Talcott. "The School Class as a Social System: Some of its Functions in American Society," *Harvard Educational Review*, Fall, 1959, pp. 297-318.

———. "Social Strains in America," *Social Structure and Process in Modern Societies*. New York: The Free Press of Glencoe, 1960, pp. 226-247.

———. *The American Social System*. (In preparation.)

———, and Robert F. Bales. *Family, Socialization and Interaction Process*. New York: The Free Press of Glencoe, 1955.

——— and Winston White. "The Link between Character and Society," in Seymour M. Lipset and Leo Lowenthal (Eds.), *Culture and Social Character*. New York: The Free Press of Glencoe, 1961.

———, E. Shils, K. D. Naegele, and J. R. Pitts (Eds.), *Theories of Society: Vols. I and II*. New York: The Free Press of Glencoe, 1961.

Pope, Liston. *Millhands and Preachers*. New Haven: Yale University Press, 1942.

Radcliffe-Brown, A. R. *Structure and Function in Primitive Society*. London: Cohen and West, Ltd., 1952.

Rainwater, Lee. *And the Poor Get Children*. Chicago: Quadrangle Books, 1960.

Reichley, James. *The Art of Government*. New York: The Fund for The Republic, 1959.

Riesman, David, et al. *The Lonely Crowd*. New Haven: Yale University Press, 1950.

Reiss, Paul J. "The Extended Kinship System in the American Urban Middle Class." Unpublished Ph.D dissertation, Harvard University, 1960.

Riecken, Henry W., and George C. Homans. "Psychological Aspects of Social Structure," in Gardner Lindzey (Ed.), *The Handbook of Social Psychology*. Cambridge: Addison-Wesley Publishing Company, Inc., 1954, pp. 786-832.

Roe, Anne. *The Psychology of Occupations*. New York: John Wiley and Sons, Inc., 1956.

Schumpeter, Joseph. *Social Classes—Imperialism: Two Essays*. New York: Meridian Books, 1955.

Sears, Pauline S. "Child-Rearing Factors Related to Playing of Sexed-Type Roles," *American Psychologist*, vol. VIII, 1953, p. 431 (abstract).

Sears, Robert R. "Identification as a Form of Behavioral Development," in D. B. Harris (Ed.), *The Concept of Development*. Minneapolis: University of Minnesota Press, 1957, pp. 149-161.

———, E. Maccoby, and H. Levin. *Patterns of Child Rearing*. New York: Harper & Row, Publishers, 1957.

Shaw, Clifford R., and Henry D. McKay. *Juvenile Delinquency in Urban Areas*. Chicago: University of Chicago Press, 1942.

Shils, Edward. "The Calling of Sociology," in Talcott Parsons, et al.

(Eds.), *Theories of Society*. New York: The Free Press of Glencoe, Vol. II, 1961, pp. 1405-1448.

Simpson, George E., and Milton Yinger. *Racial and Cultural Minorities*. New York: Harper & Row, Publishers, 1953.

Spinley, B. M. *The Deprived and the Privileged*. London: Routledge and Kegan Paul, Ltd., 1953.

Stendhal (Marie Henri Beyle). *The Red and the Black*. New York: Bantam Books, 1958.

Stouffer, S. A. *Communism, Conformity and Civil Liberties: A Cross-Section of the Nation Speaks Its Mind*. Garden City, N.Y.: Doubleday & Company, Inc., 1955.

————, et al. (Eds.). *The American Soldier*. Princeton: Princeton University Press, 1949.

Strodtbeck, Fred L. "Family Interaction, Values, and Achievement," in David C. McClelland, Alfred L. Baldwin, Urie Bronfenbrenner, and Fred L. Strodtbeck, *Talent and Society*. Princeton: D. Van Nostrand Company, Inc., 1958, pp. 135-194.

Stycos, J. Mayone. *Family and Fertility in Puerto Rico*. New York: Columbia University Press, 1955.

Sutherland, Edwin H., and Donald R. Cressey. *Principles of Criminology*. Philadelphia: J. B. Lippincott Company, 1955.

Thibaudeau, A. C. *Biographie Mémoires: 1765-1792*. Paris: Niort, 1875.

Warner, W. Lloyd. *The Living and the Dead*. New Haven: Yale University Press, 1959.

———— and Paul S. Lunt. *The Social Life of a Modern Community: Volume I*. New Haven: Yale University Press, 1941.

————. *The Status System of a Modern Community*. Yankee City Series, Vol. II. New Haven: Yale University Press, 1942.

————, Marcia Meeker, and Kenneth Eels. *Social Class in America*. Chicago: Science Research Associates, 1949.

———— and James C. Abegglen. *Occupational Mobility in American Business and Industry*. Minneapolis: University of Minneapolis Press, 1955.

Weber, Max. *The Protestant Ethic and the Spirit of Capitalism*. Translated by Talcott Parsons. London: George Allen and Unwin, 1930.

————. *Essays in Sociology*. Translated by H. H. Gerth and C. Wright Mills. New York: Oxford University Press, Inc., 1946.

Wechsler, Henry. "Conflicts in Self-Perception." Unpublished Ph.D. dissertation, Department of Social Relations, Harvard University, 1958.

Weeks, H. Ashley. "Differential Divorce Rates by Occupations." *Social Forces*, March, 1943, pp. 334-337.

Weinberg, S. Kirson, and Henry Arond. "The Occupational Culture of the Boxer," *American Journal of Sociology*, vol. 57, 1952, pp. 460-469.

Whiting, John W. M., F. Kluckhohn, and Albert Anthony. "The Function of Male Initiation Ceremonies at Puberty," in E. Maccoby, T. Newcomb, and E. Hartley (Eds.), *Readings in Social Psychology*. New York: Holt, Rinehart and Winston, Inc., 1958, pp. 359-370.

Whyte, William F. *Street Corner Society: The Social Structure of an Italian Slum*. Chicago: The University of Chicago Press, 1943.

Wilson, Alan B. "Class Segregation and Aspirations of Youth." *American Sociological Review*, December, 1959, pp. 836-845.

Winch, Robert F. *The Modern Family*. New York: Holt, Rinehart & Winston, Inc., 1952.

————. *Identification and Its Familial Determinants*. Indianapolis: The Bobbs-Merrill Company, Inc., 1962.

Yinger, J. Milton. "Contraculture and Subculture." *American Sociological Review*, vol. XXV, no. 5, 1960, pp. 625-635.

Zelditch, Morris, Jr. "Role Differentiation in the Nuclear Family: A Comparative Study," in Talcott Parsons and Robert Bales (Eds.), *Family, Socialization and Interaction Process*. New York: The Free Press of Glencoe, 1955, pp. 307-351.

Index